SUNNY SKIES, SHADY CHARACTERS

SUNNY SKIES, SHADY CHARACTERS

*Cops, Killers, and Corruption
in the Aloha State*

JAMES DOOLEY

A Latitude 20 Book

University of Hawai'i Press
HONOLULU

20 19 18 17 16 15   6 5 4 3 2 1

Library of Congress Cataloging-in-Publication Data

Dooley, James (Investigative reporter), author.
    Sunny skies, shady characters : cops, killers, and corruption
in the Aloha State / James Dooley.
            pages cm
    Memoir of the author's career as an investigative reporter.
    "A latitude 20 book."
    Includes index.
    ISBN 978-0-8248-5164-4 (pbk. : alk. paper)
1. Investigative reporting—Hawaii.   2. Political corruption—
Hawaii.   3. Organized crime—Hawaii.   I. Title.
    PN4781.D55 2015
    364.109969—dc23

                                            2015000662

University of Hawai'i Press books are printed on acid-free paper
and meet the guidelines for permanence and durability of the
Council on Library Resources.

Printed by Sheridan Books, Inc.

Contents

CHAPTER ONE

"A Culture of Corruption"

Don Ho died on a Saturday.

There was a phone message waiting from a copy editor at the *Honolulu Advertiser* when I got home late that evening. "I'm writing the obit on Don Ho," Dave Koga said in the message, left four hours earlier. "Mark Platte says Ho might have had some organized crime connections and I should check with you."

I shook my head. It was too late to call back, and there was no point, anyway. Platte, the editor of the *Advertiser*, had refused to print that information before. Why would he now?

Koga's obituary was a fine, if uninspiring, summary of Ho's life. There were a few glaring omissions, however. There was no mention of Ho's five years of service as a U.S. Air Force transport pilot. The story was silent on Ho's unusual family life, which at one time had seen him cohabiting with three different women, including his wife, who together had borne him 10 children.[1]

And there was not a word about Ho's personal ties to mobsters and mob associates, including Larry Mehau, his longtime close friend and onetime business manager.

Platte certainly knew all about Mehau. A year earlier, I reported that the FBI had identified Mehau in a wiretap affidavit as "a longtime Hawaiian organized crime figure."[2]

And Platte had recently killed a series of stories I had written that concerned, among other things, Mehau's mob connections. The stories were based on sworn testimony from numerous Honolulu police officers in the department's elite Criminal Intelligence Unit (CIU).[3] The *Advertiser* spent somewhere around $100,000 in legal fees in a four-year effort to get those federal court records unsealed, then refused to publish the sections concerning Mehau and his associates, including officers inside the Honolulu Police Department (HPD). And there were numerous other archived *Advertiser* stories available to Koga and Platte that detailed the criminal pasts of some of Ho's associates, as well as the long-simmering "godfather of organized crime" allegation about Mehau.

Koga's story the next day quoted Mehau at length about Ho. He was identified in the story as a "Big Island rancher who grew up with Ho and was a lifelong friend." That was it. Nothing about the contents of the CIU files. No mention of the FBI affidavit. Just "Big Island rancher."

In the days that followed, no editors raised the subject again with me. Other media outlets touched briefly on it, but not the *Advertiser. Kapu* is the Hawaiian word. Forbidden territory.

Several reporters on the staff did stop by my desk, asking me to repeat the story of the time I met Don Ho and Larry Mehau together. I had first shared the story a couple of years earlier when the staff of the paper had gathered in the middle of the newsroom to say good-bye to Walter Wright, my former partner in investigative reporting, who was retiring.

In 1979, Walter told me he was working on a story about rape allegations made against Don Ho. The accuser was a young woman from the Midwest who said she had been assaulted in a Waikiki condo after Ho met her and a friend in a restaurant, bought them several drinks, and invited them to a party. The victim ended up naked in the streets of Waikiki, found her way back to her hotel room, and called the police. A medical examination showed evidence of intercourse and force used on the woman. Police obtained a search warrant and recovered the woman's clothing in the room where she said the assault occurred.[4]

Walter then told me that the victim's parents had convinced her to withdraw the complaint. The second woman refused to cooperate with authorities.

I was surprised to hear the allegations against Ho. He was a charming guy who didn't seem to have problems meeting and befriending women. His friends were a different matter. At various times, some of the scariest men in Hawai'i had hung out at Ho's Polynesian Palace showroom on Lewers Street in Waikiki.

"So, Walter, what do you want from me?" I said at the time.

He explained that we would never be able to write a story about the incident unless we got Ho to confirm that it had happened or at least that it was under investigation. I asked Walter how in the world we were going to do that.

"We'll just go down to the Polynesian Palace tonight and talk to him," Wright said.

"Are you sure you want to do that, Walter?" I said. "I don't know if that's a very good idea."

"Yeah," he said. "Come with me. I don't want to go down there alone."

"I don't blame you. I don't want to go down there at all," I said.

But he insisted. So we went to Waikiki.

Ho was on stage when we got there that night. Walter talked us past the door, and we were taken to one of Ho's dressing rooms to wait for him.

In those days, Ho had an upper dressing room where he held court after he finished on stage, signing autographs and kissing grandmas. He sold albums and posed for photographs until the well-wishers and admirers were eventually shooed away. There was a bigger adjoining room down

Singer-entertainer Don Ho. *HONOLULU ADVERTISER* PHOTO; *HONOLULU STAR-ADVERTISER* COLLECTION; HAWAI'I STATE ARCHIVES.

some stairs, where Walter and I were taken to wait. It was a long, low-ceilinged, gloomy room with tables and chairs spread around.

At the far end of the room were several guys watching the movie *Tora! Tora! Tora!* on television. We found a couple of chairs and sat down, maybe 10 or 15 feet away from the TV set. The attack on Pearl Harbor was underway, with all the gunfire, explosions, and bloodshed that went with it. My uneasiness increased. One of the men looked up from the television at us. I couldn't see him very well through the gloom, but he looked Hawaiian and very large.

"Who you guys?" he said.

Walter said, "It's okay. We're here to see Don."

The guy looked at us some more. This was obviously not a very satisfactory answer, but he let it go and went back to the movie. After a few more minutes, he looked at us again and said, "No, really. Who are you guys?"

Walter smiled and said again, "We're here to see Don. It's okay."

Now, this was Walter's story and I was just along for the ride, but I felt like we probably should say something more than that. I gave Walter a questioning look. He made a calming motion with one hand. By this time, the guy was staring hard at us. He got up from his chair and approached us. He was enormous. Not so much tall as very wide and solid.

He looked very irritated when he said, "WHO THE FUCK ARE YOU GUYS?"

I had had enough of playing second fiddle and blurted out, "We're from the *Advertiser*. I'm Jim Dooley and this is Walter Wright. We need to talk to Don."

The guy processed this information, then said, "Why didn't you just say so?" and went back to the movie. I whispered sharply at Walter, "What's wrong with you? Don't antagonize this guy. I think it's Cyril Kahale."

"Who's that?"

"I'll tell you later. Just don't piss him off."

I thought I had recognized the man when he approached us. Kahale was a former professional football player whose feats of physical prowess were legendary. But it was dark in the dressing room, and I had never actually met Kahale.

Ho eventually finished his show and his activities in the upper dressing room. When he came into the lower room, Walter introduced us and said something like "We're here to talk to you about the rape thing."

Ho was immediately angry. I don't remember his exact words, other than one phrase he repeated several times: "You guys got no class."

He told us to follow him, that we couldn't talk where we were. We went down more stairs, along some narrow hallways until we arrived in a small, windowless room with just one chair inside. There were generator or machinery noises in the background. I had no idea where we were. It felt like the lowest deck of a ship.

Ho sat in the chair and told us to wait. Several of his "boys" listened as Ho told us again that we had no class. Walter kept him talking and Ho opened up a bit, saying his accuser hadn't been raped, that she was a crazy publicity seeker. And it wasn't the first time he had been falsely accused, Ho said. Shortly after Ho spoke with us, *People Magazine* published a lengthy profile of the entertainer in which he readily discussed his relationships with women and alluded to rape accusations made against him. "There have always been women in Ho's life—in bizarre combinations and startling abundance," the story said. Ho joked in the story about why he enjoyed kissing grandmas after his shows: "I kiss grandmas because they're clean," he said with a twinkle. "I haven't picked anything up from a grandma yet. Besides, grandma don't yell rape; she appreciates."

Eventually, the doorway to the room darkened, and Ho popped out of the chair. I looked over, and there was Larry Mehau, a very large man in his own right. Several more even bigger men filled the hallway behind him.

"Larry!" Ho said. "These guys want to talk about that rape thing. They're from the *Advertiser*."

Mehau looked at us with a pained expression on his face. "Tell them to get out," he said to Ho.

"Yeah, you guys, get out of here," Ho said. "Get out! Get the fuck out!"[5]

I thought to myself, "Okay, that's good. We're getting the fuck out now." Even Walter the Oblivious realized it was time to go. We had to turn sideways to make it past Mehau and the men in the hallway. Once clear of them, I resisted the urge to run. But I came pretty close.

We blundered around the hallways and finally found our way outside. "God damn it, Walter," I said, "why'd you put us in a spot like that? Did you see the size of those guys? Next time, you're on your own."

"Who's Cyril Kahale?" Walter said.

Cyril Kahale Jr. worked for many years as Ho's bodyguard, bouncer, and aide-de-camp. During his shows, Ho would occasionally introduce Kahale as his "complaint department."[6] He had a lengthy arrest record but only one felony conviction, for burglary, that dated way back to 1960.

The same 2004 FBI affidavit that named Mehau as a longtime Hawai'i organized crime figure said Kahale was a pal of Mehau and of Herbert Naone Jr., a former Honolulu cop and Mehau friend who was chief of security at the state-run Aloha Stadium facility. Naone, the FBI said, held a "prominent position in Hawaii's organized crime and narcotics trafficking underworld" and "has been able to elude law enforcement action and has directly assisted others in evading arrest and prosecution."[7]

According to FBI wiretap transcripts, Naone partnered with another ex-cop, James Rodenhurst, to extort cash payoffs from Honolulu bar owners. They also engaged in a number of other illegal activities, including attempts to acquire a commercial driver's license for Kahale so that he wouldn't have to take necessary written and driving tests, according to the FBI. Kahale was never charged in that case. Naone and Rodenhurst were convicted of extortion.

Attorneys for both Naone and Rodenhurst said their clients had dedicated their lives to law enforcement. Rodenhurst's lawyer, Myles Breiner, acknowledged that his client had "made a few mistakes," but added: "We live in a culture of corruption that permeates most of our public institutions."[8]

In 1984, Kahale was indicted by a Hawai'i grand jury on a charge of participating in the kidnapping and murder of Arthur Baker, an occasional driver and office helper for Larry Mehau at Hawai'i Protective Association, Mehau's security guard company. Kahale also did occasional work for Hawai'i Protective.

The indictment was based on testimony from confessed Hawai'i mob hitman Ronald Kainalu Ching, one of the men who used to hang around Don Ho's dressing room. Baker, a drug addict and federal drug informant, was dragged out of the Sunday Lounge, a seedy nightspot on the outskirts of Waikiki, one November night in 1978 and was never seen alive again.

Ching eventually confessed to burying Baker alive in the sand dunes of a beach on the Leeward Coast of Oahu. His bones were recovered by authorities right where Ching said they'd be. But Ching recanted his accusations against Kahale, and the case against Kahale was dropped. Ching was convicted of murdering Baker.

Kahale and Mehau accused then-Honolulu Prosecuting Attorney Charles Marsland Jr. of conducting a vendetta against Mehau. They said Marsland believed Mehau was responsible for the murder of Marsland's son, Charles "Chuckers" Marsland, in 1975. The Kahale murder charge had been cooked up by Marsland to force Kahale to falsely testify against Mehau in the Chuckers murder case, the men charged.[9] Kahale filed a $35 million false arrest suit against the city, and a jury awarded him nearly $500,000 in damages, which was reduced on appeal to $400,000.

Marsland's 19-year-old son disappeared after working a shift at Infinity, a Waikiki nightclub just up the street from the Polynesian Palace. The younger Marsland was shot to death, and his body was left on a remote dirt road in the Waimanalo area of Oahu, across the Koolau mountain range from Waikiki.

Cyril Kahale Jr. and Larry Mehau, rear, flank their attorney, David Schutter, at a news conference. GREGORY YAMAMOTO, PHOTOGRAPHER; *HONOLULU STAR-ADVERTISER.*

Ching named three other men as his accomplices in the Marsland murder, including two men with ties to Don Ho—convicted felons Eric Naone and Raymond Scanlan. When Naone was questioned by police shortly after the murder, his alibi was that he had spent the night hanging out at Ho's dressing room with Ching, Mehau, and a convicted felon and city refuse worker named George Perry Jr.

Naone and Scanlan, a former Honolulu police officer, were acquitted of the Marsland murder in a dramatic state court trial. Ching was convicted.

Ching, Kahale, Naone, and Scanlan had another thing in common besides criminal histories and Don Ho's dressing room. All worked for years as Teamsters Union drivers on the sets of films and television shows shot in the Islands.

I would write many stories about the Teamsters movie drivers over the years. Some were published, but others were spiked by Platte and Managing Editor Marsha McFadden. "Readers have no interest in a story like this" was a favored Platte decree.

The spiking became so commonplace that I came up with my own name for the process: splatting. I pinned copies of spiked stories on the wall above my desk in what I called the Splatte File. At the top were the Teamsters and Larry Mehau stories. This did not improve my prospects at the newspaper.

Ho's ashes were scattered in the waves off Waikiki Beach following a daylong memorial attended by thousands of well-wishers and fans, covered in great detail by the staff of the *Honolulu Advertiser.* I was not asked to participate.

There was still no mention in any of the coverage of Ho's Frank Sinatra–like mob connections or his unusual home life. Those facets of his life were plainly secondary to Ho's accomplishments as a singer and entertainer, but they were certainly salient to an overall portrait of the man and his times. Except in the pages of the dominant newspaper in Ho's hometown.

Ho's FBI file, obtained under the Freedom of Information Act after the entertainer died, contains 40 pages of records, nearly all of them concerning Ho's dealings with Larry Mehau. All the documents appear to have been generated in the late 1970s and early 1980s, and most were heavily redacted to remove the names or other identifying information concerning individuals other than Ho. But it's a simple matter to fill in the blanks concerning Mehau.

One memo was written after the interview of an unnamed entertainment industry figure who talked about a man identified as a "close associate" of Ho, who "appears to have total control over the entertainment industry in Honolulu and has strong influence with Gov. George Ariyoshi."[10]

Mehau was a close friend of Ariyoshi's and organized entertainment at the governor's fund-raisers. He also arranged for top entertainers to perform at the annual opening day ceremonies of the state legislature.

The FBI informant was concerned about his safety and spoke about another individual who had discussed Mehau with an HPD official. "This information was leaked to someone outside of HPD," the memo said. The informant said he was willing to cooperate but was "well aware of what may happen if ever it were to become known that he is cooperating with the FBI," according to the memo. The only records in Ho's FOIA file that weren't at least partially redacted were copies of newspaper stories about Mehau, including two written by me.

Don Ho died just two days after the death of former prosecutor Marsland, whose son had been executed gangland-style by at least one of Ho's hangers-on. Marsland's death merited a story obituary in the *Advertiser,* which I helped to write. But the newspaper did not see fit to cover the funeral of Marsland, a man whose fervid pursuit of organized crime in Hawai'i and perfervid criticisms of judges and law enforcement agencies made tall headlines for decades.

Honolulu Prosecuting
Attorney Charles
Marsland Jr. ROY ITO,
PHOTOGRAPHER;
*HONOLULU STAR-
ADVERTISER* COLLECTION;
HAWAI'I STATE ARCHIVES.

Those two deaths, and the morning newspaper's treatment of them, were emblematic of how journalism in Hawai'i had changed during my three decades as an investigative reporter in the Islands.

The work was great while it lasted, taking me from the depths of the underworld in Hawai'i and Japan to top-floor corporate suites and judges' chambers. Stories I wrote led to prison terms for quite a few men and landed the colorful and combative mayor of Honolulu in court on bribery charges.

I found secret land partnerships called *huis* whose investors included politicians, criminals, business leaders, and judges.

I found contracting cronyism at all levels of government and pried open the financial and political secrets of an astounding $6 billion educational charity known as the Bishop Estate.

I interviewed the craftiest and clumsiest of con men. I found prison guards who changed uniforms on Friday nights and spent their weekends locked behind bars.

Things changed radically when Gannett Company, Inc., the nation's largest newspaper chain, bought the *Advertiser* in 1993 from local ownership.

Outside editors who knew nothing about Hawai'i, its people, and its history were brought from the Mainland to imprint the Gannett version of the news business on the *Advertiser.*

As I was writing stories in 1995 and 1996 detailing financial shenanigans committed by the trustees of the mighty Bishop Estate, I was told to stop writing about the estate. An assistant city editor told me that the publisher didn't like them.

At that point, I began thinking about another job in journalism and found one in television news at KITV, the local ABC affiliate.

In 1997, not long after I was gone, the *Advertiser* balked at publishing a lengthy essay on problems inside the Bishop Estate that was written by five prominent local residents, including a senior U.S. District Court judge. Called "Broken Trust," the essay drew heavily from some of my earlier stories and was ultimately published by the *Advertiser*'s competitor, the *Honolulu Star-Bulletin.*[11]

Broken Trust ignited a volcanic controversy that engulfed the estate and its five trustees. Investigations conducted by the state attorney general and the Internal Revenue Service forced out the trustees and imposed wholesale changes on one of the richest charitable institutions in the world.

Among the departed trustees were the former president of the state senate and the former speaker of the state house of representatives. The trustees, who were collecting nearly $1 million apiece annually from the estate, were appointed by the five members of the Hawai'i Supreme Court.

In 1989, the Broken Trust authors reported, two Supreme Court justices voted to appoint Larry Mehau to the Bishop Estate millionaires' club, but a third and decisive vote couldn't be found for Mehau.[12]

That was the Bishop Estate and that was Hawai'i.

I worked as an investigative reporter in television for five years but was eventually recruited back to print by a new team of editors at the *Advertiser.* Everyone involved learned to regret it.

Investigative reporting in the 50th state, particularly long-form newspaper projects, was like working in a journalism hothouse, a news laboratory where all the stories seemed to be part of an organic whole. The stories stood on their own, but like stands of bamboo, there was a dense root system underneath that stretched over time and distance, producing new shoots in surprising places.

It was a fantastic job. I'm sorry it's over.

CHAPTER TWO

Kukui Plaza

A Greek bearing gifts called me in 1976.

His name was Stamatios Mertyris—Mike the Greek to his friends—and he had been working as a waterproofing subcontractor on a Honolulu housing redevelopment project called Kukui Plaza.

The Greek and two employees of the Kukui Plaza development company, Oceanside Properties, Inc., shared information with me that ultimately led to state bribery charges against Mayor Frank F. Fasi and sent Oceanside president Hal Hansen to federal prison for fraud.

I nearly dismissed Mertyris as a crackpot after his first call. He wouldn't tell me his name, and he had a strange accent I couldn't place. He wouldn't specify any of the dark secrets he claimed to know about city government.

But it was early 1976. Watergate was still echoing through the land. I was young and eager, new to the city hall beat. I had been a reporter as long as I'd lived in Honolulu—about three years. I would play Woodstein to my Deep Throat caller, at least for a little while.

When Mertyris first called, I had never heard of Kukui Plaza. Fresh out of college, I arrived in Honolulu in 1973 and worked eight months as a wire service drudge with United Press International (UPI) before landing a job as a general assignment reporter at the *Advertiser* in mid-1974.

I had a degree in English literature from the University of California at Davis, a former agricultural college outside Sacramento that back then was still mostly surrounded by tomato fields.

I had no formal training in journalism, just summer jobs and school newspapers. But my father, Edmund, was an accomplished newspaperman.

He was managing editor of the *San Francisco Examiner* and the *Denver Post* before that. My sister Nancy was a reporter, too, first for *Newsweek* in New York and later for the *Examiner.* I figured it must be in the blood. UPI in San Francisco said I could work four days a week in Honolulu if I would pay my way out there. It was the only offer I had, and it was Hawai'i. I could stay for a year or two, rack up some experience, learn to surf, meet some *wahines,* and maybe work out an assignment in Asia. What did I know?

Print journalism even then was a dying business. Just a few years before I arrived in the Islands, Congress had enacted the Newspaper Preservation Act, intended to stem the alarming rate of closures and consolidations that were occurring in metropolitan areas around the country.

The act allowed competing publications to combine under joint operating agreements (JOAs) that merged certain aspects of their individual operations—advertising sales, printing facilities, and deliveries—but still allowed the papers to employ separate editorial staffs that produced independent and competing publications. The federal law waived antitrust prohibitions that would otherwise have blocked such mergers.

When I arrived in Honolulu, a JOA between the *Advertiser* and *Star-Bulletin* was in full force. Like many other afternoon newspapers, the *Star-Bulletin* had fallen on hard times as customers arriving home from work increasingly cancelled subscriptions because they could get their evening news free of charge from the television.

Similar JOAs were fashioned around the country. My father and sister worked at one that combined the San Francisco *Examiner* and *Chronicle.* The *Examiner* itself was the survivor of a series of earlier mergers that had seen the amalgamation and eventual disappearance of at least five other newspapers: the *San Francisco Call, Evening Post, Bulletin, News,* and *News-Call Bulletin.*

In Honolulu, the staffs of the two major papers each occupied half of the second floor of the stately old news building at the base of Kapiolani Boulevard, within easy walking distance of the state capitol, city hall, and the downtown business district.

The first floor was devoted to sales staff who sold advertising for both papers. On the third floor were the publishers and executive staffs. I found that the UPI bureau was a windowless, closetlike space accessed by a set of stairs in the middle of the *Advertiser* city room. It was filled with clattering teletype machines and had cramped working spaces for a reporter and the bureau chief. The job was nothing like I imagined it might be. My principal duty was to rewrite newspaper stories into wire service copy for UPI's radio station clients: 5 a.m. to 1 p.m., boiling down story after story into one or two paragraphs each, updating police blotter items and weather reports.

I was instructed to change the newspaper verbs from past to present tense whenever possible, making the stories sound more immediate to radio listeners. "A 29-year-old man is in fair condition this morning following a single-car freeway accident last night"—that sort of thing.

I did learn to type fast under pressure. I learned to wheedle basic information out of Honolulu police over the phone. And I found that asking ignorant questions is an occupational imperative.

By that time, UPI had begun its long, agonizing slide into oblivion. In 1974, employees of the company went on a nationwide strike. A similar strike earlier by Associated Press workers had shut down the news building in Honolulu, so UPI's tenancy agreement there required the bureau to move out of the news building in the event of a work stoppage. My two "Unipresser" colleagues and I found ourselves walking a picket line a half mile away from the news building outside an electrical supply firm, Territorial Electronics, where the UPI chief had set up shop. Because there were only three reporters in the bureau, we had to walk solo picket shifts, marching for a cause that had no apparent connection to Territorial Electronics. It was pathetic. The strike lasted, as I recall, several weeks, until the union totally capitulated and we returned to work, minus a lot of dignity and some desperately needed income.

In mid-1974, UPI phased out my job and offered me a transfer to Buffalo, New York. I declined with alarm and managed to hire on at the *Advertiser* as an entry-level reporter, paid $14,000 per year. I figured I would give it a year or so and then head back to California. What did I know?

My first bylined story was a timeless prose picture of a circus parade. I worked general assignment, wrote obituaries, and filled in on the police beat during my first several months. The cops, I found, were only slightly more accommodating in person than they were on the phone, and the pidgin they spoke frequently baffled me.

I had no idea, for instance, that when a sergeant said what sounded like "Da bolo head bugga wen' mawkay," he was actually telling me, "The bald guy died." (Make—pronounced MAW-kay—means dead in pidgin. Putting went (wen') in front of it turns the verb to past tense.)

It took me way too long to figure out that the "sippadee" charge police frequently spoke of was actually criminal property damage, or cpd for short.

When veteran *Advertiser* political reporter Douglas Boswell jumped to the competing afternoon newspaper in late 1974, shortly before the annual start of the Hawai'i legislature, I was sent to the *Advertiser*'s government bureau to help out. The office was in the basement of the state Capitol. I had never set foot in the building before.

When city hall reporter Douglas Carlson jumped to television news in 1975, I was told to watch city hall while more permanent arrangements were made.

Not too long after that, the Greek called, asking to speak to the city hall reporter. I tried to hide my ignorance and inexperience from him, but he told me later that he had me figured for shallow right away. The only reason he talked to me, he said, was that he couldn't get anyone else to listen. The only reason I listened was that I didn't know any better.

Les Whitten, a very fine reporter and legman for Washington, D.C., columnist and muckraker Jack Anderson, once advised me and other young reporters to *always* hear what tipsters had to say. He told a story about the time he and Anderson were visited in their D.C. office by a disheveled man who had a length of tinfoil tied to the back of his belt. "Like a tail," Whitten said.

He and Anderson looked dubiously at each other but heard the man out. He explained that he knew damaging secrets about a sitting U.S. senator, divulging some convincing details in the process. When asked to explain the tinfoil, the tipster explained that he had first shared his information with the FBI, but agents told him he should talk to Jack Anderson. They said he needed to be "grounded" first, so they attached the tinfoil tail to his belt and gave him directions to Anderson's office.

The man's information turned out to be golden and led to a great series of stories about the senator's tangled personal finances, Whitten said.

So I listened to Mertyris. He was reluctant to detail the nasty secrets he claimed to know. He and the friends he represented were frightened, suspicious, and maddeningly elliptical. They were prone to melodrama and manipulation.

I soothed and reassured, coaxed and cajoled. I sought names and dates and developed an omnivorous appetite for paperwork that plagues me to this day.

Some of the hoops they jumped me through were preposterous, culled from cheap spy fiction. They would leave documents for me in hard-to-find places. "On the front seat of the brown Datsun parked under the banyan tree behind the state Capitol" was one such instruction.

"Listen," I answered. "It's pouring rain outside. Why don't you just come to my office? I'm alone here for a couple of hours."

"Too risky" was the reply.

So out I went to find the brown Datsun. The banyan tree in question covered at least an acre of property, and there were two brown Datsuns in the large parking lot beneath it. Both cars had papers on the front seat, and both were unlocked.

Which one? I had no way to call the Greek to inquire. I looked around, but no one else was out in the downpour. If I picked the wrong car, at least the driver wouldn't be around to protest. I picked the closest car and found what I was looking for.

The gist of the allegations was that Oceanside Properties president Hal Hansen was being squeezed for favors and political support by Fasi and his chief fund-raiser, Harry C. C. Chung.

In return, Hansen had demanded and received a three-year extension of control of the public parking concession at Kukui Plaza, an arrangement that should have been approved by the city council but was not. There were 900 public stalls at the project, and the extension meant that as much as $1.2 million in revenue had been diverted from the taxpayers to a private company.

Armed with the basic allegations and guided by government bureau veterans Gerry Keir and Jerry Burris, I began some discreet checking at city hall.

I had to be careful in my nosing around. Relations between Frank Fasi and reporters were never warm. When I took over the beat, a partial cease-fire was in effect: occasional border clashes but no open hostilities. During this period, I covered a speech by Fasi in which he pointed me out to the assembled Rotarians, identifying me as the representative of a worthless rag of a morning newspaper. I dutifully scribbled notes while the crowd looked me over.

Fasi's press secretary, Jim Loomis, advised me after the speech not to take it personally. "Actually, Frank likes you," Loomis said.

A few questions around city hall told me that the city council knew nothing about the parking stalls deal. Then I went to the Department of Housing and Community Development, the city agency responsible for oversight of Kukui Plaza, and sought access to the project files.

After some skirmishing with bureaucrats—I tried to blunt their questions with bland explanations—I was shown the files. And there, right near the top, was the parking stalls agreement. Finding the document where it was supposed to be, and saying what it was supposed to say, was a cosmic event for me. It satisfied serious misgivings I had about Mertyris and company. It meant I had what looked like a very good story in hand. And there was something about finding the paperwork and laying my hands on it that was deeply satisfying. A ratchet turned, and parts of my life fell into place.

Other paperwork in the file told me more about the origins of the deal and discussions between the administration and Oceanside about it. I sought and received copies of the agreement and other documents. From there, it was simply a matter of questioning responsible officials about the implications of the deal and writing the story.

Honolulu Mayor
Frank F. Fasi. ALLAN
MILLER, PHOTOGRAPHER;
*HONOLULU STAR-
ADVERTISER* COLLECTION;
HAWAI'I STATE ARCHIVES.

I lived in dread during that period that another reporter would stumble on the story before I got it in print, or that the mayor would deliver a pre-emptive speech about it. That didn't happen, though. My first story about Kukui Plaza and its troubled history was published in March 1976.[1]

The story was not a major sensation when it appeared, but it did make some waves at city hall. None of my competitors rushed to match it, however. The afternoon *Star-Bulletin* eventually published a knockdown story, quoting city and Oceanside officials who pooh-poohed the *Advertiser* report. None of the three television stations or the news radio station covered it.

This was standard fare in a competitive news market. If you didn't have a story, better to ignore it or knock it down, if at all possible. If you can't do that and the story is too good to ignore, then match it. Only under the most grievously compelling circumstances would a reporter write, and an editor sanction, a story that quoted and credited a competitor.

This worked to my advantage. The lack of response irritated Mertyris and his two friends, who I finally learned were Oceanside vice president Joseph Zbin and Oceanside employee Eleanor Shinno.

That was when they sent me to the Datsun under the banyan. On the front seat, I found a bill for legal services submitted to Oceanside by Paul Devens, the recently resigned number-two man in the Fasi administration. The invoice showed that Devens' law firm wanted $65,000 for helping Oceanside finalize its parking stall deal with the Fasi administration. We printed a copy of the invoice with the next story, and the Kukui Plaza fun-house ride was underway.[2]

I found that Fasi fund-raiser Harry Chung's home furnishings company had received the no-bid contract to supply all the carpeting at Kukui Plaza, a massive, twin-towered condominium project that combined market-priced units with price-controlled units for low- to moderate-income buyers. Another Chung company was given a concession to supply coin-operated clothes washers and dryers at Kukui Plaza.

The low- and moderate-income units in the development were supposed to be set aside first for residents of the area who had been displaced by the construction project, but city record-keeping was so shoddy that many of the individuals on that list couldn't be located.

Then the same units were to be made available to qualified buyers via a lottery drawing, but many of the apartments were instead sold to an insider list of buyers who had political and personal connections at city hall.

One of the units went to the secretary of Ralph Aoki, head of the city's urban redevelopment agency. When Aoki was called before the city council to testify on the issue, he was asked if it was equitable that his secretary was given the inside track on a Kukui Plaza unit.

"Sometimes in our system, the people who have the right kind of friends, they get what you might call equity," Aoki answered.[3]

Years later, I wrote a series of stories that found Aoki pursuing his personal version of equity when working as a federal bankruptcy court trustee. Aoki was convicted of fraud and sent to federal prison.

In the early stages of the Kukui Plaza scandal, my sources kept telling me that Harry Chung's son had received the contract to write insurance coverage for the project, but they had no paperwork to back up the charge.

I spent long hours chasing that down but kept hitting walls. Neither Chung nor his son would talk. The city files had no paperwork on the subject. But I finally noticed that fine print in the development contract specified that copies of insurance policies had to be filed with the city. I demanded to see the required public records, and they were finally retrieved from Oceanside. Chung's son Gary was the agent. The cosmic ratchet clicked again.[4]

The Honolulu City Council decided to take the unprecedented step of conducting its own investigation of Kukui Plaza. They hired a private law

Kukui Plaza development at the corner of Beretania Street and Nuuanu Avenue in Honolulu. *HONOLULU STAR-ADVERTISER.*

firm, equipped it with subpoena powers, and then held a series of public hearings on the subject.

This occurred after the mayor directed his newly appointed prosecuting attorney, Maurice Sapienza, to conduct a criminal investigation of the case.

Mertyris and friends insisted to me that Sapienza, after arriving in Honolulu from the Mainland, had lived rent-free for several months at another Oceanside Properties development. Sapienza wouldn't talk to me when I called him about it. Oceanside said officially it knew nothing about it.

Finally, in checking records of Fasi's political campaign organization, I found that Sapienza had donated money and listed the Oceanside apartment as his residence.

Armed with that information, I called Sapienza again. When he took the call, he was eating an apple. A big, juicy one, by the sound of it. I told him I'd found the campaign records listing his residence at an Oceanside project. Sapienza chomped on the apple for a few seconds and mentally chewed over the implications of the campaign records. I waited patiently for a response.

"Well," he eventually said, still chewing away, "I guess you've got me." He went on to say that he thought Harry Chung actually owned the apartment because Chung made the arrangements for Sapienza to stay there.[5]

I always had a soft spot for Maury Sapienza after that. He would shuck you for as long as he could, but at a certain point, if he had to, he would level with you. If he happened to be eating an apple at the time, well, hell, he'd talk to you with his mouth full. I certainly didn't care. In fact, I liked and appreciated him for it.

After the city council finished its look at Kukui Plaza, the state attorney general's office stepped into the act. They brought in a Los Angeles attorney, Grant Cooper, to head a new investigation that eventually indicted Fasi and Chung on bribery charges. The chief prosecution witness was to be Hal Hansen.

At the time, Fasi was mounting another campaign to be elected governor, running against incumbent George Ariyoshi, the attorney general's boss. That dropped a heavy political overlay on the court proceedings. Fasi, a consummate politician, made hay with it, scoffing at Ariyoshi and his "hired gunslinger" Grant Cooper.

At the same time, Hal Hansen had been indicted by the federal government on fraud charges, and serious friction developed between the federal and state prosecutors. Hansen wanted an immunity deal with the feds if he was to testify in the state case. The feds wouldn't play ball.

Hansen eventually refused to testify when the state case went to trial, even after he was locked in prison during the Christmas holidays for contempt of court. The state was forced to drop the charges.

Kukui Plaza lasted two years. The final legal installment was written when Hansen was packed off to a federal penitentiary for fraud.

Fasi ran and narrowly lost to George Ariyoshi in the 1978 gubernatorial Democratic primary election; he blamed his defeat on the Kukui Plaza case. He later lost three more tries for the governor's office.

The Kukui Plaza years were a maelstrom of investigations, charges and countercharges, speechifying and court proceedings. I learned a great deal during this period about people, politics, journalism, lawyers, and life. For my craft, I learned the indispensable value of documentary research and how to go about it. And I learned that documents mean little without people to explain, or explain away, their contents. I learned that courts are imperfect places to find the truth, and political chambers even less so.

And I learned that investigative reporting is tedious, glorious, and a hell of a lot of fun.

CHAPTER THREE

Organized Crime

An unusual group of "security guards" was hired to protect cooperating witnesses in the city council's Kukui Plaza investigation. Where the chairman of the investigating committee, Councilman Kekoa Kaapu, found the guards, or exactly why their employment was necessary, was never made clear.

What was clear, though, was that some of the guards were downright menacing.

Several had past and future connections to Honolulu's underworld. One, a man with the unlikely name of Francis Scott Key, was later murdered in prison. Another, Richard "Chico" Avilla, had his nickname tattooed prison-style across the backs of his fingers. He later served time for narcotics trafficking. A third, Sherwin "Sharkey" Fellezs, had previously worked as an informal investment counselor to one-time Hawai'i organized crime boss Wilford "Nappy" Pulawa and testified as a prosecution witness when Pulawa was convicted of federal tax crimes.

In an encounter with Fellezs one evening at city hall, we shook hands, and he pressed a fat little joint of "pakalolo" (the pidgin term for marijuana) into my hand. I didn't want to offend him by giving it back, so I held onto it. It was just his way of saying hello, I figured. What did I know?

I changed my mind about that after Fellezs called me several days later.

"You know, when I wen' see you da odda night, was Tuesday, yeah?" he said.

"No," I said, "it was Wednesday."

"No, brah, was Tuesday. You rememba?"

"I remember. It was Wednesday."

20

"You shua?"

"Positive."

"Cuz, some guys like know whea I was Tuesday. I tot I was witchu."

"Not me," I said, getting the message that he wanted me to alibi him. "I saw you Wednesday."

"Oh, okay. Catch you layta."

I didn't know what he was doing Tuesday night, but I was glad I wasn't there. Later, though, I decided that he probably wasn't doing anything at all that night but was just sizing me up. First, I hadn't said anything when he passed me pakalolo. Then he sounded out my willingness to tell a lie for him. I'm not sure if I failed the test or passed it, but he never tried to slip me weed after that.

We stayed on friendly terms, however. Fellezs later helped me out on several stories, including one about his days as a protected witness in the Pulawa case. He and other witnesses had been housed in a building at the Makapu'u Light House, built on a remote headland hundreds of feet above the Pacific Ocean on Oahu's southern shoreline. Protected by U.S. Marshals, the witnesses were ferried by helicopter to and from the courthouse.

Francis Scott Key, Chico Avilla, Sharkey Fellezs, Nappy Pulawa . . . just the names alone made good copy.

When Kukui Plaza finally wound down, I had developed a taste for investigative journalism and thought it was time for a move.

I was still nominally assigned to the city hall beat, but the atmosphere there was a bit tense. During a break in the bribery trial, when I was standing outside the courtroom on what is now the second floor of the supreme court building, Fasi came out of court, saw me, and quickly walked up. My back was against a balustrade that circled the central rotunda, and I braced myself when the mayor advanced on me so quickly.

He didn't say anything, but the expression on his face, and the look in his eyes, made me think that he really wanted to push me over that railing. When I flinched defensively, he smiled, shook his head, and walked away.

Also during the trial, my colleague Gerald Kato and I went to the office of mayoral spokesman Jim Loomis, seeking follow-up reaction to a story we had run that morning.

Loomis hadn't wanted to say much the day before, when special prosecutor Grant Cooper accused Loomis in court of perjuring himself during earlier testimony before the city council.[1] (No charge was ever filed against Loomis.)

When Kato and I walked into Loomis' office, we found him literally speechless with anger. He had a copy of the newspaper on his desk, and he grabbed it, jumped up, and began waving it at us, shouting incoherently.

Then he threw the paper on the floor and kicked it into a corner. Gerry and I watched as Loomis yelled imprecations and stomped the newspaper. We took it as another "no comment" and made ourselves scarce.

So I thought the timing might be right for a move to another beat. The switch to investigative reporting was complicated because the *Advertiser* had only recently hired Walter Wright from the *Seattle Post Intelligencer* to do full-time investigative work. But when I asked for the chance to try it myself, Editor George Chaplin, Managing Editor Buck Buchwach, and City Editor Gerry Keir agreed on a trial basis. The decision would give all of us occasional heartburn in subsequent years. Investigative reporting is by its nature aggressive. Editors are cautious creatures. The mixture makes everybody bilious at one time or another.

But my overall experience with editors when the *Advertiser* was locally owned was that, even when a story troubled them, they wanted to find a way to fix it and get it in the paper. Too often in later years, editors looked for reasons to keep stories out of the paper.

I wanted to take a look at organized crime in Hawai'i. Kukui Plaza had given me a glimpse of criminals and the criminal justice system, and it was fascinating.

The *Advertiser* had a rich tradition of crime reporting, thanks primarily to Gene Hunter, an associate editor of the paper who was in failing health by the time I was hired. Hunter had come within a whisker of winning a Pulitzer Prize in the early 1970s for his detailed and colorful coverage of Hawai'i's often violent underworld. I pored over the stories Hunter and his contemporaries had authored about Hawai'i's criminals and soon found myself writing about some of the same men and a central theme of much of their work: gambling.

Illegal gambling has always been a linchpin of Hawai'i organized crime and is likely to remain so for the foreseeable future.

Here's the lead from a story I wrote two decades ago about the local syndicate: "The recipe for organized crime in Hawaii has been a simple one, first written in the 1960's: Take gambling revenue and mix it with liberal amounts of bloodshed. The recipe has been seasoned along the way with other traditional ingredients of organized crime activity—narcotics trafficking, prostitution and pornography, labor racketeering—but gambling has always been the traditional mainstay."[2]

The Hawai'i Crime Commission in 1978 pegged the beginning of organized crime in the state to the early 1960s, when "a group of thugs, known as the Pakes [pronounced paw-KAYS] or Orientals, led by Yobo Chung, began to extort professional gamblers on Oahu who sponsored gambling events."[3]

"Organized criminals rely on terroristic threatening and violence to establish monopolistic gambling territories for themselves, or to prey on smaller gamblers for protection money," the commission reported.[4]

Once in control of gambling, the report said, organized criminals extended their reach into other criminal endeavors, such as narcotics trafficking.[5]

Hawai'i is one of two states in the union without any form of legalized gambling. (Utah is the other.) Every year bills are introduced at the state legislature to approve some form of gaming. They fizzle every year.

Just a few years ago, when I was working for the online news publication *Hawai'i Reporter*, I wrote a story about last-minute, backroom legislative maneuvering for passage of a bill allowing casino gambling in Hawai'i.

A bill that had nothing to do with gambling had been gutted and replaced with pro-gaming language. But the measure was short-lived.

"Like Frankenstein, the bill-with-a-new-brain lived only briefly," I wrote.

"Senate Bill 1247 proposed creation of a gambling casino in Waikiki. It died today but one of its backers, lobbyist John Radcliffe, said it is sure to rise again."[6]

Radcliffe later told me, à la Gene Wilder, to refer to him in the future as "Fronkenshteen."

He has reanimated the creature annually for decades, and I am confident he will continue to do so.   :

Lacking legal outlets for their love of wagering, planeloads of local gamblers regularly jet off to Las Vegas, where they are valued customers at casinos like the California Hotel, which makes sure that food favorites from Hawai'i like Spam *musubi* and boiled peanuts are on the restaurant menus.

The appetite for gambling is so strong in the Islands that underground casinos, chicken fights, and sports books are always in operation.

To a certain extent, the attitude of local law enforcement and lawmakers toward illegal gambling has been rather laissez faire—the allure of illicit gaming is durable and recognized as an essentially ineradicable activity that is legal elsewhere in the country. And professional gamblers—the people who make a living at it by operating games, paying protection, collecting debts, and washing money—are a very valuable and reliable source of intelligence to law enforcement about more serious felonies like drug trafficking that flourish in the shadows of illegal gambling.

As waves of immigrants arrived in Hawai'i from Asia and the Pacific region, they commonly brought with them more relaxed attitudes toward gambling. Japanese, Chinese, Korean, Filipino, and Samoan immigrants have successively moved into positions of authority in the local underworld through gambling activities.

In the late 1960s, things got out of hand in the gambling dens of Hawai'i.

The local underworld, as Hunter and others described it, had been controlled following statehood in 1959 by a succession of men—George "Yobo" Chung, John Sayin "Seni" Kim, Alema Leota, and Wilford "Nappy" Pulawa—whose authority rested on control and exploitation of gambling.

Honolulu witnessed an alarming increase in violent incidents associated with turf wars over control of gambling and, to a lesser extent, other vices. There were murders, spectacular car bombings, beatings, and kidnappings.

Yobo Chung, identified by Hunter and others, including the Hawai'i Crime Commission, as the first true head of local organized crime, was shot to death in 1967 at a gambling game he operated on Maunakea Street in Chinatown.

The murder, which was never solved, occurred shortly after a powerful bomb had mangled the legs of Seni Kim and destroyed the brand new Cadillac Kim was driving on a Chinatown street. Kim recovered and began a short-lived reign as boss before voluntary retirement.

Numerous other bombings, shootings, and violent incidents followed in succeeding years as warring underworld factions struggled for control of gambling and related crime.

In 1971, federal authorities combined with Hawai'i law enforcement to try to crack down on illegal gambling in the Islands. The campaign, which involved dozens of police officers, federal investigators, undercover agents, prosecutors, and court personnel, resulted in an indictment of seven men on charges of violating newly enacted federal laws covering large-scale gambling operations.

The case centered on a gambling casino operated in Club International, a Chinatown nightspot run by career criminal Walter W. C. "Hotcha" Hong, who had a record of more than 60 gambling arrests. Three years after Hong and the others were indicted, the case had fallen to pieces. Hunter reported that one prosecution witness refused to testify, saying he "didn't want to spend the rest of his life on crutches."[7]

Hong pleaded guilty to a misdemeanor charge and was fined $50. Another defendant, Benjamin "Benny" Madamba, was acquitted outright. A third, Joseph "Chocolate Joe" Kang, was murdered while the case was pending. The remaining defendants paid fines totaling $90.

Official statements made at the outset of the case that it was a blow to organized crime were never validated in court. A law enforcement official told Gene Hunter in the aftermath of the trial, "What we know to be true because of our intelligence system can't always be substantiated in court."[8]

I studied Hunter's archived stories of past crimes and criminal trials, annotating them like a graduate student. I started making more contacts inside and outside law enforcement and became a regular visitor to the basement of the supreme court building, where old trial records were stored. In those days, security in the file room was virtually nonexistent, and visitors had the run of the stacks, free to choose whatever files struck their fancy. It was Aladdin's cave to me.

The building, on King Street just a 10-minute walk from the News Building, is a Honolulu landmark and features a large statue of King Kamehameha outside the front entrance.

In 1977, one of my newfound law enforcement sources tipped me to a big story on the Big Island. Organized crime figure Benny Madamba—the defendant who was acquitted in the Club International case—had disappeared from a Hilo bar several weeks earlier. A body believed to be Madamba's had been found in a sugarcane field. Two other sources, one a criminal and the other a Big Island bail bondsman, confirmed to me that the body was Madamba's, and I was able to piece together a detailed story of the murder, tying it to a turf dispute between syndicate factions led by former Nappy Pulawa lieutenants Alvin Kaohu and Henry Huihui. The story ran before an autopsy formally confirmed the identity of the victim.

Four men—Kenneth Lendt, Henderson Ahlo, James Palama, and James Kealohapauole—were subsequently charged with the murder. Prosecutors and police said Madamba was killed after he switched allegiance from Kaohu to Huihui. I had met Lendt several months earlier. He had been introduced to me in a bar by one of the people I met while covering Kukui Plaza.

When the case went to trial in Hilo, I was assigned to cover the first week of testimony because our Big Island reporter, Hugh Clark, was tied up with other matters. Lendt became a prosecution witness, testifying that he helped murder Madamba on the orders of Kaohu. Lendt owed Kaohu $600, and the debt was forgiven after Madamba was murdered, Lendt testified. He admitted stabbing Madamba but said that happened only after Ahlo had caved in the victim's head with a rock.

Ahlo, known as "Henny Boy," was so strong that he could "tear quarters in half," Lendt told the jury. During breaks in the trial, assembled reporters asked Ahlo if it was true about the quarters. He said it was. When we gave him a quarter and asked him to prove it, he did. Several times. Ahlo didn't actually tear the coins in two. He bent them in half with his bare hands, back and forth, until they fractured. It was very impressive.

Ahlo and the others were convicted and sent away for long prison stretches. Kaohu was convicted of manslaughter.

More than 20 years after the trial, after I had moved to television reporting, KITV news anchorman Howard Dashefsky told me one day that he
had met a guy in a bar the night before who tore quarters in half with his
bare hands. Dashefsky hadn't caught the guy's name, but when I checked
with the parole board, I found that Ahlo had been released from prison.
Henny Boy was out and about.

Several years after that, I found myself writing more stories about
Henderson Ahlo, the Honolulu Police Department, and Larry Mehau.

When the Madamba murder trial ended, I helped to cover another
high-profile homicide case, this one in state court in Honolulu. Nappy Pul-
awa, Henry Huihui, Alvin Kaohu, and another alleged syndicate lieutenant,
Robert "Bobby" Wilson, were in court on charges of murdering two men,
Lamont "Monte" Nery and Dennis "Fuzzy" Iha, in 1971 over control of Las
Vegas gambling junket revenue.

A deputy prosecutor on the case was Charles Marsland Jr., who in later
years was elected Honolulu prosecuting attorney. Marsland had been a
deputy corporation counsel for the city, handling civil court matters, but
moved to criminal prosecutions after his son "Chuckers" was murdered
in 1975.

The murder turned Chuck Marsland into a crusader against organized
crime with a personality that combined John the Baptist with Eliot Ness. If
you didn't agree with him, you were likely a fool or corrupt and probably
both. He would tell that to your face in profane and very personal terms.

At one time when Marsland was on particularly bad terms with *Advertiser* editors, I was asked to arrange a meeting between him and personnel
of the editorial page, including the dignified and professorial John Griffin.
It didn't take long before Marsland was verbally attacking and insulting
the astonished Griffin, calling him a "flapping twat" before stomping out
of the meeting.

Marsland once got into a fistfight in the hallway outside his office with
a colorfully named local criminal, Penrod Fanene. Fanene (whose friends
called him Tommy) was angry because Marsland had called Fanene's
uncle, former syndicate boss Alema Leota, "total scum" in a speech to the
Chinatown Chamber of Commerce the previous day. (Penrod Fanene, by
the way, is one of my all-time favorite local names. Heidi Ho is still at the
top of the list. Sterling Silva is way up there.)

The Nery-Iha murder case was a reprise of a 1974 state court proceeding
that had ended in a mistrial. During the first trial, the main prosecution
witness, former Pulawa lieutenant Roy Roosevelt Ryder, was given immunity from prosecution and testified that Nery and Iha were killed in retaliation for the 1970 slaying of Las Vegas gambling junket operator Harry

Otake. Marsland and other prosecutors charged that Otake had been paying "appreciation" money to Pulawa—part of the $800,000 haul that Pulawa's gang collected from gambling operators, bookmakers, and others from 1969 to 1971.

In the first trial, Ryder implicated Pulawa and the other defendants in the Nery-Iha murders, but he told a radically different story the second time around. Like Hal Hansen in the Kukui Plaza bribery trial, Ryder turned out to be a truly terrible witness for the prosecution. Instead of implicating Pulawa and the other defendants, Ryder said nothing about them but claimed to have slain Nery and Iha with another underworld character, George "Fat George" Arashiro. Arashiro was no longer alive to confirm or deny. His girlfriend had shot him to death in 1972.

It wasn't the first time Ryder had assigned posthumous blame to Arashiro for a notorious underworld slaying. In Pulawa's 1974 federal tax trial, Ryder testified (under immunity) that he arranged to have Arashiro and another man, Paul Kea Lono, shoot Pulawa competitor Francis Burke to death in the middle of an October 1970 day in the Chinatown district of Honolulu.

Burke reportedly had close ties to Mainland mafia figures and had served prison time for narcotics offenses. He was shot in the head and died in the gutter of Maunakea Street near a gambling den he reportedly controlled. The killer fled the scene so quickly that he ran right out of his rubber slippers. A $5 bill was clutched in Burke's hand when police covered his body from the view of passing pedestrians.

Arashiro and Lono were tried but acquitted of the Burke murder in 1971—before Ryder had turned state's evidence.

The 1978 Nery-Iha murder trial reprise was Ryder's last stand as a government witness. In fact, city prosecutors desperately tried but failed to revoke his immunity deal before he took the witness stand. With complete aplomb, Ryder told the jury in detail how he and Arashiro kidnapped Nery and Iha at gunpoint and took them to a lonely stretch of beach near the end of Farrington Highway on Oahu's North Shore. The victims were stripped naked and forced to kneel in a grave dug about 10 yards from the shoreline before each was shot in the head. Ryder expressed admiration for Nery, who submitted quietly to his execution. Ryder used a pidgin word for a local male, "blalah," in testifying about Nery's dignity.

"Those kine blalahs, they go straight like that. Everybody else screams," Ryder said. Iha tried to escape and was felled with a shovel before he was shot, Ryder said. The bodies were coated with a mixture of lime and seawater before they were covered with sand. The skeletons were exhumed after Ryder led police to the gravesite.

During the retrial, Pulawa refused to stand for the judge or jury because he said that, as a Native Hawaiian, he was not subject to the laws or jurisdiction of state and federal courts. Pulawa had already been convicted in the federal tax case and was transported in chains from federal prison to face the state murder charges. Based on Ryder's new version of events, Pulawa and his codefendants were acquitted, and he returned to federal prison. Ryder was never charged with perjury because he testified under immunity in both the 1974 and 1978 trials, and there were no other witnesses available to refute his version of events.

Covering the two murder trials, as well as Kukui Plaza before that, had helped me begin to develop a network of sources and contacts in and out of law enforcement. Those connections began to pay off after the Nery-Iha case imploded. I began to hear rumblings about the kidnapping and murder of an underworld character named Arthur Baker.

I located family members and friends of Baker and began piecing together a story about who he was and what had happened to him.

Baker was a drug user with a criminal record of two felony firearms convictions. He had served time at a federal prison in California and was awaiting sentencing for the second conviction when he disappeared.

He was a casual employee at a sleazy hostess lounge on the outskirts of Waikiki called the Sunday Lounge when two or three burly men entered the bar about 11 p.m. on the night of November 12, 1978. They beat Baker, handcuffed him, and dragged him outside to a dark-colored station wagon. The car exited Sunday Lounge's parking lot on Kalakaua Avenue, turned right on Kapiolani Boulevard, and disappeared into the night.[9]

Baker had also been working part-time for Hawai'i Protective Association, Larry Mehau's security guard company, occasionally acting as a driver for Mehau himself, sources told me. One friend said Baker worked at HPA as an errand boy and general gofer. The company and Mehau declined to discuss Baker but later said Baker was fired for bad work habits and because he refused to remove a "Leota for Governor" bumper sticker from his car.

Mehau was a big wheel that year in the reelection campaign of his close friend, Governor George Ariyoshi. And Alema Leota, former syndicate boss, had mounted one of the most improbable gubernatorial election campaigns in the history of Hawai'i politics. Leota's run for office was possible because he had never been convicted of a felony. He had misdemeanor convictions for drug sales and several brutal assaults, but nothing that would bar him from public office.

The son of a devout pair of Mormon immigrants from American Samoa, Leota grew up in the Kahuku area of Oahu. In 1950, he and his brother Reid first made news when they were involved in a violent altercation with the elderly owners of a Windward Oahu bar. They broke one man's jaw and beat the other man's face black-and-blue—all because the proprietors had repeatedly asked the brothers to tone down their profane language.

The following year, the Leota brothers were arrested after they allegedly threatened to kill an African American pimp in Chinatown. The victim, Henry T. Scott, refused to press charges, but Reid Leota was carrying a gun and was convicted of a weapons charge. A police officer testified that Reid Leota said when he was arrested, "If you guys had come five minutes later, there might have been four dead Negroes."

Reid Leota was sentenced to six months in jail but appealed and was out on bail when he and his brother committed more mayhem. Another pimp, Charles Levy Nelson, was shooting pool in a Chinatown dive when Alema Leota attacked him with a pool cue. Nelson was struck on the head and forced onto the sidewalk outside, where Reid Leota stomped him to death.

Gene Hunter reported: "Nelson suffered a ruptured heart, a skull fracture, bruises to both lungs and numerous broken ribs. It was then that police described the Leota brothers as having a 'wild hatred' for Negroes."[10]

While awaiting trial in that case, Alema Leota was arrested on federal drug charges. Police described him in that case as an underworld thug known for beating drug dealers, leading the presiding federal judge to tell Leota he was "one of the worst criminals I have ever had before me. You are vicious."

Leota was later tried but acquitted in the same federal tax case that ensnared Nappy Pulawa. Two months before Leota declared his candidacy for governor, the IRS filed a $26,221 lien against him for taxes owed when he reputedly ran Hawai'i organized crime with Pulawa.

Leota's run for governor was a short-lived but entertaining chapter in the Islands' political history. His campaign manager was Ofati "Al Ofati" Malepeai, a Waikiki fringe figure who had been manager of Don Ho's showroom for years. I would deal with Malepeai on other stories in later years.

I was present when Leota took out his official campaign papers at the Capitol. Asked why he was running, Leota said, "There's so much bullshit going on, it's just incredible."[11]

He later discussed organized crime in a television interview, using words that were to be incorporated into a Hawai'i Crime Commission report on "linkages" between the syndicate and the government. "To say that we have organized crime involves great government participation and sanction," Leota said. "It means that government is guilty because it takes government help to make organized crime work."[12]

Alema Leota, who ran
the syndicate and
then ran for governor.
*HONOLULU STAR-
ADVERTISER* COLLECTION;
HAWAI'I STATE ARCHIVES.

In addition to helping out on the Leota campaign, Arthur Baker was also working as an informant for the U.S. Drug Enforcement Administration. One family member denied that assertion, saying Baker had been approached by DEA to be a snitch. Another acquaintance said Baker was snitching to the feds. Court records and documents later obtained under the Freedom of Information Act stated categorically that Baker was an informant.

DEA Agent Robert Aiu, a personal acquaintance of Baker's, refused to discuss the man when I asked. He said he couldn't talk about "a pending investigation" and referred me to his boss, who also declined to comment.

Honolulu Police Detective Manuel "Manny" Rezentes likewise told me he couldn't talk about Arthur Baker. I had tried to ask Rezentes about persistent reports that a professional killer named Ronald Kainalu Ching had been involved in Baker's disappearance.

Rezentes warned me about asking too many questions about Ronnie Ching. Others also told me to watch my step because Ching was a very dangerous man.

I didn't have a phone number for Ching, but I did know that he lived in a unit at the Chateau Blue apartment building on Kapiolani Boulevard, near the Ala Moana shopping center. I spoke with the manager of that building, a sad little man named Thomas K. W. Wong, about reports that he and Ching had been involved in an altercation in the Sunday Lounge parking lot shortly before Baker's abduction. Wong was uncommunicative but agreed to tell Ching that I was interested in talking to him.

Ronnie Ching called me at my office not long after that. It was my first and last interview of a working hit man.

Ching was polite and well-spoken. He told me that he knew I was asking a lot of questions about him but I should be careful not to believe everything I heard. He said he had had nothing to do with Arthur Baker's disappearance. He denied being a contract killer in a matter-of-fact and even pleasant tone.

Ching said he didn't like people asking questions like that about him but understood that I had a job to do. That was it. He wasn't interested in answering any more direct questions about Baker but said he would be around if I wanted to talk with him again. End of discussion.

Ching spoke no threatening words, but he succeeded in completely creeping me out. Up to that point, I had regarded him as a concept more than a reality, but he clarified my thinking in a direct way. Ching was to use the same matter-of-fact tone in court several years later when he admitted to committing some of the most heinous homicides in modern Hawai'i history, including the Arthur Baker slaying.

But that was in the future. I tucked Ching's name away for future reference.

For the time being, I had new fish to fry: the yakuza.

CHAPTER FOUR

Yakuza

While I was covering the Pulawa murder trial in 1978, a law enforcement source asked me if I knew anything about the yakuza—Japanese organized crime. I didn't have a clue. The source said I should check out a guy named Takeshi Takagi, a Japanese national living and working in Honolulu.

I was busy at the time and dubious. Who ever heard of Japanese mobsters?

But I was told that Takagi and the yakuza would be worth finding out about. So I made contact with Clarence "Japan" Handa, a Japanese-born criminal who had been a prosecution witness in the Pulawa murder and tax trials. "Japan" had a heavy accent that grew even thicker whenever he was asked about someone or something that he really didn't want to talk about. When I asked him about Takagi, the only word I could understand was my own name.

"Jimmy, Jimmy, Jimmy," Japan said sorrowfully, shaking his head and lowering his eyes.

"What, Japan? What's the matter? Tell me about Takagi."

"Oh, Jimmy, no," he said. He lapsed into Japanese and finally a brief phrase in pidgin: "I no can say." I couldn't get anything more out of him, but that was enough for me. Takagi was definitely worth checking out.

Takagi, I learned, was a Japanese citizen, living in a rented luxury home on a hillside that overlooked Waialae Country Club and the posh Kahala neighborhood of Honolulu. He owned a company that staged sex shows in a subterranean theater in Chinatown, catering primarily to Japanese tourists. Takagi was good-looking and a very sharp dresser. He drove expensive cars, and he was missing half the little finger on one hand and the tip

Yakuza gang member Takeshi Takagi, smoking a cigarette, departs Honolulu District Court. Half of his left-hand little finger is missing. *HONOLULU STAR-ADVERTISER.*

of the other. He was also reportedly heavily tattooed on his back. The physical characteristics were classic signs of a yakuza.

Missing digits and dragon tattoos! Here was a story that would write itself. The more I looked, the better it got. Takagi was not the first yakuza in Hawai'i. There were others before him and more working with him. The dimensions of the subject and the possibilities of a series on yakuza in Hawai'i were taking shape in my mind when Takagi was busted by Honolulu police on a gun possession charge. The lead story of my planned series was about to become public property when Takagi appeared in court to answer the gun charge against him.

There were no other reporters in court when I showed up at Takagi's hearing at the old district court building on the edge of Chinatown. I probably could have held back on publication, but the decision was taken out of my hands by a picture shot by *Advertiser* photographer Roy Ito as Takagi emerged from court that day.

Framed in the courthouse doorway with his girlfriend and an associate, Takagi looked like he had been centrally cast for the part of a high-powered international hoodlum. He was handsome and impeccably dressed. His girlfriend was very attractive, and his companion was menacing. The photo was just too good not to use immediately.

Coupled with court testimony from HPD officer Donald Carstensen identifying Takagi as a yakuza, the photo and story ran after the first day of the court hearing.[1]

Takagi and his lawyer had had nothing to say when they left court that day, and when the story ran the next morning, I went back to court to cover the continuation of the hearing. I had gone considerably beyond the courtroom testimony in the story, naming Takagi as a member of a Tokyo-based yakuza gang called the Sumiyoshi-ringo.

Before the hearing began, I approached Takagi and his interpreter in the hallway. How did Mr. Takagi like the story this morning? Did he wish to make a statement now?

The interpreter translated my questions, and Takagi answered.

"Mr. Takagi says you have made a serious error," the interpreter said.

I don't care how ironclad you think your information is, those words will freeze a reporter's blood. I asked what the error was, expecting him to say something like "I'm a businessman, not a mobster, and I'm going to sue you for every penny you've got."

But the interpreter said, "The name of his group is Sumiyoshi-rengo, r-e-n-g-o, not ringo."

I assured him that I would correct that error in the paper the next day, and I was happy to do so.

I wrote another story that focused on two local syndicate figures who accompanied Takagi to both days of the court hearing.[2] One, Wallace S. "Wally" Furukawa, achieved notoriety in 1970 when his brand-new Lincoln Continental automobile was destroyed by five sticks of dynamite planted in the engine compartment. Furukawa was a Nappy Pulawa lieutenant and frequently used the car to ferry Pulawa around town. Furukawa miraculously survived, suffering injuries to his feet and lower legs. The bombing was widely seen as a warning, and a headline on one Gene Hunter story about it said, "Wally Gets the Word."

The car bomb was detonated on the same morning that high-level officials of federal, state, and county law enforcement had convened on the Big Island for a first-ever summit on combating organized crime in the Islands.

Furukawa was later a prosecution witness in the Pulawa tax trial. Not long after that, he pleaded guilty to participating in a massive bookmaking operation busted by federal investigators.

Furukawa drove to and from the Takagi court hearing in a yellow Corvette owned by the defendant.

The other man with Takagi at court was John "Haole John" Deems, identified in the Pulawa tax case as a bagman who collected tribute money for the syndicate from gambling operators. I watched Deems carry on lengthy conversations with Takagi in Japanese during breaks in the court case. I reported that Deems had become a close associate of Seiji Nakahara, a top official of Sumiyoshi-rengo in Tokyo.

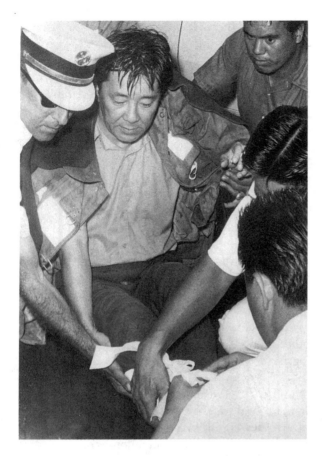

Organized crime figure Wallace Furukawa is treated by emergency workers after his car was bombed. *HONOLULU STAR-ADVERTISER.*

I was always very interested in Deems and tried hard over the years to get him to talk to me. He was the only Caucasian who ever occupied important positions in both the Hawai'i and Japanese underworlds. We would occasionally talk by phone and later by e-mail, and Deems always seemed to be on the verge of opening up to me. He was plainly proud of his achievements and wanted to share.

But it never quite happened. Deems died in 2011 after moving home to the Mainland. I learned after he died that he had recorded a series of video reminiscences about his underworld activities that have been posted on YouTube. I recommend them. He was a funny, profane man with fascinating stories.[3]

As I looked into Takagi and the yakuza story, I found that Japanese mobsters had been living and working in the Islands since at least the early 1970s and were connected to local and Mainland syndicate figures in a variety of ways.

They were smuggling drugs into the state and guns out to Japan, as well as supplying prostitution, pornography, and gambling services to Japanese tourists.

I found that one *kobun*—a soldier in the huge yakuza gangs known in Japan as *boryokudan*—named Wataru "Jackson" Inada had been murdered in his Honolulu apartment shortly before he was scheduled to go to trial in a federal drug-smuggling case that was linked to Los Angeles mafia figure Peter Milano.[4]

Yakuza and their associates had been operating bordellos in Waikiki hotels. One establishment, named Utamaro after a famous Japanese erotic artist, had employed runners to pass out business cards on Waikiki Beach to Japanese tourists.

"The Toruko [Turkish bath] Utamaro is like the enjoyment of watching the 11 p.m. T.V. program," the card said in Japanese.

The reference was to surprisingly raunchy television shows aired nightly in Japan. (A colleague of mine who was an occasional traveler to Japan told me that he was taken aback by the programming when he turned on late-night television in his hotel room on a Tokyo visit. "It seemed to be some kind of game show but the contestants—men and women—were seminude and were riding each other around like it was a rodeo," my friend said. "Everybody was squealing and whooping and the audience was roaring with laughter. It was amazing.")

The Utamaro flyer continued: "You can be proud to say this is the best setup in the U.S. You can drink and watch porno movies and have the services of a beautiful blond girl for your enjoyment," the card said.[5]

Waikiki civic leaders complained about the operation, which was in a detached annex of a major hotel. Utamaro was eventually closed, but I found another operation, Hotel Tsuru, going strong in a different location just a block from Waikiki Beach. The building was across Kapahulu Avenue from the Honolulu Zoo, so I spent several evenings in my car in the zoo parking lot, watching the activities at the Hotel Tsuru.

Those were strange evenings. Occasionally I could hear lions roaring and chimps screeching in the night behind me while I watched a raging hormone show in front of me. In the background, waves washed placidly over Kuhio Beach.

There was a steady flow of taxicabs and white Cadillacs with red roofs that dropped off and picked up customers at the hotel, the same private cars that had earlier serviced Utamaro.

At one point, *Advertiser* colleague Mike Keller and I inquired at Hotel Tsuru about checking in for the night. We were told that was impossible by the front desk staff. When we persisted, we were told that all the rooms had been booked five years into the future.

A friendly cabdriver explained the Hotel Tsuru operation to me. The price per customer was $70, $20 of which was kicked back to the driver who delivered the customer. The proprietors were very suspicious of non-Japanese johns, I was told.

Eventually I found a Japanese exchange student from the University of Hawai'i campus, paid him $70 to get laid, and then interviewed him about the experience. I was probably guilty of criminal pandering and had to really finesse that particular expense past the *Advertiser*'s editors. But the story ran, and Hotel Tsuru was closed not long after.[6]

Two months later, Honolulu police busted another prostitution operation in a condominium rented by three Japanese "students" in a very expensive residential building at the base of Diamond Head. When the cops raided the unit, they found a dozen male Japanese tourists and three Caucasian women inside. Although a cache of X-rated videocassettes was available for customers' viewing, police found three of the tourists in a room watching a Japanese-dubbed copy of the *Lassie* television show.

When I checked with the apartment owner's agent, I found that one of the men who had rented the condo for $2,000 a month was an officer of the company that had operated Hotel Tsuru.[7]

The initial yakuza series generated a variety of new story lines that I followed in later months. One involved yakuza connections in professional boxing. Kuwashi Shimizu, a former featherweight boxing champion in Japan who had emigrated to Honolulu, had business ties to both Takeshi Takagi and to Takatsugu Yonekura, a yakuza convicted of smuggling guns from Hawai'i to Japan.

Shimizu told me he had known Yonekura since high school in Japan, when both were amateur boxers. Asked if he knew Yonekura was a yakuza, Shimizu said, "You know, he don't have a finger, he have a lot of tattoos, [he] looks like the yakuza, but inside, he's not. I like his heart, he so good."[8]

Shimizu admitted he had worked as a bouncer for nearly a year at Utamaro because the management there was having "syndicate" problems. Asked if there was prostitution at Utamaro when he worked there, Shimizu said, "I cannot say. This is a custom, you know." Shimizu said he eventually quit Utamaro because "I don't like the syndicate. I don't like the drugs."

Shimizu explained to me that the boxing world in Japan was heavily influenced by the yakuza. When Shimizu was learning the ropes as a young boxer, yakuza would frequently give him clothes and money. "I cannot say no," Shimizu told me.

A Honolulu boxing promoter who was in business with Shimizu and Takeshi Takagi, Sukeji "Skippy" Miyashiro, told me that yakuza were deeply involved in the sports and entertainment industries in Japan.

"Look at Japanese sumo wrestling," Miyashiro said. "Whenever they win a bout, they have an envelope that's all kinds money. They [yakuza] give them thousands of dollars, Japanese ways, you know. I hope the Americans do the same thing."

Another story line I followed led me to a yakuza affiliate named Takehiko Nozaki who had worked as a federal informant and eventually became the first Japanese national to be enrolled in the U.S. Witness Protection Program.

Nozaki's role as a snitch surfaced when the feds went to court to revoke the probation of Hawai'i syndicate figure John Chang Ho Lee.

Lee had made headlines several years earlier when he was sentenced to 20 years in state prison for a robbery conviction but was given day passes almost immediately so that he could attend high school football games and go shopping.

Police were outraged when they spotted Lee out and about in the community. So was the judge who sentenced Lee. "I know the man, his record, and I sentenced him to 20 years—no conditions," said the judge, Allen R. Hawkins.[9]

But prison officials said Lee qualified for the conditional release program, saying that he was being "intensely supervised." Police and the judiciary had no say in the matter.

While under that 20-year sentence but out and about in the community, Lee turned up as the star of an undercover audiotape recorded by law enforcement. The hour-long tape recorded a meeting between Lee and Nozaki. Its contents, plus testimony at the revocation hearing, made for a mother lode of information for an enterprising reporter.

In addition to his state court charges, Lee had also pleaded guilty to a heroin-trafficking charge—the same case that connected to the Milano crime family in Los Angeles and ended with the murder of Lee's codefendant Jackson Inada. It turned out that Lee had been cooperating with the feds and police in that case but never had to testify because Inada and Inada's girlfriend had been murdered shortly before the trial was to start.

In court, a federal drug agent said Lee "tacitly admitted" to murdering the pair because he didn't want to testify in the case.[10] The girlfriend died because she disobeyed orders from her killer not to look at him, the agent said.

On the audiotape, Lee bragged about his organized crime connections. Among the names he dropped was Marcus Lipsky, a reputed former Chicago syndicate figure who later moved to Los Angeles and invested heavily in the Don Ho show. Lee also repeatedly mentioned Ofati "Al Ofati" Malepeai, the Waikiki denizen who had worked for years for Don Ho and had managed Alema Leota's short-lived foray into politics.[11] Malepeai had been partners with Lee and Nozaki in an importing business that brought fresh tuna to Hawai'i from Western Samoa. Federal authorities alleged in court papers that the business was actually a "front for narcotics smuggling activities." In a long interview, Malepeai admitted to me that he had been in the tuna venture with Lee and Nozaki but said it was a legitimate business that faltered because of licensing problems with the government of Western Samoa.[12]

Malepeai also was close to Lipsky but didn't know why Lee mentioned Lipsky on the undercover tape. "John does not know Mr. Lipsky," Malepeai said. He speculated that Lee may have been trying to impress Nozaki because of Lipsky's reputation "from his younger days."

Lipsky was once named by a U.S. congressional committee as a member of the Al Capone mob in Chicago, where Lipsky was born and raised. Lipsky was also identified by federal authorities as a one-time associate of Jack Ruby, the fringe mob character who murdered John F. Kennedy's assassin, Lee Harvey Oswald, on national television in Dallas. Lipsky had lived for years in Southern California, staying clear of the law and pursuing philanthropic interests and business investments.

Malepeai told me Lipsky was "a very influential man" but said Lee's words on the audiotape were "a lot of big talk about nothing." Malepeai acknowledged knowing many of the mobsters and felons named by Lee on the audiotape but said that was because of his work for the Don Ho show and other entertainment ventures.

"They come in, I buy them rounds, you know, buy them drinks, known hoodlums, known guys," he said. "Ever since I got involved in the nightclub business, I take care of the [hoodlums]," he continued. "Nothing illegal about that, but because of me doing that, I'm indirectly involved. That's a sad state of life. I'm indirectly involved and all I wanted to do was help."

Malepeai was very unhappy with my subsequent news story and threatened legal action over it. He never followed through on the threat.

Years later, Malepeai was convicted in federal court of smuggling hundreds of pounds of cocaine and crystal methamphetamine into the Islands.[13] He received a lengthy prison sentence and was dubbed "a local organized crime figure" by the U.S. Justice Department.[14]

Yakuza stories continued to develop for me, as state and federal law enforcement began paying increased attention to the subject.

Four Japanese nationals carrying pounds of heroin concealed in duty-free cigarette cartons were stopped by Customs agents at Honolulu International Airport. In Japan, police searched the apartment of one of the mules and found detailed instructions on how the courier was to carry the contraband from Thailand and how he was to behave when he arrived in Hawai'i.

Then there were the yakuza who disguised their severed fingertips by wearing false rubber pinkies when passing through airport immigration checks. One successfully cleared immigration but removed the ersatz digit before he hit the Customs inspection line. When he was asked to empty his pockets at Customs, the phony fingertip tumbled into view, and he was taken into custody.[15]

In 1982, a court source tipped me to a lawsuit filed in federal court that concerned a proxy fight then underway for control of a local financial institution, City Bank. One of the parties in the suit had enlisted the aid of a Japanese racketeer named Kaoru Ogawa for his help in the proxy fight.

I had been collecting information about Ogawa for a year or so after I learned that he maintained a home in Honolulu and was friends with Larry Mehau, former HPD officer and convicted drug trafficker Raymond Scanlan, and local businessman Charles Higa.

On one visit to Honolulu in 1978, Ogawa, who owned a large chunk of stock in Japan Airlines, received VIP treatment at the airport, where a special Customs line was opened for him and where he was met by Mehau, Higa, and Maurice "Mutt" Matsuzaki, a state law enforcement officer who moonlighted as an official of Hawai'i Protective Association, Mehau's company that held the contract to provide security services at the airport.

Ogawa told Customs that he was carrying $10,000 in cash and *omiyage*—gifts for friends—that included live koi, the ornamental carp whose breeding and hybridization had developed into a virtual art form in Japan.

Ogawa technically was not a yakuza, but a type of businessman peculiar to Japan called *sokaiya*. The *sokaiya* made their living by squeezing "donations" from Japanese corporations by gathering, then suppressing, embarrassing secrets about the companies. For a fee, the *sokaiya* also kept embarrassing questions from being asked at annual stockholder meetings of major Japanese companies.[16] Ogawa published a magazine called *J&A* that he used as part of his *sokaiya* activities.

I got my hands on a 1980 Tokyo Metropolitan Police report that called Ogawa "Japan's most influential racketeer" and detailed his criminal history, which included a conviction for extortion in 1979. For that offense, he received a five-year suspended prison sentence that was still running when the City Bank suit was filed and Ogawa came to town in August 1982 to testify in the case.

The Tokyo police report said that in 1980, Ogawa had collected between $6.8 million and $12 million from as many as 1,000 of Japan's most important companies.[17]

Through an interpreter, I contacted Ogawa at his *J&A* office in Tokyo and asked for an interview the next time he came to town. To my surprise, he agreed. Ogawa came straight to the News Building from the airport, and we talked in a conference room for 45 minutes or so.[18]

He was quite candid in the interview, acknowledging his criminal problems in Japan and elaborating on a $1.2 million claim pending against him by Japanese tax authorities. He said he was not a yakuza but knew many of the gangsters, explaining that they wielded considerable influence in business, sports, and entertainment in Japan. He also spoke of his friendship with Mehau, saying that he had once incorrectly identified Mehau as Hawai'i's "godfather" in *J&A* magazine.

In the middle of the interview, one of the clerks from the city desk interrupted and said I had an important telephone call. I left the room to take the call, which turned out to be from a Customs agent who demanded to know if I was talking to Kaoru Ogawa.

"Yeah, I am," I said. "Why?"

"Because there are a half-dozen of us who followed him from the airport outside in the street right now, trying to figure out why this joker stopped by the newspaper for an hour or so," the agent said.

I laughed and told him to read the paper the next day.

In a twist of irony, Ogawa complained in the interview that attorneys for City Bank "had dug up this dirt on me" and were trying to use it against him in the proxy fight—the same sort of business tactics that had made Ogawa a fortune in Japan.

After the story of Ogawa's visit and background was published, attorneys in the bank suit successfully petitioned the court for an after-the-fact sealing of many of the records that had been filed in the case. The court's acquiescence in the sealing request rankled me and *Advertiser* editors, but I had already copied the paperwork and publicized its contents so there didn't seem much point in fighting the closure of the records. But I didn't forget it.

Businessman Charles Higa, Ogawa's Honolulu friend, had frittered away a family fortune amassed by his father and grandfather. He was later convicted in a state court extortion case. Higa and two codefendants had attempted to extort protection payments from the operator of a Waikiki X-rated book and video store that catered to Japanese tourists.

In court, Higa said he had first met yakuza in Japan in the late 1950s. The Higa family trucking business in Japan depended on a labor force controlled by the yakuza, and Higa said he followed local customs by giving gifts—money or sake—to yakuza representatives. After that, he said, he met with yakuza leaders and was personally acquainted with the top three bosses of the Sumiyoshi-rengo. Higa also said he had met twice in Hawai'i with Kazuo Taoka, boss of the biggest yakuza gang, the Yamaguchi-gumi, and also acknowledged his acquaintance with Kaoru Ogawa.

The biggest yakuza story of all came in 1985, when DEA agents busted two very high-ranking officials of the Yamaguchi-gumi in Hawai'i on charges of conspiracy to import drugs into the Islands and export an arsenal of weapons, including military rocket launchers, to Japan.

It was a huge coup for the DEA and the U.S. Justice Department. But the case eventually disintegrated into a major disaster for the government. The case foundered on problems with the main prosecution witness.

The charges depended in large part on an informant named Hiro Sasaki, a part-time professional wrestler and so-called entertainment promoter who met with the Yamaguchi-gumi officials in Japan and Hawai'i. A naturalized citizen whose real name was Tsuneo Soranaka, Sasaki had mixed personal business with government work during the yearlong investigation, testimony and evidence showed.

While acting as an intermediary between the yakuza and undercover drug agents who posed as Hawai'i syndicate members, Sasaki was separately talking to the yakuza about a plan to stage concerts in Japan by American entertainers, including Michael Jackson.

How much the federal agents actually knew about Sasaki and the concert plans was never made clear. But they plainly didn't know enough. Sasaki was paid $550,000 by the yakuza for the Jackson deal. The U.S. government paid Sasaki $102,000 for his informant work. And the government also paid to relocate members of Sasaki's family from Japan to the United States.[19]

The yakuza defendants testified at the trial that the main purpose of the visit to Hawai'i that ended in arrests and headlines was to retrieve the $550,000 they had invested in the Jackson deal, which never came close to completion.

Clearly, they were also interested in gun and drug deals. At the time, the Yamaguchi-gumi was involved in a violent turf war in Osaka and Kobe with a splinter gang, the Ichiwa-kai, formed by Hiroshi Yamamoto after he was passed over for ascension to the *oyabun*—boss—position of Yamaguchi-gumi.

In January 1985, Ichiwa-kai assassins had murdered the new Yamaguchi-gumi boss, Masahisa Takenaka, older brother of Masashi Takenaka, one of the defendants in the Hawai'i case.

Takenaka and his codefendants, who included the Yamaguchi-gumi's financial officer, Toyohiko Ito, "seemed rather amazed" when they met in a Honolulu hotel room with the undercover DEA agents and were shown an array of weaponry that included automatic weapons, rockets, and rocket launchers available for purchase, DEA Special Agent Robert Aiu testified.

Takenaka picked up a rocket launcher "and suggested that this be used to kill" Yamamoto of the Ichiwa-kai, Aiu said.[20]

"We agreed that in the near future we would kill this leader," Aiu testified.

The case had created immense media interest in Japan, and a large number of reporters from that country were on hand for the trial. The yakuza defendants even had on hand their own attorney from Osaka, Yukio Yamanouchi, to informally advise them and handle media matters.

I discovered that while the investigation was underway, Sasaki had been arrested by Honolulu police for allegedly trying to extort $120,000 from a Waikiki restaurant operator.[21]

During one of his visits to the restaurant, Sasaki was accompanied by Todd Ariyoshi, the son of Governor George Ariyoshi. Todd and Sasaki were partners in a short-lived ice cream business in Honolulu that had used Washington Place, the governor's mansion, as its mailing address.

Todd Ariyoshi was never arrested, and he told me that although he had accompanied Sasaki to the Waikiki restaurant, he did not know what Sasaki had discussed with the owner during the visit. He said he had met and become friendly with Sasaki while taking a martial arts class.[22]

The federal case was further undercut when a shipment of 18 pounds of amphetamines and four kilos of heroin bound for Hawai'i was seized by Hong Kong authorities who were supposedly cooperating in the investigation. The seizure actually short-circuited the entire Honolulu case and caused the DEA to arrest the defendants early—before the planned arrival of the narcotics.

The federal court jury in the trial acquitted the main defendants of all charges. When I interviewed some of the jurors later, they ridiculed the government's case.

"How much money did they spend on this case? A million dollars? They got almost nothing out of it," foreman Russell McLain said. He called Sasaki "a crook to the max, a scammer. If there was a scam, he'd do it."[23]

Another juror, April Lum, said the jury simply didn't believe the testimony of Sasaki and defendant Koichi Maruyama, who turned prosecution witness.[24]

"They contradicted themselves. They didn't help the government's case at all."

One of the defendants, Yamaguchi-gumi underboss Toyohiko Ito, told me in an interview before he returned to Japan that he was dying of liver cancer and wasn't expected to survive the next six months.[25] Liver disease is a common ailment among yakuza, attributable to their hard-drinking lifestyles and perhaps to the toxicity of the traditional inks and needles used in the tattooing process. In 2008 and 2009, the *Los Angeles Times*, *Washington Post*, and *60 Minutes* produced stories, based on the reporting of Tokyo-based journalist Jake Adelstein, on four liver transplants that had been performed on yakuza gang leaders at the UCLA Medical School.

Ito of the Yamaguchi-gumi was not among the transplant patients. He told me in 1985 that he was resigned to his imminent death. "It is my fate," he said.

He complained about the undercover nature of the investigation mounted against him, part of which was conducted in Japan. Such tactics should have been "unthinkable" in his home country, Ito said.

"I intend to discuss this matter when I return home with Mr. Shintaro Abe, the Minister of Foreign Affairs, who is an acquaintance of mine," Ito said.

Ito was serious. The yakuza wielded enormous political influence in Japanese society, operating from public offices that were emblazoned with their gang names and logos.

The Japanese National Police compiled a list of more than 100,000 officially recognized yakuza gang members and distributed the list to Japanese media. I was given a copy, complete with an English translation of the names and gangs, by one of the many reporters who covered the trial for Japanese media.

I became good friends with one reporter, Naoji Shibata of the *Asahi Shimbun* newspaper, and also maintained contact with Yukio Yamanouchi, the Yamaguchi-gumi lawyer based in Osaka. Both men would be very helpful when I finally visited Japan on more yakuza-related stories that focused on the sport of golf.

CHAPTER FIVE

Yakuza, Inc.

The tsunami of Japanese investment that washed over Hawai'i and much of the world in the late 1980s brought with it a multitude of new yakuza stories.

It was really a fish-in-the-barrel exercise for me. Over and over again, I found yakuza connections or criminal histories in the backgrounds of men and companies investing in real estate, particularly golf courses, and other businesses in Hawai'i and on the Mainland.

To a large degree, these connections were a function of the role the yakuza played in Japanese society, particularly in real estate development, construction, and speculation, which produced many of the biggest players in this new wave of investments. Repeatedly, when I asked these men, or their advisers, about their yakuza connections, they said yes, they had them, but they were unavoidable.

The president of the company that bought the beautiful Turtle Bay resort on the North Shore of Oahu had been a member of the Yamaguchi-gumi. He was deported home after his background was made public.[1]

The developer of a brand-new golf course in the Mauanawili Valley area of Oahu, who made his fortune in the *pachinko* parlor warrens of Osaka, likewise was sent home after it was discovered that he had failed to disclose a criminal history when he applied for a U.S. visa.[2]

The man who bought picturesque Coconut Island in Kaneohe Bay, multimillionaire Katsuhiro Kawaguchi, was repeatedly identified by respected Japanese news media as a *jiage-ya*, a type of real estate speculator who used yakuza to evict tenants from commercial and residential properties he had acquired.[3]

Kawaguchi was fined $100,000 and deported to Japan in 1988 for visa fraud violations. Coconut Island, which was filmed in the opening shots of the *Gilligan's Island* television series, was eventually acquired by the University of Hawai'i and is now a marine research center.

Kitaro Watanabe, a Japanese businessman whose Azabu companies spent $500 million acquiring Hawai'i real estate in the 1980s, was connected to the Sumiyoshi-rengo Tokyo yakuza group through a right-wing nationalistic group called *Nihon Seinensha* (Japanese Youth Company), a Tokyo Metropolitan Police official told me.[4] Watanabe's Hawai'i lawyer, Jon Miho, told me the yakuza had "no connection" to Azabu's investments in the Islands. Miho added that yakuza-business ties were "a fact of life in Japan and I think that many, many, many large corporations, especially those that deal with the public, have to deal with these guys."

Saying that yakuza had "control or major influence" over the corporations would be wrong, Miho continued. "But if you want to say that they have to deal with the yakuza, or have dealt with them, or do deal with them, I think that's probably true."[5]

I found that Leo Orii, a member of the Sumiyoshi-rengo who was living in a rented house on the Waialae golf course, had opened a furniture business in Honolulu with the son of Sumiyoshi-rengo official Kusuo Kobayashi. The company had sold rattan furnishings to the Ala Moana Hotel, one of Azabu's Hawai'i holdings.

When I knocked on Orii's door seeking an interview one afternoon, he answered it with a six-pound sledgehammer in one hand. "I have nothing to do with Sumiyoshi Rengo-kai," he said. "As a matter of fact, I hate those kind of people."

When I pointed out that David Kaplan, a friend and reporting colleague of mine who had coauthored the book *Yakuza*, had quoted Orii as saying he was a member of the Sumiyoshi Rengo-kai, Orii denied ever talking to Kaplan. "I didn't say anything to nobody," he said.

But he went on to tell me that he was personally acquainted with Sumiyoshi vice chairman Kobayashi and acknowledged being in business with Kobayashi's son.

"Right-wing man, yes," Orii said of the elder Kobayashi. "A nice man, I know him. From my point of view [there's] nothing wrong with him. I don't have anything to do with him, that's all," Orii said. Throughout the interview, which took place on his doorstep, Orii kept the sledgehammer at his side. He never brandished it, but he never put it down, either.[6]

The family of Ken Mizuno, purchaser of the Olomana golf course on Oahu, strenuously argued to me that Mizuno had repeatedly fought attempted yakuza incursions into his golf course developments in Japan.[7]

Mizuno was later convicted of perpetrating a massive fraud in the sales of country club memberships in his home country.

I turned out stories about the enormous pressure being placed on local golf courses and country clubs by the influx of Japanese investors. One local farmer, who was being threatened with eviction by a new Japanese landlord intent on developing the property as a golf course, said in an interview with another reporter, "No can eat golf balls." That phrase became a rallying cry for antidevelopment protestors in Hawai'i.

Country club memberships were marketed as securities in Japan but were nontransferable at most American clubs, which led to a dual-tier membership structure at clubs like the Honolulu Country Club, where local members paid $19,000 to join but "international" members paid $150,000.

By 1988, most privately owned golf courses on Oahu were Japanese-owned.

Virtually all proposed new courses were controlled by Japanese interests. Some of them were on property ill-suited for commercial development. But that sort of problem, and even the insanely inflated prices the investors were willing to pay for raw land, didn't blunt the buyers' enthusiasm.

After much cajoling, *Advertiser* editors approved my proposal for a trip to Japan to explore generally the new golf course investors and specifically their yakuza connections.

It was a very hard sell. There was considerable expense involved, and I was proposing a different sort of trip than, say, sending a reporter to cover a football game or political convention. In those instances, you know you've got a story before you get on the plane. In this case, I was positive the stories were there, but I couldn't absolutely guarantee them. I had amassed a great deal of information and lined up numerous interviews ahead of time, so the prospects looked good. The trip was finally approved amid dire warnings that I was mortgaging all future travel possibilities of *Advertiser* staffers and I had better produce. Ten years after I had begun writing about yakuza, I was finally going to Japan.

The highlight of the trip was an interview with Masaru Takumi, the number-two boss of the Yamaguchi-gumi, in Osaka. Arranged months in advance through Yukio Yamanouchi, the Yamaguchi lawyer I had met during the federal guns-for-drugs trial in Honolulu, the interview almost didn't come off at the last minute.

Underworld violence had broken out in Osaka shortly before I arrived. Three police officers watching the home of Ichiwa-kai boss Hiroshi Yamamoto had been shot and seriously wounded during an attempted assassination of Yamamoto by rival gang members. After firing automatic weapons at the policemen's car, the assassination team then tried to explode a bomb at Yamamoto's house, but the device misfired.

Police then made a week's worth of wholesale arrests, raiding the headquarters of various yakuza groups and subgroups. While I was still in Tokyo, attorney Yamanouchi told me by telephone that it looked like the Takumi interview would have to be cancelled. But I had other research to pursue in Osaka, so I went ahead.

While visiting with Yamanouchi and *Asahi Shimbun* reporter Naoji Shibata at Yamanouchi's office the day after I arrived in Osaka, the lawyer took a phone call from Takumi, who had changed his plans and was willing to do the interview.

Takumi was being chauffeured around Osaka with nowhere to go because police were raiding his office, Yamanouchi explained to me. Takumi would come to Yamanouchi's office if I still wanted to talk. Of course, I said, but I noticed that my interpreter, a local woman I had hired for the day, was clearly discomfited by the prospect of translating for a yakuza boss. I wasn't going to lose out on a chance at the interview, and I figured that between all of us, we would be able to figure out what was being said.

It was like the arrival of a head of state when Takumi's car pulled up. He travelled in a chauffeur-driven black Mercedes Benz limousine, and two other carloads of his soldiers arrived in Jaguar sedans. With horns blaring, the Jaguars barricaded each end of the block where Yamanouchi's office building was located, a block away from Osaka's main courthouse. I gawked out the window and saw Osaka office workers doing the same thing, peering down at the street scene from high-rise windows and doorways.

Takumi wasn't what I expected. Discreetly and expensively dressed, he was quite handsome and self-assured. Except for the fact that his right pinkie had been chopped off at the middle knuckle, he seemed more like an entertainment celebrity than a gang boss.

An underling who accompanied Takumi was more the part. Stocky, with a brush cut and gaudy clothes, the man told me he very much wanted to visit Hawai'i but was concerned that he would not get past the airport inspectors. Did I have any advice? Rather nonplussed, I outlined the procedures for obtaining a visa, explaining as delicately as I could that a criminal record was not necessarily grounds for exclusion from my country. Most individuals who were refused entry, I said, suffered the indignity because they failed to disclose their criminal records, not because they had them. The man's physical appearance positively screamed yakuza, so I advised him to dress as much like a typical tourist as possible if and when he arrived in Hawai'i.

Takumi insisted throughout the conversation that the Yamaguchi-gumi was a fraternal organization, whose members were considered outsiders in

Japan's rigidly stratified society. Yamanouchi asserted that his client's remarks were accurate. No one denied that the gang members lived outside the law, but they were given little choice in the matter, the lawyer said.

"We are different from the mafia," Takumi told me, "like Japan is different from America."[8]

Takumi readily confirmed to me that Kitaro Watanabe, head of the Azabu Corporation, "has good friends among the yakuza." He was puzzled by my interest. "That he has such friends is not unusual. He has no yakuza on his 'brain staff,' his business staff," Takumi said.

He also confirmed that Kizo Matsumoto, head of the company that bought the Turtle Bay resort on Oahu, was a former member of the Yamaguchi-gumi. "That was a long time ago and there might be some speculation that he still has something to do with Yamaguchi-gumi, but that is not so. He has nothing to do with it," Takumi said.

I asked Takumi about the truth of police reports that there were nearly 86,000 yakuza gang members in Japan. He said police badly undercounted the membership rolls. "They only enter the names on the membership lists after individuals have been arrested," he said. "The police can't keep track of the lower-level members. In reality, the total yakuza membership figure should be more than 200,000," Takumi asserted.

He also verified for me that a businessman named Yasumichi Morishita, who at the time was busily buying golf courses in Southern California as well as making other American investments, had very close ties to the yakuza. Morishita, widely identified in Japanese media by the nickname "Mamushi" (Viper), was a moneylender whose main company, Aichi Corporation, charged astronomical rates of interest on its loans. Morishita at one time had tried very hard to buy First Hawaiian Bank's Japanese subsidiary.

"Mr. Morishita has used the yakuza to collect debts owed to his company, but that is only to make things go smoothly," Takumi said. "In Japan, if you have a friend who is a yakuza, that might work beneficially for you. Just to mention that you have such a friend may be enough to make things go smoothly for you," he explained.[9]

Takumi and I had exchanged business cards at the outset of the meeting, and when it was over, he asked what hotel I was staying in. When I told him, he advised me to show the staff his business card when I checked out and I would not be charged for my stay.

I later asked my journalist colleague if that was true. He assured me that it was. For the hell of it, I showed Takumi's card to the hotel staff after I had paid my bill and was checking out. They were thunderstruck by the card and fell all over themselves to assure me that I wouldn't be charged for the room, but I insisted and the charges did go through.

A precondition of my interview with Takumi had been that I could not use his name in the stories I wrote. Normally, he said, he wouldn't mind, but relations with police and government authorities were so tense at the time that he didn't want to further aggravate the situation by being quoted on the record.

I did not quote him by name in my stories, but the pledge of confidentiality was dissolved in 1997 when Takumi was shot to death by rival yakuza while walking through an Osaka hotel.

After the Takumi interview was over and the yakuza boss and his convoy of underlings had swept away, I went out for drinks and dinner with Yamanouchi, a lawyer colleague of his, and my friend from the *Asahi Shimbun*.

Before we left Yamanouchi's office, the lawyer opened a walk-in safe built into one wall and emerged with multiple stacks of yen. He stuffed the money in various pockets as I tried my best not to goggle. Cash was king in those days in Japan, and I was consumed with worry about how I was going to cover my end of the tab.

We went to a seafood restaurant, and I was at their mercy when it came to ordering. One dish consisted of some small dumplinglike objects with an unrecognizable flavor. I asked what they were. "Very expensive" was the response.

"These come from a fish?" I asked.

Yamanouchi searched for the English words. "Yes, fish, fish . . ." and his eyes brightened when he thought of the right word. "Fish sheman!" he announced.

"Fish sheman," I thought. What the hell is that? Yamanouchi's friend produced a large Japanese-English dictionary and searched for the translation.

"Go-nads," he read. "Fish gonads!"

I took another slug of sake.

The main course was a pale-fleshed raw fish. I love sashimi, so I ate heartily. I asked what kind of fish it was. "Like catfish" was the response. "Very expensive."

"Catfish is expensive in Japan?" I asked.

"Not catfish. Fugu."

"Fugu!" I nearly shouted. I had heard about fugu. It is the highly poisonous blowfish, considered a delicacy in Japan. It is quite lethal if not prepared correctly. The best quality gently tingles the palate. The worst numbs all of you permanently. My mouth did feel a bit numb, but after all the sake, what did I know? My extremities were functioning. I smiled and said it was delicious and had another bite.

After dinner, I feebly offered to pay the bill, or at least part of it. The tip, maybe. They laughed me off. I doubt if I could have covered a tenth of the tip.

On February 24, 1991, three years after my trip to Japan, attorney Yamanouchi was arrested by Osaka police and charged with attempted extortion of a man trying to build a small commercial building near the offices of the Takumi-gumi, the yakuza subgroup headed by Masaru Takumi.

Yamanouchi beat that rap and went on to become quite a well-known novelist, regularly turning out books that featured yakuza and ex-yakuza protagonists. Three of his books formed the basis for *Another Lonely Hitman*, *A Yakuza in Love*, and *The Fire Within*, movies directed by Rokuro Mochizuki that are considered to be yakuza noir classics.

I returned to the Islands and wrote a series of stories about golf courses and the yakuza, later turning out additional stories about Yasumichi "Viper" Morishita and Ginji Yasuda, another Japanese investor with long-standing Hawai'i ties, who had wasted a $100 million personal fortune by buying the Aladdin Hotel Casino in Las Vegas and running it into the ground.

Friends described Yasuda "as a proud but naïve businessman whose silver-spoon youth and lavish lifestyle were better suited to the role of gambler than gambling czar," I wrote.[10]

After finding direct financial and yakuza ties linking Yasuda to Morishita and to another Japanese investor named Tomonori Tsurumaki, I tried many times to obtain comment from Yasuda, who by then was seriously ill in Los Angeles. The allegations about him were extremely serious, he had access to a great deal of money, and my editors were very nervous.

I didn't know it at the time, but Yasuda was terminally ill and would pass away several months later. I sent certified letters to him and to several of his executive employees and advisers, laying out my findings about his yakuza ties and requesting comment.

The only response I ever got was from a television reporter in Las Vegas, who had somehow gotten a copy of my detailed letter to Yasuda. This guy informed me that he was preparing a story about the contents of my letter and had the chutzpah to ask me for additional backup information.

I was appalled. Where had this clown gotten my letter? How could he possibly contemplate doing a story based on my work, my years of research? He primly informed me that he couldn't reveal his sources and said he was going to do a story whether I talked to him or not. Didn't I want my viewpoint represented?

The guy was trying to muscle me and was using some of the same tactics that I had used on other people in the past. It made me squirm. I eventually told the guy that I had learned that some of the information contained in the letter was inaccurate but I wasn't going to specify what it was. He could use the contents of the letter at his own risk. That seemed to cool him off, and his subsequent story focused on Yasuda's financial predicament at the Aladdin and only mentioned my letter in passing.

My final foray into things yakuza was an interview with Tomonori Tsurumaki, the yakuza-connected businessman who had partially financed Yasuda's venture into Las Vegas. The catch was that the interview had to take place in Chicago. Tsurumaki had travelled there to buy classic and vintage automobiles for display at Autopolis, a bizarre $300 million museum-racetrack he was building on a mountaintop on the island of Kyushu.

I pitched the trip to *Advertiser* management and was turned down. Get real, I was told, there's no budget for this, and it doesn't have much to do with Hawai'i. I blustered and sniveled, but it was no sale. Finally, I hit on an alternative. I would use "mileage plus" benefits generated by my previous work trips for a quick flight to Chicago. A red-eye flight would get me there by 10 a.m., and I'd talk to Tsurumaki and catch a return flight the same day. I could do the whole thing in 24 hours.

The editors threw up their hands. It's not worth it, they said, but go ahead.

It all would have worked out if Tsurumaki had stuck to my plan. But he had other things in mind besides talking to me. Most of them involved spending a great deal of money on cars.

I talked my way into accompanying Tsurumaki, his Honolulu-based attorney, and other advisers on a van ride to Old Volo Village, some 50 or 60 miles outside of Chicago, where acres of old cars were on sale in warehouses built in the middle of Illinois cornfields.

Tsurumaki and his associates selected 10 automobiles, including a 1930 Packard, three vintage Corvettes, and a 1963 Cadillac convertible. The sticker prices totaled $605,000, but after some old-fashioned used-car haggling, Tsurumaki pried cash, volume, and "international goodwill" discounts out of seller Greg Grams to get the final price down to $540,000.

"I'm getting slaughtered in this deal," Grams complained in mid-haggle.[11]

By the time we got back to the city, I still hadn't been able to ask my questions of Tsurumaki and had to rebook a flight home. I arranged a pricey overnight room at the same Swiss Air–owned hotel where Tsurumaki was staying and was invited to accompany Tsurumaki to dinner.

It turned out to be a business meal at a lovely Italian restaurant owned by car fancier Joseph Marchetti. Over pasta, Tsurumaki told me that he had come from a humble "country" background and made his money in steel, agriculture, real estate, and stock investments. One of the purposes of the Autopolis facility, he said, was to provide a recreational outlet for Japan's growing motorcycle gangs.

He acknowledged personal acquaintances with yakuza leaders, particularly Kakuji Inagawa, boss of a large Tokyo-based gang called Inagawa-kai.

Tsurumaki said he had played golf twice with Inagawa, once as part of a group that included former prime minister Kakuei Tanaka.

But he was not a yakuza and was pressing defamation charges against a Japanese newspaper that had labeled him a financial adviser to Inagawa-kai, he said.

Although he had been charged in Tokyo with extortion three years earlier, he had not known that the collection agency he hired to collect a $500,000 debt was run by an Inagawa-kai member, Tsurumaki said.

He had done business deals in the past with "Viper" Morishita, Tsurumaki said, but no longer worked with the man because he did not care for some of his business methods. Morishita got his nickname "because three years after he bites you [lends you money], the interest payments kill you," Tsurumaki said.[12]

After dinner, the group repaired to a riverfront warehouse where Marchetti stored part of his automobile collection. Tsurumaki and Marchetti began dickering over prices for some of the machines, but that all stopped when Marchetti unveiled what he called his "pride and joy," a replica Ferrari P4 race car.

Marchetti refused to take any offers for the vehicle, saying that only three of the originals had ever been built and were worth up to $15 million apiece.

Then he fired the car up, and the roar of those 12 cylinders in that enclosed warehouse space made my hair stand on end. I told Marchetti I wanted to buy it.

My stories about Yasuda, Morishita, and Tsurumaki ran in August 1989 and pretty much closed out my explorations of Japan investors and their yakuza affiliations.

I did produce one more, several months later, after Tsurumaki and Morishita made international news when they spent more than $100 million each on European artwork. Tsurumaki laid out $51.3 million for a single Picasso painting. Morishita paid $55 million for works by Monet, Renoir, Gauguin, and Picasso. He even spent another $53 million to buy a major share of Christie's International, the London auction house. I was the only reporter in the western world, as far as I knew, who had already publicly connected these two men to each other and to the yakuza.

On one buying trip they made, they stayed in a Trump Tower apartment in Manhattan, took in the Kentucky Derby, sported at Yasuda's Las Vegas casino, and finished the trip at one of Morishita's Palm Springs golf courses.

I wrote a summary of my findings about the two, noting that they were "better known for collecting bad debts than fine art."[13] The artwork was eventually seized by Japanese banks after the borrowers defaulted on loans.

CHAPTER SIX

Vegas

In mid-1978, a man straight out of the movie *Casino* called on his friends in Hawai'i for help with gambling regulators in Nevada.

The Nevada Gaming Control Board had denied a "key employee" casino license to Irving "Ash" Resnick at the Aladdin Hotel, listing among its reasons Resnick's ties to organized crime figures in Hawai'i and his associations with "undesirables" in organized labor.

At one time in his life, Resnick had been a semiprofessional basketball player in New York, where he grew up, but when I encountered him, he was a gambler and self-promoter par excellence. Resnick had moved from casino to casino in various Las Vegas management positions, always battling gaming authorities who had concerns about his murky past and shady associates.

Resnick helped pioneer the production of big-time boxing matches in Nevada, at one time working as Sonny Liston's manager. The FBI investigated allegations that Resnick helped fix the championship bout that Liston shockingly lost to Muhammad Ali, according to FOIA files.[1] There are even stories out there on the Web suggesting that Resnick had a hand in Liston's death.

Resnick put Joe Louis to work as a greeter at Caesars Palace, saying the two had been friends since they first met in an Army lunch line in 1942.

The FBI identified Resnick as an associate of several notorious New York–based mafiosi, including Charles "Charley the Blade" Tourine and Vincent "Jimmy Blue Eyes" Alo.[2]

Resnick was a regular visitor to Hawai'i, collecting gambling debts and cultivating high rollers. He annually hosted a golf tournament on Maui called "Ash's Whip Out" that attracted gamblers from around the country as well as the Islands.

In 1973, somebody stitched Resnick's car with bullets while he was driving in Vegas. The following year, police removed eight sticks of dynamite wired to blow up his vehicle when he turned the ignition.[3]

Like I said, Ash was straight out of *Casino*.

In 1978, his problems with the Gaming Control Board came to a head when he was denied a license to work as casino manager at the Aladdin. Honolulu police had surveilled Resnick during visits to the Islands and seen him in the company of undesirables, including organized crime members like Masato "Tramp" Kawakami, a Honolulu illegal gambling operator who was also working as a Teamsters Union driver for the *Hawaii Five-0* television show, Gaming Control Board investigators reported.

United Press International then moved a story in May that Resnick had appealed the license denial to the politically appointed Gaming Control Commission, which reversed the control board's decision after hearing from influential friends of Resnick in Las Vegas and Hawai'i.[4]

Among Resnick's backers were Hawai'i Governor George Ariyoshi and Honolulu Mayor Frank Fasi. Ariyoshi said he wrote his letter at the request of Don Ho.[5] The governor's letter said he had a "slight" acquaintance with Resnick but knew that he helped Hawai'i entertainers and "enjoys a high reputation here." Fasi went further, calling Resnick "a close personal friend" who "would be an asset to any employer."

But the letters were nothing compared to in-person testimony delivered to the commission by Hawai'i state senator Duke Kawasaki.

To refute the control board's information about Resnick's ties with Tramp Kawakami and Maui organized crime figure Takeo Yamauchi, Kawasaki said the Hawai'i State Crime Commission knew nothing bad about Resnick or his friends in the Islands. Kawasaki also assured gaming commissioners that he was a friend of the Honolulu Police Department and had been advised that Resnick had not been followed by HPD officers.[6]

Resnick also received glowing personal references from such notables as entertainer Wayne Newton and Jerry Tarkanian, at the time the head coach of the University of Nevada at Las Vegas "Runnin' Rebels" basketball team.

Walter Wright and I began looking into Resnick and his activities in Hawai'i. In June, we broke a story that when Kawasaki testified for Resnick, his airfare and hotel room at the Aladdin had been "comped" by Resnick. He had substantial gambling markers outstanding at the Aladdin and other Vegas casinos when he testified and paid $32,000 in gaming debts in June.[7]

Resnick was the source for much of that information, although Kawa-saki acknowledged some of it, saying he was a regular player in Las Vegas and had been staying at the Aladdin when he heard about Resnick's li-censing problems. He extended his visit to testify for Resnick, he said, because he believed the casino executive had been unfairly accused of wrongdoing.

Walter and I pitched and won approval for a trip to Nevada to further explore stories about Kawasaki and Hawai'i's love affair with Las Vegas.

We spent a week in the desert, eventually turning out a three-part se-ries that covered the massive numbers of Island residents who regularly junketed to Vegas and the ugly history of violence that was associated with the junket trade.

Nappy Pulawa and Alvin Kaohu had won the dubious distinction of getting enrolled in the gaming industry's black book, a roster of mobsters who were never allowed to set foot in a Nevada casino.

The timing of our visit landed us in the middle of the period covered by the *Casino* film. Frank "Lefty" Rosenthal, the man whose life formed the basis for Robert De Niro's Ace Rothstein character, was a contemporary of Resnick's and active in Las Vegas at the time. So, too, was Anthony Spilotro, the murderous, diminutive Chicago mobster portrayed by Joe Pesci as Nicky Santoro in the film.

Walter and I noted in one of our stories that federal authorities at the time were investigating Spilotro's possible ties to casino company Argent Corporation and its chief executive, Allen Glick, who was transformed in the film into Philip Green, played by Kevin Pollack. Argent had just been fined $100,000 because of cash-skimming operations at two of the com-pany's Vegas casinos.

At the Aladdin, two executives (not Resnick) were under indictment for allowing hidden ownership by Detroit mobsters affiliated with Motor City mafia don Anthony Giacalone.

And the chairman of the Gaming Control Commission when Resnick got his license was Harry Reid, later to become majority leader of the U.S. Senate. In *Casino*, the Gaming Control Commission chairman was named Harrison Roberts, and the character, played by Dick Smothers, was mod-eled after Reid.

A Vegas character named Joe Agosto, whom Walter Wright knew per-sonally from Seattle, was once caught on an FBI wiretap referring to Reid as "Mr. Clean Face," and I can remember Walter talking to Resnick about the commission and "Mr. Clean Face."

Lefty Rosenthal/Ace Rothstein didn't get his license from the commis-sion, but Ash Resnick got his, thanks to Duke Kawasaki and friends.

The centerpiece of our series was all about Duke Kawasaki and Ash Resnick.

When we arrived, we had major questions about the markers Kawasaki had amassed at Vegas casinos and what had become of them. Walter and I spent five days chasing down the facts. In my memory now, I spent much of that time in our hotel room listening to Walter work the phone. The man was a magician on the telephone. I worked closely with Walter on that story and others, sharing a room in Vegas and later an office off the *Advertiser* city room. I learned a lot of things from him, mostly the values of patience and politeness and perseverance, especially on the telephone.

He joked, he rambled, he got people to talk about anything and everything, and in the process he absolutely wrung them dry of information.

I marveled at the process, and it very nearly drove me crazy. "Why are you wasting our time on that shit?" I told Walter at one point in our Vegas stay. "We're under the gun here. We've gotta get this information and you're blabbing on the phone with some secretary about her sick kids."

"You never can tell," Walter said, as he got ready to make another call.

I quit the room in disgust, and when I came back a half hour later, Walter was on his way out the door. "I think I've got it," he said. "I'll be back in an hour or so."

When he came back, he had a copy of Duke Kawasaki's gambling records, straight out of Central Credit in Las Vegas. We had our story. I have an idea about where Walter got the numbers, but he never told me for sure.

The records showed that during the period Kawasaki was in Las Vegas, including the day he testified, his Resnick-approved markers at the Aladdin increased from $38,000 to $80,000.[8]

Kawasaki and Resnick insisted that there was no connection between the debts and the testimony. The senator told us that the experience had caused him to swear off gambling forever. "I figured that the Good Lord never intended that I be halfway lucky at gambling," Kawasaki said.

Walter and I spent two of our nights in Vegas loitering around the Aladdin until Resnick made time to talk to us. We were finally shown into his office at 2 a.m.

"How ya doin', fellas?" he boomed at us as we sat down.

It was the middle of the workday for him. He was busy, taking care of customers, clearing credit requests, and trying to arrange personal wagers on professional basketball games. He had one of his aides calling around town to different casinos and sports books, trying to get the best odds for him. The aide, who looked like an ex-boxer, was extremely harried because he couldn't get the numbers Resnick wanted.

"The fuck you mean, he won't give it to you?" Resnick bellowed.

"You tell him it's for me? Awright, awright, call the other guy, all I need's half a point. That's all, half a point."

A very attractive woman found her way into the office. "Ash," she said, "I need your help. I need a physician."

When she left, Resnick wondered if we were in the market for some female company. We regretfully declined.

Several times during our meeting, a little man straight out of Damon Runyon—purple shirt, yellow tie, pointy shoes—burst through the door to Resnick's office.

"Ash, Ash, I need my money, Ash," the man said. "Gimme my money, Ash."

"You told me to hold it, I'm holding it," Resnick roared. "Now get the fuck outta here and quit bothering me. Can't you see I'm busy?"

The little guy, who also had the look of an ex-pug, glanced at us as he backed out of the room, still asking for his money. "He's a degenerate gambler," Resnick told us. "We go through this every time he's in town. Pretty soon I'm gonna have to give him his money."

Eventually he did, that very night, pulling open a desk drawer and removing stacks of cash totaling $50,000 for the supplicant.

"Don't come back crying when it's gone," Resnick said.

Then he turned to us. "Now look, you guys, I told you, Duke's clean, he don't owe nothing, how many times I gotta tell you this?"

As Resnick told it, he had personally borrowed $30,000 from another Aladdin customer to pay the balance that had been outstanding on Kawasaki's account. So, no more marker, no more problem. We tried to point out that, if anything, Resnick's solution only worsened the senator's apparent conflict of interest. Resnick waved us off. It was Vegas. Things were different there.

It was an entertaining evening. Walter and I asked ourselves later if Resnick might not have staged the whole thing to meet our expectations of a night in the life of Ash Resnick, Casino Manager. We decided no, that Resnick played his life like it was theater.

Resnick took his show on the road to Hawai'i once or twice a year, and he usually called to let us know he was in town. If he didn't, I would hear soon enough that Ash was around and give him a call. "How ya doin', pal?" he would boom on the phone. "How about dinner?" Or breakfast or lunch or whatever meal suited him. Meetings with Resnick were always arranged around food.

One of Resnick's purposes in visiting Hawai'i was to check on the progress of a lawsuit he had filed against the exclusive Waialae Country Club after he was banned from the club's premises. The club, which hosts the

Hawaiian Open golf tournament annually, never said precisely why Resnick had been banished, but members indicated it was because he was conducting debt collection sessions there. The lawsuit was eventually dropped, and Resnick moved his activities to another golf venue where he was more welcome, the Honolulu International Country Club.

He summoned Walter and me to meet with him one evening at the HICC to discuss a story we were working on about his planned employment of Norman "Katsu" Yoshino as the Hawai'i representative of the Aladdin.

Walter and I had already met with Yoshino at a business he operated, a secondhand precious metals business on Kalakaua Avenue just outside of Waikiki.

Yoshino had a history of association with local organized crime figures, including one-time gambling czar Earl K. H. Kim, but no criminal record to speak of. He was nervous about talking to us, but did so on the advice of Resnick. We told him it would be like a dry run for questions Nevada gaming authorities were sure to ask him as part of the licensing process.

When Resnick heard about the kinds of questions we were asking Yoshino, he called us to the Grill Room of the HICC to straighten us out. Yoshino was there, and he wasn't happy. A lot of other people were there—it was early evening—including some well-to-do and influential members of Honolulu society.

Resnick told us Harry Chung, Mayor Fasi's chief fund-raiser, was supposed to be there to meet friends but couldn't make it because he had been in a car accident the night before. Yoshino told us that William Chung, Harry's brother and the chairman of the Honolulu Police Commission, was a business associate of Yoshino's.

Yoshino would periodically excuse himself from our table and leave the room. I finally asked Resnick where Yoshino was going. "Oh, he's got Jerry Kaichi's wife in the next room. She's waiting for Jerry. He's coming to pay off a marker," Resnick said.

Kaichi was a well-known Honolulu drug dealer, in and out of prison on a regular basis. I began to understand why Waialae had eighty-sixed Resnick.

Yoshino, who is the *hanai* brother (an informal adoption practice rooted in Hawaiian culture) of former Honolulu mayor and congressional and gubernatorial candidate Mufi Hannemann, told us in our initial interview, "I'm a gambler. I just never got caught."

He later changed that statement to "I used to be a gambler" and amended it again by saying he had never been anything more than a social gambler. We included all three quotes in our stories about Yoshino.

The Clark County Sheriff's Office in Las Vegas later found Yoshino to be unsuitable for employment as the Aladdin's casino representative in Hawai'i.[9]

The last time I saw Ash Resnick, he was holding court poolside at the Halekulani Hotel, one of Waikiki's poshest venues. I got there just in time to see Larry Mehau and another man I could only see from the back leaving Resnick's table.

"Who was that with Larry?" I asked Resnick.

He gave me the man's business card. It was Tom Enomoto, a local real estate developer and the chief political fund-raiser for Governor John Waihee.

"What'd they want?" I asked Resnick.

"They didn't want nothin'. I'm trying to sell the Dunes, and they maybe got access to Japanese money," he said.

"But Ash, you don't even work at the Dunes."

"I'm just trying to put something together," he said.

Resnick died in 1989. I wrote an obituary that didn't do him justice.

I kept turning out Vegas-related stories, some of the best ones about an intriguing, Indonesian-born, Hawai'i-based businessman named Sukarman Sukamto, who made big news in Vegas in 1992.

A legal dispute between the Caesars Palace Hotel-Casino and Nevada gaming regulators led to the public disclosure in January 1992 that the casino had written off $4.2 million in gambling debts owed by Sukamto.

The casino didn't forgive the debts because it believed Sukamto couldn't pay them. Instead, the markers were written off as an inducement for Sukamto to repay some of an even larger amount owed and because Caesars wanted Sukamto to keep coming to Vegas and losing money.

A baby-faced real estate developer and investor, Sukamto owned the Bank of Honolulu, a nationally chartered, federally insured American financial institution that he had purchased with his father-in-law, Atang Latief. The Caesars Palace legal settlement also revealed that the casino had written off $2.8 million in gambling debts owed by Latief. It's not every day that you find the owners of an American bank losing millions of dollars at Vegas gaming tables.

A year and a half after the markers were written off, sources in Vegas that I developed while researching the Resnick and yakuza stories told me that Sukamto's debts at Caesars had risen again to $3.5 million. He also owed $3 million at the Mirage Hotel-Casino.[10]

In a three-year period, Sukamto visited Caesars Palace nearly two dozen times, and more than $300,000 in room, food, beverage, and entertainment expenses charged by him and his friends were comped—given free of charge—by Caesars.

In Honolulu, Sukamto bought Aloha Motors, a defunct car dealership on the outskirts of Waikiki, then flipped the property over to the state for more than $130 million and a tidy profit. It is now the site of the Hawai'i Convention Center.

Across Kalakaua Avenue from the convention center is a monstrous high-rise residential condominium developed by Sukamto called the Waikiki Landmark.

In 1994, I found that Sukamto's companies and employees were lavishing campaign donations on a select group of Island politicians.[11] A total of $55,525 was given to the campaigns of Mayor Fasi, Lieutenant Governor Ben Cayetano, city councilwoman (and future state senate president) Donna Mercado Kim, and others. The donors included Sukamto corporate officials and staffers, including secretaries, Sukamto's bodyguard, and the travel agent who booked all of Sukamto's Vegas forays.

Sukamto's friend, former Honolulu police lieutenant Manny Rezentes, gave money to the same politicians on the same days as the other Sukamto donations. Rezentes had left the public payroll and was working at the time as Caesars Palace marketing representative in Hawai'i. Even Caesars had given $2,000 to the Fasi campaign. An executive told me that the casino bought four $500 Fasi fund-raiser tickets "at the request of a customer."

The campaign donations were legal because all the donors said they gave the money voluntarily. Sukamto said his employees could afford the donations because they were paid well and received "attractive bonuses."

Sukamto at the time was under investigation by the FBI on suspicion of attempted bribery of state senate president James Aki in connection with proposed development of Aki-owned real estate. Sukamto was never charged, but Aki was later convicted of felony promotion of gambling at his family property.

During a visit to the federal building around this time, I was about to enter a courtroom to sit in on a trial when I was grabbed and pushed against a wall by federal Drug Enforcement Agent Robert Aiu, the husband of councilwoman Donna Kim.

When I protested and tried to get free of him, Aiu pushed harder and said, "I hear you're asking questions about my wife and Sukamto."

One of the court security personnel came over and pulled Aiu away.

I knew Aiu slightly—he was one of the lead agents in the disastrous guns-for-drugs yakuza trial, and I had talked with him once or twice about other cases, including the murder of his snitch, Arthur Baker.

I told Aiu I didn't know what he was talking about and that he had no right to manhandle a reporter in the federal courthouse. I said that I had asked no such questions about his wife and Sukamto, and even if I had, they were both public figures and fair game for reporters' questions.

When I asked him who told him I was asking those questions, he said, "Manny Rezentes." I also knew Rezentes slightly—I had interviewed him about the Sukamto donations story. Years before, when Rezentes was still with HPD, he had warned me about talking to Ronnie Ching about the Arthur Baker murder. He also figured prominently in the 1984 trial of Ching and three other men accused of murdering city prosecutor Charles Marsland's son.

Ching accused Rezentes of complicity in the Marsland murder, something Rezentes adamantly denied. He was never charged in the case.

When I called Rezentes after my courthouse encounter with Aiu, he claimed that someone using my name had called him and asked about a supposed personal relationship between Sukamto and Kim.

When I told him that I made no such call, Rezentes said that, on second thought, the caller didn't sound much like me, but he hadn't made that realization when he told Aiu about the call. To this day, I don't know who was impersonating me or why. As far as I know, Kim and Sukamto were never anything more than acquaintances.

But the incident illustrates the small-town nature of Honolulu.

Sukamto moved to Singapore in the 1990s and legally changed his name to Sukamto Sia. For continuity's sake, I will continue to refer to him as Sukamto. He maintained an extensive business presence in Hawai'i, including his ownership of the Bank of Honolulu, and was a regular visitor to the Islands as well as to his favorite haunts in Las Vegas.

In October 1998, the high-flying Sukamto crashed to earth. He was arrested in Vegas for writing bad checks to cover massive gambling losses there: $8.5 million at Caesars and $6 million at the Rio.[12] A month later, Sukamto filed personal bankruptcy papers in federal court in Hawai'i, listing more than $300 million in debts and $9 million in assets.

In retrospect, Sukamto would have been much better off if he'd just flown home to Singapore and stayed there. But he pursued the bankruptcy action in Hawai'i, filing extensive details of his business activities and personal finances.

I began poring over the records and comparing them with other publicly available documents that concerned the Bank of Honolulu and Sukamto's business ventures. The outlines of a possible story about fraudulent misuse of bank assets began to take shape. When I bounced my suspicions off an FBI agent I knew, I struck a nerve.

The agent told me, off the record, that the bureau was actively investigating Sukamto and asked me to hold off on my story. Sukamto was in

Singapore but would be arrested the next time he came to town for a Bankruptcy Court meeting with his creditors. I could have the arrest story exclusively if I held off until then.

I was by that time working as an investigative reporter for KITV, the local ABC television affiliate, and the promise of exclusive video of the arrest of Sukamto by FBI agents was very hard to pass up. I talked the matter over with Wally Zimmerman, news director at KITV, and we decided to go along with the FBI.

On the appointed day, I arrived early to scope out the creditors' meeting room with chief cameraman Bob Guanzon. The room was in a private office building in downtown Honolulu, but it was technically part of U.S. Bankruptcy Court, so no cameras were allowed inside. One of the side doors to the room had a window in it, so Bob was able to unobtrusively set up outside the window with a view into the room.

Sukamto arrived with his legal team, entering the room through another door. After they were settled in, a door behind us burst open, and a team of FBI agents brandishing guns rushed out, shouldering me, Bob, and his camera out of the way to get into the creditors' meeting.

By the time we recovered, the feds were ushering the handcuffed Sukamto out of the room. We got only some brief footage of that part of the arrest.

We were bitterly disappointed by how things worked out. The agents were apologetic but said we were in the way and had to be moved. I don't know if they did it on purpose. But we did get an exclusive beat on the arrest and some footage of it. Nobody else had that.

Sukamto was indicted on 20 counts of wire fraud and bankruptcy fraud, eventually pleading guilty to two main charges. Additional counts of fraud and money laundering against his lovely girlfriend, Kelly Randall, and a brother, Sumitro, were dismissed as part of the plea deal.

The Bank of Honolulu, teetering on the edge of insolvency, was seized by federal regulators.

While the criminal case was pending, friends of Sukamto, including Manny Rezentes, put up their residences as collateral for his $1.5 million bail. Sukamto and Randall moved to a rented mansion in the exclusive Bel Air enclave of Los Angeles. Sukamto told the court that he needed specialized treatment there for a thyroid condition while he and Randall awaited trial.

Before Sukamto was sentenced, some of his friends wrote letters to the court urging leniency. I got my hands on one of those letters, written on official letterhead of the University of Hawai'i by head football coach June Jones. (Jones was also a good friend of Manny Rezentes.)

In the letter, written to U.S. District Court Judge David Ezra, Jones referred to Sukamto as "SS" and called him "one of the most wonderful persons I have associated myself with" in Hawai'i.[13] Jones told Ezra he didn't think his friend deserved to go to prison.

Sukamto "could be a great asset to the University of Hawai'i by giving instructional lectures to our students. I make this suggestion as part of a rehabilitation sentence, in lieu of custody time," the letter said. When I talked to the coach about the letter, he was chagrined to learn that it was a public record. He declined to discuss its contents, saying it was "a private letter to the judge."

Ezra turned aside the recommendations of Jones and other Sukamto supporters, sentencing him to three years in federal prison. Sukamto was deported after his release and is forbidden to return to the United States.

In late 2007, Sukamto still owed more than $200 million to his creditors. Randall owed more than $1 million.[14]

The pair married in mid-2007 and were back to living the high life. The wedding, I found out, was staged at the plush Hotel De Paris in Monaco with guests flown in from around the world to celebrate the event. Among the guests were prominent Waikiki entertainer Danny Kaleikini and Donna Kim, by then the vice president of the state senate.[15]

CHAPTER SEVEN

Bishop Estate

When things got slow at work, the Bishop Estate was always a source of inspiration.

Created under the 1884 will of Hawaiian Princess Bernice Pauahi Bishop, the estate had developed over the next century into the richest and most influential private institution in the Islands and one of the wealthiest charities in the world.

The princess had endowed her estate with more than 400,000 acres of land in the Hawaiian archipelago and required that the assets be administered by five trustees for the benefit of the Kamehameha Schools, an educational institution for children of Native Hawaiian ancestry.

Among the land holdings were large swaths of beachfront property, including tracts in Waikiki that became some of the most precious real estate on the planet. By the 1990s, the estate's investment portfolio was worth billions of dollars and included a $500 million ownership stake in Goldman Sachs, the Wall Street investment banking behemoth.

That investment was engineered by a wily and astute trustee of the estate, Matsuo "Matsy" Takabuki, and earned the institution a 400 percent return when the Goldman shares were sold in 2002 for $2.5 billion.

Bishop Estate also had another close connection to Goldman through the bank's former chairman, Robert Rubin. When Rubin became U.S. treasury secretary in President Bill Clinton's administration, he placed his personal Goldman Sachs holdings in a blind trust whose minimum value was guaranteed, for a fee, by the Bishop Estate. The unusual arrangement brought both Rubin and the estate plenty of criticism.

Rubin's cabinet position gave him oversight of the Internal Revenue Service, which the five Bishop Estate trustees assiduously lobbied to protect both the size of their annual compensation and the institution's tax-exempt status. The tax exemption and the trustee pay were regularly questioned by critics who said the financial activities of the estate and the Hawaiians-only admissions policy of the Kamehameha Schools violated federal tax and civil rights laws.

Rubin's spokesman at Treasury assured me that the secretary would take no official action involving the estate.

In writing her will, Princess Pauahi and her haole husband, Charles Reed Bishop, included a clause that eventually made the job of Bishop Estate trustee the juiciest political patronage plum in the state. The will decreed that the five trustees would be selected by members of the Hawai'i Supreme Court.

Given that the supreme court justices were in turn appointed by the governor and approved by the state senate, that brief sentence in the will guaranteed that many rivers of influence in Hawai'i—money, land, politics, justice, and Native Hawaiian rights—converged at the Bishop Estate.

I wrote my first Bishop Estate story in 1984, a time when its financial activities were largely ignored by the public and the press.[1] I found that the estate, which for decades had been land-rich but cash-poor, was overflowing with money.

The reason was a change in the state's laws of land ownership. For generations, those laws had concentrated control of residential Hawai'i real estate in the hands of a few oligarchies. The Bishop Estate was the largest of them.

Constrained by the terms of the will and by state and federal tax laws, the estate trustees had rarely sold residential house lots but instead leased them for 55-year terms. After the legislature passed land ownership reform laws in the 1960s and '70s, the land barons were forced to give leaseholders the chance to buy their property outright.

As a result, a tidal wave of dollars engulfed the estate by the early 1980s. Yearly financial accounts that had to be filed with the state probate court showed that the trustees collected annual commissions based on a percentage of estate income and had become very rich men.

In 1983, the five trustees of the estate collected $238,000 apiece in commissions. One of the trustees collecting that money was William S. Richardson, the former chief justice of the Hawai'i Supreme Court, who left the court in 1982 to take a seat on the Bishop Estate board of trustees. He was given the job by his colleagues on the supreme court.

Another trustee was Henry H. Peters, a state legislator who happened to be the speaker of the state house of representatives. Also serving were Takabuki and Myron "Pinky" Thompson, businessmen who had been close advisers to former governor John Burns, as well as Richard "Papa" Lyman, another former politician who was both a descendant of missionaries and a Native Hawaiian. Thompson, Peters, and Richardson were also Native Hawaiians. A later appointee to the board was Richard "Dickie" Wong, longtime president of the state senate.

As more and more land sales were recorded, trustee commissions rose accordingly, to the point that the trustees had an embarrassment of riches. They decided to refuse to accept some of the commissions—after receiving an opinion from the IRS that the waivers would not be taxable—and stopped disclosing their commission income in annual financial reports filed by the estate in probate court. The trustees simply stopped talking about their annual pay.

I learned that federal law required that tax returns of charities like the Bishop Estate be open to the public. Charles Memminger, a competitor at the *Honolulu Star-Bulletin*, and I each invoked the federal disclosure law and forced the estate to give us its tax return, which disclosed that in the 1987 fiscal year, trustee commissions had ballooned to $920,000 each. They also voluntarily waived another $112,000 that they were legally entitled to collect.

That was the high-water mark of commissions accepted by the trustees. The following year, each trustee accepted $648,000 and waived another $906,416. The next year, the commissions were $659,558, and waivers were $690,000.

In 1989, a friend told me that Hawai'i Supreme Court Chief Justice Herman Lum had an interest in a restaurant called the Great Wok of China that operated in the Bishop Estate–owned Royal Hawaiian Shopping Center on Kalakaua Avenue in Waikiki.

Lum rose to chief justice after William Richardson resigned from the court to become a Bishop Estate trustee. Lum voted to appoint Richardson to the estate job.

I verified Lum's investment, which was made through a partnership called Lumleong Enterprises.[2] The partnership invested $210,000 in the restaurant and signed a commercial lease with the estate trustees in 1980, after Lum was appointed to the supreme court. Lum's wife and son were officers of the restaurant company, and each had put $10,000 into the venture.

I further found that Lumleong Enterprises had a long history of other dealings with the Bishop Estate. It held two commercial leases of estate land in Honolulu from the 1960s until 1984–1985, when the partnership sold the leases for $2.4 million.[3]

Before and after Lum became a supreme court justice, he presided over Bishop Estate cases. Once on the high court, he participated in the appointment of estate trustees. When I asked Lum about these apparent conflicts of interest, he told me in a written statement that the estate had a "unique" relationship with the supreme court that required the justices to act in a "private capacity" when selecting trustees. And the estate was so large that it exerted an inescapable and "pervasive influence" at all levels of Hawaiian society, including the supreme court, Lum said.

When Lum was still a circuit court judge in 1972, he ruled in favor of the Bishop Estate in a lawsuit that challenged the propriety of the state supreme court's involvement in the trustee selection process. Lum did not disclose to the Native Hawaiian plaintiffs in that case, called *Kekoa v. Supreme Court*, that he had personal business ties to the estate worth hundreds of thousands of dollars.

Lum was a circuit judge at the time of the *Kekoa* case but served as a substitute justice after all members of the high court disqualified themselves from hearing the matter. Lum and the substitute panel ruled that the selection process was permissible because supreme court justices had no "personal stake or interest in the trustee appointment decision."

When researching the story, I located Curtis Kekoa Sr., the lead plaintiff in the 1972 case, who had been a U.S. Air Force colonel at the time of the decision and later had become a lawyer. He told me he had no idea that Lum had interests in two large commercial Bishop Estate leases when Lum ruled in the *Kekoa* case. He said he thought Lum's participation in the case was "inappropriate."

"I believe that a justice of the supreme court who has an existing or foreseeable interest in a Bishop Estate business lease or arrangement has a personal stake or interest in the appointment of a Bishop Estate trustee," Kekoa told me. And Lum's later participation in trustee selections after he rose to the supreme court was likewise inappropriate, Kekoa said.[4] A justice involved with the estate in a commercial lease could pick a trustee "who would not be a threat but might be an ally" in later lease negotiations, Kekoa said.

In fact, when the Great Wok restaurant ran into financial problems in the mid-1980s, the estate granted a two-year deferral of its lease rent obligations, a Royal Hawaiian Shopping Center executive told me.

Lum's entry into the new Bishop Estate commercial deal after he became a supreme court justice was "tantamount to flouting" the state code of judicial conduct, which forbade judges from engaging in improprieties or even the appearance of improprieties, said Kekoa.

Native Hawaiian attorney Mililani Trask told me that Lum had violated the "personal stake" standard established in the *Kekoa* case when he participated in the 1982 selection of Chief Justice Richardson as a new Bishop Estate trustee.

The Richardson appointment created a vacancy in the top job at the supreme court and gave the remaining justices "a chance to become chief justice and to have not only the additional pecuniary benefit but the added prestige and political power as well," said Trask.

In researching the Lum story, I found a recent supreme court decision in a civil lawsuit filed against the Bishop Estate. In the decision, signed by Lum, the court reversed a lower court ruling that had found the estate liable for damages suffered by the plaintiff.

The attorney representing the estate, former state bar association president James Ventura, was a $50,000 partner with Lum in the Great Wok of China.[5]

The attorney for the losing side in that case said he knew nothing about the Lum-Ventura connections to the estate. "I can't believe your facts are correct," the lawyer said.

Lum told me that his business ties to Ventura and the estate were not enough to create an apparent conflict of interest.

The Code of Judicial Conduct required judges to personally decide if they had a conflict in a case, and if they found no conflict, they could not disclose the situation to the parties in the case, Lum said. So he had not disclosed the situation to the plaintiff in the suit.

"The procedure is designed to minimize the chance that an attorney or party will feel coerced" into agreeing to waive the judge's potential conflict of interest, Lum said.

But federal judges operated under almost identical ethical canons and routinely disclosed potential conflicts to parties in cases they were handling. "If you make the disclosure properly, you're not coercing the parties into agreeing to let you hear the case," U.S. District Court Judge Harold Fong told me. "You can never go wrong by disclosing it."

In his defense, Lum told me that he had previously ruled against the Bishop Estate in two landmark decisions that upheld the legality of the state's land reform laws that forced the estate to begin selling house lots to residential lessees.

In one of those cases, I found that the estate tried to disqualify Lum, saying that his personal dealings with the estate raised questions about his "objectivity and impartiality." But the court found that because Lum's estate deals involved commercial and not residential leases, he was not in a conflict of interest.

Lum's rulings in those cases may have run against the interests of the estate, but they made the trustees, including Lum's former colleague and mentor William Richardson, extremely wealthy men. In the nine years Richardson served as a trustee, he was paid some $4.5 million in commissions by the estate.

In the aftermath of my stories, and of increasing public outcry over trustee compensation and the court's unseemly alliance with the estate, Herman Lum recused himself from new Bishop Estate cases and from cases involving Ventura and his law firm. The entire supreme court later disqualified itself from further trustee selections.

In November 1994, the Bishop Estate received unwelcome national attention when CNN network business reporter Casey Wian revealed that trustees had mixed personal investments with estate money in a troubled Houston-based energy company called McKenzie Methane. The company was undergoing bankruptcy reorganization in Houston and was trading charges of fraud and bad faith behavior with the trustees in court proceedings there.

I found out what I could about the case on the ground in Honolulu and by phone with lawyers and McKenzie officials in Houston, but I couldn't manage to advance the story much beyond what Wian had reported.

I did learn that personal investments had been made not just by estate trustees but also by employees and officers of the estate and the Kamehameha Schools, as well as by high-powered, nationally known businesses and executives who had partnered with the estate in other ventures.

The specifics were available in bankruptcy court records, but I would have to go to Houston to look at them. The editors balked. I had already wrung approval from them to cover a criminal trial scheduled to begin in early 1995 in Tacoma, Washington, that centered on a $10 million "prime bank note" investment scam that I had uncovered in Honolulu in 1993 and 1994.

So I proposed continuing on to Houston when my work in Tacoma was finished. That leg of the trip was very reluctantly approved, so I hit the ground running when I got to Texas.

When I met with the McKenzie Methane lawyer who had all the records, he told me that he had recently retrieved the files from storage to show to a *Wall Street Journal* reporter who was researching a big story on the Bishop Estate.

Great. Now I was competing with the *Wall Street Journal* on the story.

The records were fabulous. Not only were there lengthy transcripts of sworn testimony delivered by trustees and estate employees but also there were videotapes of the testimony. A year later, after I had moved to television, those tapes would have been priceless.

The court documents demonstrated that not only had the trustees mixed their personal money with estate funds in a disastrous business venture, but so had other top employees of the estate. They all used financial analysis commissioned by the estate to make the investments.[6]

Takabuki, who had led the McKenzie Methane investment decision, turned out to be not so astute after all. He and his family members invested $1.5 million in the deal. Three trustees also participated: Pinky Thompson put in $510,000, Richardson ponied up $210,000, and Henry Peters (a former state house speaker and still a powerful legislator) invested $220,000.

The remaining trustee, Oswald Stender, wasn't on the board when the investment was made. But in deposition testimony Stender delivered in Texas, he described the personal investments by trustees as inappropriate "self-dealing."

Thirteen estate employees, including its asset manager and tax manager, personally invested sums ranging from $100,000 down to $10,000.

All the investments were made through a series of partnerships organized and administered by the estate's financial assets manager, Mitchell Gilbert, who invested $72,000.

The investment vehicles were called the HAK Partnerships, which stood for the Hawaiian words *hu aina koa*, Gilbert said in a sworn deposition. The translation of the Hawaiian phrase, Gilbert said, was "an effervescent production up from the ground."

In addition, Gilbert used estate stationery to solicit influential "investment affiliates" of the estate to join in the partnerships with the trustees and employees.

Some of the affiliates who put in personal money were Dave Thomas, founder of the Wendy's chain of fast-food restaurants; former U.S. Treasury Secretary William Simon; Ted Field, heir to the Chicago-based Marshall Field department store fortune; and even the estate's high-powered tax lawyer and lobbyist, Mark McConaghy, who worked in Washington, D.C.

Gilbert said he wrote the solicitation letters in a personal capacity and not as an estate employee, acknowledging in his deposition that he should not have used estate stationery. And he should not have signed them as the estate's financial assets manager, he said.

Copies of the letters were cc'd to Takabuki, who apparently raised no objection but did say under questioning later that Gilbert should not have sent the solicitations. "It's not a Bishop Estate investment," Takabuki said.[7]

A Bishop Estate Texas lawyer said that the estate could hope to recover only $20 million of its $85 million investment.

"Disaster . . . is the only word for it," the lawyer, D. J. Baker, said in court papers.

Estate lawyers and press representatives stoutly defended the propriety of the deal but admitted that a new policy had been put in effect that prohibited employees' personal investments in estate ventures.

Other estate watchers harshly criticized the mixture of personal and professional interests. And the McKenzie deal would later play a significant role in the "Broken Trust" essay and subsequent cataclysms that engulfed the estate.

I continued turning out significant exclusives about the estate and its far-flung and peculiar investments. One involved trustee Lokelani Lindsey, whose tyrannical behavior at Kamehameha Schools later sparked a wholesale revolt against the estate by school employees, teachers, students, and alumni.

Lindsey, while pulling down $850,000 in annual estate compensation, had used estate staff to handle zoning and building permit work for a small beach home she owned on Windward Oahu.[8]

Later, I managed to play a background role in a criminal case that sent Lindsey and her sister to prison. It wasn't meant to be a background role. I was just after a story.

I had moved to television when *Advertiser* reporter Sally Apgar wrote a lengthy story about Lindsey's personal finances, mentioning in passing a significant investment she shared with her sister Marlene.

I knew that Marlene, a hairdresser and real estate agent, was going through personal bankruptcy at the time. When I checked her bankruptcy filings, I could find no mention of that financial holding.

I hadn't written the story and didn't know enough of the background to write knowledgeably on the issue, so I called an official at bankruptcy court and alerted him to the contents of Apgar's story. He was interested and said he would check into it and try to let me know what he found out. Months later, I was surprised to learn that the Lindsey sisters had been indicted for bankruptcy fraud. They had conspired to hide the asset mentioned in Apgar's story from Marlene's creditors.

I called my contact at bankruptcy court and said, hey, I thought you were going to keep me in the loop on this. What happened? He apologized but said the FBI had taken control of the investigation and left him in the dark, too. I never had much luck when the FBI got involved in bankruptcy cases.

The Lindsey sisters were each sentenced to six months in prison.

While still at the *Advertiser* in 1995, I noticed a cooling of interest by the editors for Bishop Estate stories. I continued to turn them out, however.

Here's the lead from one, written in April 1995: "Just past the rural Virginia town of Gainesville on Highway 29, an hour's drive from Washington, D.C., sits a little corner of Hawaii's mighty Bishop Estate.

"Like some other estate investments spotlighted by *The Advertiser* this year, the Robert Trent Jones Golf Club has struggled financially."[9]

The story went on to say that the estate had initially guaranteed a $40 million loan to build a championship course on 210 acres of land on the shores of man-made Lake Manassas.

I found members of the club who complained to me about the estate trustees' management of the club after they assumed direct control of the project in 1994. Construction of 100 cottages on half-acre lots was far behind schedule, as were sales of club memberships, priced at initiation fees of $50,000 to $70,000. Club members wanted to buy out the remainder of the loan, pegged then at a value of about $18 million. One complained to me that members were "totally in the dark about what's happening and we know nothing about any purchase options."

I had heard very similar complaints over the years from Honolulu residents trying to buy the land under their homes from the estate.

Trustee Henry Peters later came in for very harsh legal criticism because he simultaneously managed to negotiate for both sides in the golf course sale talks. Critics wondered why a charity dedicated to the education of Hawaiian children was building playgrounds for the rich and powerful 5,000 miles from home.

The estate refused all comment on the RTJ investment. We were rebuffed when we asked permission for a photographer to take a picture of the ornate Pauahi Room inside the clubhouse. They wouldn't let us on the property.

Not long after that story ran, an assistant city editor at the newspaper took me aside and said that the *Advertiser* publisher had directed that we back off the Bishop Estate.

"Readers are tired of them," I was informed.

I wasn't told which readers, but I suspected some of them worked across South Street from the News Building, in the headquarters of the Bishop Estate.

Gannett Corporation had recently bought the *Advertiser* and dumped ownership of the rival *Star-Bulletin*. Newsroom gossip said that Gannett officials—known to some as Gannettoids and to others as Gannettalia—first delivered the bad news to *Star-Bulletin* workers, then donned official

Advertiser aloha shirts before crossing the hall to assume control of the morning paper.

I began thinking about looking for another job.

I finished up a number of pending projects, including a series cowritten with reporter David Waite about horrible conditions in Hawai'i prisons and wholesale criminal activities by prison guards.[10]

Dave and I found that guards were raping and assaulting inmates when they weren't dealing drugs to them. We found several guards who had been convicted of criminal offenses and had been allowed to serve their prison sentences on weekends so that they could continue working as guards during the week. They just changed uniforms and stepped to the other side of the bars when Friday night rolled around.

I also worked hard on a story about an organized crime figure who was doing business locally with the Teamsters Union. After the story was done and turned in, it languished for more than a month. I was repeatedly told that newly installed editor Jim Gatti was "looking at it."

David Waite, a caustically funny man and great reporter, took to referring to Gatti as "Captain Hazelwood," after the infamously inept seafarer responsible for the *Exxon Valdez* oil spill in Alaska. Eventually the story ran, basically unchanged, and I never could figure out the delay.[11]

In 1996, editors at the paper began distributing personnel evaluations that were a hallmark of Gannett management. I was shocked by my report, prepared by the same assistant city editor who had called me off the Bishop Estate stories.

I wasn't productive, I was argumentative, I needed to seriously change my attitude . . . and so on. The little toady who wrote the report said editors were under orders to emphasize the negative.

I picked up the phone and asked KITV news director Wally Zimmerman for a job. "When can you start?" he said.

Two notable events occurred at the *Advertiser* not long after I left.

One was that the prison guard series won the Gannett chain's national award for public service reporting. The editors had to call me back from KITV to pick up the award with Dave Waite.

The other was the publication, in the rival *Star-Bulletin*, of the "Broken Trust" essay, which tore huge holes in the Bishop Estate and eventually led to the ouster of all five estate trustees.[12]

The authors drew heavily from my earlier reporting on the estate in marshalling their damning facts about the estate and its trustees. The essay was written by four respected and eminent Native Hawaiian professionals and a university law professor who specialized in trust law. They first offered it to the *Advertiser* for publication.

But Jim Gatti dithered and delayed, so the authors took their work across the hall to the *Star-Bulletin*, which published it almost immediately.

A cascading series of investigations, public protests, and lawsuits, provoked in large part by "Broken Trust," then consumed the estate, which nearly lost its federal tax exemption and had to jettison the five trustees.

I covered some of those events for KITV, where I worked for the next five and a half years. Two Bishop Estate trustees, Oswald Stender and Gerard Jervis, filed a civil suit in state court to have a third trustee, Lokelani Lindsey, removed from the trust. At the same time, Attorney General Margery Bronster was pursuing an action in probate court to remove all five estate trustees from office, alleging wholesale breaches of fiduciary duty.

While all that was going on, I learned some disturbing information about Jervis. He had been carrying on an affair with an estate lawyer that was so reckless the couple had been caught having sex in a public restroom at the Hawai'i Prince hotel near Waikiki. They were discovered by hotel security, escorted off the property, and told not to return.

The following day, the woman, Rene Ojiri-Kitaoka, committed suicide. Her body was found in a car parked in the garage of her home.

It was a tragedy that also spoke volumes about the quality of the trustees appointed by Hawai'i's high court to direct a multibillion-dollar charitable institution. Jervis was Ojiri-Kitaoka's supervisor. She was 39, married, and working as a lawyer for Kamehameha Investment Corporation, a wholly owned subsidiary of the Bishop Estate. The affair took place while state and federal authorities were closely scrutinizing the activities of Jervis and his colleagues.

After confirming the details of the hotel incident and suicide, I talked the matter over with my editors at KITV. We had the story to ourselves at that point and knew that we had to go with it.[13]

I found Jervis at the Lindsey removal trial. During a morning break, I pulled him and his lawyer, Ronald Sakamoto, out of the courtroom. In the hallway outside, I quietly told them what I knew. I said we would be airing a story on the subject that evening and asked for comment from them.

Jervis looked like he'd been poleaxed. He must have known the roof was going to fall in on him, but he didn't seem prepared for it. He and Sakamoto said they had no immediate comment and hurriedly left the courthouse. The trial proceeded without them.

Then I had to call Ojiri-Kitaoka's husband to tell him that we would be running a story that night. I told him I was sensitive to the pain this would bring him and his family but that publicity on the subject was unavoidable. He said he had nothing to say.

The following day brought news that Jervis had been hospitalized after taking an overdose of sleeping pills. He recovered quickly and returned to his job at the estate. Five months later, he resigned.

Fellow trustee Oswald Stender also stepped down. Lindsey, Henry Peters, and Dickie Wong were forced from the board by the courts.

Another set of Bishop Estate stories I wrote at KITV concerned business deals between trustees Peters and Wong and a real estate developer named Jeff Stone. While simultaneously doing personal condominium deals with Peters and Wong, Stone was also involved in a large purchase of property from the estate.

All the parties involved protested that the deals were unrelated and perfectly legitimate, but their timing and nature caused the state to investigate and ultimately charge Stone, Peters, and Wong with criminal offenses. The charges were later tossed out of court because of serious procedural defects in the state's case.

The stories did not endear me to Stone, Peters, or Wong. Stone had purchased and expanded a huge resort and residential development on Oahu called Ko Olina, and I later found him doing more real estate deals with Colleen Hanabusa, the politically powerful woman who succeeded Richard Wong as president of the state senate.

Back at the *Advertiser*, a new batch of editors had taken charge of the newspaper, and they began trying to recruit me back. Friends at the paper urged me to consider returning, and eventually I did. I truly enjoyed working in television, but I'm a long-form prose guy at heart.

Things hadn't really changed at the morning newspaper.

And they hadn't changed all that much at the Bishop Estate under a new batch of trustees installed by the courts. The same attitude of secrecy and press hostility was still there.

When I asked one of my Bishop Estate sources for an opinion of the new trustees, the response was "Same stew, different vegetables."

That about summed up the *Advertiser*, too.

My second run at the newspaper is dealt with in detail later in these pages. Let me just say here that by 2008, I was no longer an investigative reporter and had been consigned to what *Advertiser* management considered a gulag beat: the state courthouse.

I actually quite enjoyed covering courts, even though the editors unaccountably cared little for stories originating there. That attitude seemed to have little to do with who authored the stories or how they were written. They just didn't think much of court stories.

So I was kicking back in my office one morning when a lawyer named John Goemans cold-called me.

I'd known John for a long time and had mixed feelings about him. He was personally very likeable but a bit off-kilter. He never really had an office or a thriving law practice and operated instead from Starbucks lounges and bookstore reading rooms. He frequently pursued civil rights cases and had long targeted the Bishop Estate, challenging the legality of its tax exemption and the constitutionality of its admissions policy that favored children of Native Hawaiian ancestry.

John had been involved in a long-running federal court lawsuit, filed on behalf of a Caucasian mother and child on the Big Island, that claimed the admissions policy violated federal civil rights laws. The case lingered in the courts for four years, eventually rising all the way to the U.S. Supreme Court. In 2007, days before the high court was due to announce whether it would hear the case, the parties agreed to settle it.

The estate agreed to pay an undisclosed amount of money to the plaintiffs, who agreed to drop the case. Terms of the settlement had been a very closely guarded secret for more than a year. The estate was extremely sensitive to the issue of its admissions policy and certainly did not want to say or do anything that might encourage new lawsuits about it.

The plaintiffs in the suit were bound by court confidentiality, and leakage of the settlement amount might lead to litigation against them by the estate. No one had breathed a word about it until Goemans called me.

I do not know what prompted him to do this. He was in ill health and close to penniless, living with relatives on the Mainland.

He was also unhappy about how the settlement money had been distributed. Goemans originated the idea of the lawsuit and found the plaintiffs, but it was litigated by a California lawyer named Eric Grant.

Mostly, though, Goemans expressed outrage that the settlement figure was never made known to the public. He said the estate was legally obligated to disclose the settlement amount on its open-to-the-public federal tax return and in the annual financial report that had to be filed with state probate court.

Goemans told me he wanted to talk about the settlement on the record, and he knew the potential consequences of such a disclosure.

I said, okay, how much was it?

"Seven million dollars," he said.

Holy crap, I thought, that's a hell of a lot of money. I asked Goemans if he had any paperwork to support what he was saying.

He did, indeed, and he eventually faxed it to me.[14]

It was a great story, and it brought John Goemans and his former clients a world of grief. Bishop Estate sued them and Grant for breach of confidentiality, demanding return of $2 million of the settlement.

That case was settled before trial in 2011. Terms of the settlement are secret. The identities of the two plaintiffs have never been revealed. They were always identified in court papers as Jane and John Doe, arguing successfully that public disclosure of their names would expose them to personal danger and force them to leave Hawai'i.

The last time I saw Goemans was in 2008, when he had been flown into town for meetings with lawyers. He stayed at the YMCA during that trip.

Goemans died of pancreatic cancer in 2008. He was 75 years old.

His contention that the estate was legally obliged to disclose the $7 million number in tax returns or probate filings fell on deaf ears. I looked hard for the number but could never find it. It was apparently consolidated with larger line items in the tax return and broken up into smaller payments to various law firms in the more detailed probate papers.

I protested this lack of disclosure to the state attorney general's office and to the outside master appointed by the probate court to review the estate's annual accounts. They ignored me.

Secrecy prevailed.

CHAPTER EIGHT

Ronnie, Henry, and Royale

In the early 1980s, two big names in Hawai'i's underworld started singing.

Ronald Ching and Henry Huihui had a lot to tell. Each was deeply involved in organized crime and organized labor. Both had committed notoriously public murders that shook Island society to its foundations. And both were connected to Larry Mehau.

By the time Ching and Huihui were done testifying, they had provided at least partial solutions to enduring criminal mysteries. Ching admitted to four homicides, including the 1970 slaying of state senator Larry Kuriyama and the murder of the son of city prosecutor Charles Marsland Jr. in 1975. He also confessed to burying federal informant Arthur Baker alive in 1978 and to fatally shooting another informant, Robert "Bobby" Fukumoto, in 1980.

The Kuriyama homicide had, in the words of *Advertiser* reporter Vickie Ong, "hit the community like a punch in the stomach."[1] The 49-year-old senator was shot to death in the carport of his home after attending a political rally with Governor John Burns and other colleagues. The gangland-style slaying was committed by a gunman using a silenced pistol. Kuriyama's wife and four of the couple's five children were inside the house when he was shot, and the senator's 17-year-old son, Stanley, cradled his dying father in his arms while waiting for medical help.

Well before Ching began talking, two men, including longtime Ching associate Alexander "Aku" Sakamoto, had been tried but acquitted of killing Kuriyama.

The 1970 murder, with its syndicate-style overtones, occurred as the violent struggles for control of the underworld were heating up and bodies were

The body of slain Senator Larry Kuriyama lies in state at the Capitol. Governor John Burns led the line of mourners. ROY ITO, PHOTOGRAPHER; *HONOLULU STAR-ADVERTISER* COLLECTION; HAWAI'I STATE ARCHIVES.

dropping around the state. The murder focused intense interest on organized crime by law enforcement, news reporters, and political leaders.

Huihui, who had regularly been identified as a syndicate leader but had never been successfully prosecuted for mob-related crimes, pleaded guilty to another notorious homicide: the lunch-hour shooting of union leader Josiah Lii in 1977. An official of the Inland Boatmen's Union with mob ties of his own, Lii was shot to death in a hallway outside his office in downtown Honolulu, within sight of the Aloha Tower waterfront landmark. Lii's wife and several children were in his office and rushed to his aid when he was shot.

Huihui, a Fagin-like figure who surrounded himself with a feral band of acolytes, also admitted to personally murdering one of his followers, David Riveira, outside a posh private residence in Nuuanu Valley where the group was staging casino gambling.

Like earlier high-profile syndicate singers who performed in court, Ching and Huihui hit a lot of sour notes, ultimately raising as many questions as they answered. Their testimonies, delivered in separate courts and different cases, were peppered with lies and inconsistencies.

RONNIE CHING

Ching's turn on the public stage began after a 1981 raid by federal agents and police of his apartment in the Chateau Blue apartment building. Inside the unit, the raiders found a chunk of C-4 plastic explosive in a box taped under the kitchen sink. Cached inside a safe was $28,000, as well as five pounds of "Thai stick" marijuana and smaller quantities of heroin and cocaine.

From Ching's storage closet down the hall, agents seized semiautomatic rifles, a small-caliber "pen gun," a .32-caliber handgun silencer, a state deputy sheriff's badge, .223-caliber ammunition, and a set of handcuffs.[2]

The last items intrigued investigators. The apartment building was three blocks from the Sunday Lounge, where Arthur Baker had been handcuffed before being dragged away by his kidnappers in late 1978.

And the Chateau Blue was one block away from the Brass Door bar, where just months earlier, syndicate figure and police informant Robert "Bobby" Fukumoto had been murdered. Fukumoto's assailant walked into the tavern at 12:20 a.m. and fired 10 .223-caliber bullets into the victim with a semiautomatic rifle, blowing him off his barstool. The assailant fled on foot, and witnesses saw him run down Kona Street and into the parking lot of the Chateau Blue.

Less than a half hour after the shooting, Ching called the Honolulu Police Department with a strange story. He claimed that he had been in his apartment watching television when there was a knock at his door. Ching said that when he looked out the peephole, he saw "a man in dark clothing" who then ran away from the door. Minutes after making the call, Ching walked to the scene of the Fukumoto murder, where his presence was noted by police officers.

Honolulu Police Chief Francis Keala and prosecutor Charles Marsland were present when Ching's apartment was searched, a highly unusual occurrence.

Marsland and Keala were neighbors in the Portlock neighborhood of Honolulu, and the chief had identified the murdered body of Marsland's son after it was discovered on a lonely road in rural Waimanalo in 1975. Ching was a suspect in the murder of the younger Marsland.

At a bail hearing held days after the apartment search, Ching said he recently had been working as a Teamsters Union driver on the *Magnum, P.I.* television series, earning some $1,300 per week. That was good money in those days, but it covered only a fraction of the $1,000-a-day heroin habit that Ching said he had at the time.

I learned that before Ching had landed the driver job, he had worked at Unity House, a labor services organization run by Arthur Rutledge, head of the Hawai'i Teamsters Union. While working at Unity House, Ching had delivered "a veiled threat" to one of Rutledge's union foes, Richard Tam, who had recently won control of the Hotel-Restaurant Workers Union local that Rutledge had also been running.

Tam was working in his office one day when Ching paid him an unannounced visit. "It wasn't a social call," Tam told me.[3]

"Ching came in, shook hands and said he's a friend of the Old Man [Rutledge] and that I should stop leaning on the Old Man," Tam said.

Tam knew Ching's reputation and took the visit as a threat. "There was nothing overt," Tam said. "But the message was there—a veiled threat that I better watch out."

When I interviewed Rutledge immediately after the raid on Ching's apartment, he admitted that it had been a violation of federal labor law to hire Ching at Unity House but said the *Magnum* job was legal and part of Rutledge's efforts to help rehabilitate convicted criminals. And Rutledge said he had nothing to do with Ching's visit to Tam.

I was personally amazed that a heroin-addicted syndicate hit man was working on the set of one of the most popular shows on American television, a program that showcased Hawai'i to the rest of the world. That was the beginning of my decades-long fascination with the men and women who drove vehicles on Hawai'i film and television sets. I found that literally dozens of the drivers had long, varied, and sometimes very violent criminal careers. Drivers regularly shuttled between film sets and prison, keeping up with their union dues while locked behind bars.

At Ching's initial detention hearing, the government argued that Ching was a danger to the community and should be held without bail. HPD officer Don Carstensen testified that Ching told him the year before that he had first "made his bones"—committed a murder—when he was 16 years old.[4] Carstensen said Ching was under investigation for other crimes but declined to elaborate.

At a subsequent hearing, Ching was asked pointed questions about his knowledge of organized crime in general and the "syndicate hits" of Baker and Fukumoto in particular. Ching took the Fifth Amendment to those questions, posed by U.S. Organized Crime Strike Force attorney Daniel Bent.

Ching's lawyer, David Bettencourt, asked Carstensen during the second hearing if he was also investigating Larry Mehau. Bent successfully objected, saying those questions were irrelevant to a bail hearing. Carstensen was not required to answer.

Bent had been part of a joint federal-local criminal investigation of Mehau called Operation Firebird that was ultimately closed without charges.

Bent went on to become U.S. attorney for Hawai'i and later testified in a state court civil case that he believed the Firebird investigation of Mehau

Professional killer Ronald K. Ching. CARL VITI, PHOTOGRAPHER; *HONOLULU STAR-ADVERTISER* COLLECTION; HAWAI'I STATE ARCHIVES.

would have resulted in criminal charges if witnesses hadn't been frightened into silence. Bent said in that state case that Mehau was "a significant organized crime figure."[5]

Ching was ordered held without bail at the close of the detention hearing.

Present in the courtroom that day was Aku Sakamoto, who had been tried but acquitted in 1975 of state charges that he murdered state senator Larry Kuriyama in 1970. Ching had been an interested courtroom observer during Sakamoto's murder trial.

Ching later admitted to murdering Baker and Fukumoto and being present at the murder of Kuriyama. He said all three murders were committed "at the request of others."

Those guilty pleas came three years after Ching was convicted in the federal guns and explosives case. He was sentenced to 21 years in prison and had begun serving that time at Lompoc federal prison in Southern California when he opened new plea bargain negotiations with law enforcement. Records produced under the federal Freedom of Information Act show that Ching spoke with federal agents about his knowledge of murders and labor corruption, but the discussions were preliminary, and law enforcement was leery of him.

At one point, an FBI agent working with the U.S. Senate Permanent Subcommittee on Investigations arranged to speak with Ching about Unity House, the Hawai'i labor organization where he had briefly worked for Teamsters boss Art Rutledge. The content of those talks is classified.[6]

Ching also indicated to the FBI that he had information to share about one of his fellow inmates at Lompoc, notorious New Jersey mafia figure Anthony "Tony Pro" Provenzano.

One of the entries in the FOIA file said that investigators and prison officials doubted the extent of Ching's knowledge of Provenzano's activities.[7] But the two convicts did have a common trait besides lifetime involvement in violent, bloody crime: both were past members of the International Brotherhood of Teamsters.

Their union experiences were far removed by both geography and levels of influence. Provenzano was a past vice president of the IBT and was long suspected of involvement in the disappearance and murder of IBT president Jimmy Hoffa, still one of the nation's most infamous unsolved crimes.

Ching was never more than union muscle in a remote outpost of the Teamsters empire, although Hoffa and Hawai'i Teamsters boss Art Rutledge knew each other well.

The talks with federal authorities ultimately amounted to nothing. The FOIA files show that Frank Marine, who replaced Dan Bent as Strike Force attorney in Hawai'i, didn't trust Ching and believed he was playing games with investigators.

But Ching had also entered into discussions with former police officer Don Carstensen, by then a full-time member of Chuck Marsland's staff, and he eventually was returned to the Islands to begin his work as a witness for the prosecution.

Ching was born in 1949 in Honolulu, attending Kaimuki High School until the 10th grade—when he reputedly made his bones as a contract killer.

He told investigators that he had killed as many as 20 people but took credit in court for just four of them, beginning with the 1970 Kuriyama homicide. "Larry Kuriyama was shot by another with my aid and support," Ching told Honolulu Circuit Judge Robert Won Bae Chang in an August 1, 1984, court hearing. He added that he had "agreed with others" to murder the senator.

Neither Ching nor prosecutors ever uttered another word about who else was involved or why Kuriyama was slain.

Ching's longtime pal, Aku Sakamoto, had earlier been tried but acquitted of killing Kuriyama. The murder was allegedly committed because of a business dispute between Kuriyama and a Leeward Oahu dairyman named Alfred Ruis, according to prosecutors in that 1975 trial. Ruis was separately tried and acquitted of murdering Kuriyama.

In the 1975 proceedings against Sakamoto and Ruis, prosecutor Maurice Sapienza alleged that Ruis had used syndicate figure Harold "Biggie" Chan to put out a murder contract on Kuriyama. Chan, who was shot to death in 1972, had run a gambling operation with Ruis, according to trial evidence in 1975. There was no evidence implicating Kuriyama in illegal activities.

The Sakamoto and Ruis trials were typically plagued by shaky prosecution witnesses. One admitted on the witness stand that he had lied to a grand jury about the case. Another, who supposedly drove Sakamoto to and from the murder scene, was unable to identify Sakamoto in court. Another witness, Fred Hammond, described himself as a professional killer and said he had been offered but refused the Kuriyama murder contract. Years later, I found Fred Hammond working as Teamsters movie driver.

Sakamoto, a shade-tree auto mechanic in Ching's old Kaimuki neighborhood, took the witness stand in his trial and denied any involvement in the crime.

No mention was made of Ching in the Sakamoto and Ruis trials. Ching attended the Sakamoto trial and was sitting in the gallery when the principal prosecution witness failed to identify the defendant.

Sakamoto could not be retried for the Kuriyama killing due to double jeopardy protections, but testimony from Ronnie Ching as part of his 1984 plea deal did result in the indictment of Sakamoto in a separate murder case. Sakamoto was accused of killing airport worker Herman S. C. Kam, who disappeared in mid-July 1970.

Kam's body was never recovered, and his family managed to have him legally declared dead seven years after he disappeared. Acting on information later provided by Ching, authorities excavated a remote beach site in a futile effort to find his remains. Less than a year after the Kam murder indictment, prosecutors withdrew the murder charge against Sakamoto and revoked the plea deal they had reached with Ching.

The move was prompted by new evidence from a friend of Ching's that undercut Ching's grand jury testimony about the Kam murder. I wrote at the time: "The evidence, coupled with Ching's ongoing reluctance to disclose information about some friends and associates and Ching's growing dissatisfaction with his role as a prosecution witness, prompted a mutually agreeable decision among the parties to dissolve Ching's plea bargain."[8]

Another murder charge brought on the basis of Ching's testimony, against parolee Robert Reyes, was also dropped after Ching's plea deal collapsed. Reyes was accused of killing Chinatown gambler George Chiu in 1980.

Other murder cases mounted on the basis of Ronnie Ching's testimony ended badly:

- Charges against Cyril Kahale Jr. for allegedly participating with Ching in the kidnap-murder of drug informant Baker were dismissed. Kahale—a close associate of Don Ho and Larry Mehau—later won a $400,000 judgment against the city.
- Charges against three different men subsequently accused by Ching of helping in the Baker murder were also dismissed outright by the prosecutor's office.
- Three codefendants charged with murdering Robert Fukumoto pleaded guilty to reduced charges. Two of them, Rudolph Na-o and Gary Murata, were convicted of hindering prosecution. The third, Glenn Ii Jr., pleaded guilty to manslaughter. Ching never testified in the case.
- Three men named by Ching as accomplices in the murder of Prosecutor Marsland's son—Eric Naone, Raymond Scanlan, and Gregory Nee—were acquitted in a jury trial.

The "Chuckers" Marsland murder case was the only Ching-generated prosecution that ever went to trial. The court proceedings were highly theatrical: a hit man's testimony, allegations of police corruption, behind-the-scenes looks at the seedy and often violent world of nocturnal Waikiki. The father of the victim, exuding Old Testament rectitude, listened from the gallery as his deputies tried to prove who had kidnapped and murdered his teenage son nine years earlier.

The trial featured not just long-awaited testimony from Ching but also a dramatic Perry Mason moment of surprise evidence that badly undermined Ching and the prosecution's entire case.

Charged with Ching was Raymond Scanlan, a former Honolulu police officer who had left the force after the Marsland murder and shortly before he was arrested on a heroin trafficking charge. The heroin case generated the godfather allegations that bedeviled Larry Mehau for years. Scanlan later worked for Don Ho and had a long career as a Teamster movie driver. He also worked as a driver and dogsbody for Japanese white-collar criminal Kaoru Ogawa during Ogawa's periodic visits to the Islands.

Another defendant in the Marsland case was Eric Naone, a former Teamsters business agent and Art Rutledge bodyguard who was a regular hanger-on at Don Ho's dressing room.

The third defendant, Gregory Nee, was a former Don Ho doorman who by the time of the trial was working as a lumber salesman in the Pacific Northwest.

At the time of his murder, the younger Marsland was attending college and working part-time at a nightspot called Infinity on the grounds of the Sheraton Waikiki hotel, just up Lewers Street from Don Ho's Polynesian Palace showroom.

Naone had befriended the younger Marsland and was interviewed by police after the murder. Naone told police that he knew Chuckers Marsland and was "very good friends" with Ching. He was best man at Ching's wedding.

He said that he and Ching had gone to the Infinity the night of the murder and talked to Marsland there. Naone said he and Ching left about 3:30 a.m. and walked to the Polynesian Palace, where they spent time with other "friends": Larry Mehau and George Perry Jr., a convicted felon and longtime close associate of Mehau. Also present at Ho's dressing room was a young man identified only as "Greg," Naone told police.[9]

Naone and Ching left the showroom about 5 a.m. and drove to Naone's family home and then to the residence of Ching's girlfriend in the Kalihi neighborhood of Honolulu, Naone told police in 1975.

Marsland was shot to death at approximately 6 a.m. Ching said on the witness stand that he and Naone shot Marsland because they believed he was talking to police about drug activities in Waikiki.

Ching had "turned on" Marsland with cocaine, and Naone had given Marsland the same drug "for distribution," Ching testified.

And Marsland had "dealings" with a pimp and drug dealer named Louis Matias who was later murdered in prison, Ching said. (When Ching first started talking plea deals with law enforcement in 1981, he claimed that Matias and another by-then deceased criminal, Dennis Galarza, had killed Marsland.)

Ching testified in the trial that the murder was sanctioned by HPD officer Manny Rezentes—the same officer who had warned me in 1978 that Ching was a very dangerous man. Rezentes was never charged in the Marsland case and heatedly denied Ching's allegations about him. He did not testify at the trial.

According to Ching, the younger Marsland had talked to Rezentes about his dealings with Matias. "Manny was concerned . . . with what other law enforcement . . . he [Marsland] might mention it to," Ching testified.

Rezentes and Naone agreed that Marsland had to die, according to Ching. Naone asked Ching to help in the murder and also recruited Greg Nee to help in the crime, Ching said.

Scanlan provided two weapons used in the homicide, a handgun and a shotgun, according to Ching.

The prosecution said Marsland believed he was being taken to a meeting with Rezentes when he was picked up on the main drag of Waikiki, Kalakaua Avenue, by Naone and Ching in a car driven by Nee. The men drove Marsland to a Windward Oahu location, where he was shot to death, Ching said.

When Nee stopped the car, Ching said he got out and removed a shotgun from the trunk, then told Marsland he had something to show him. When Marsland left the car, "I told him this was it, he was going. He was surprised. I guess he was shocked," Ching testified.

"I shot him twice. After the first round, he took a step back. I shot him again and he went down," Ching told the court.[10]

After Ching and Naone moved the body off the road, Naone shot Marsland five or six times, according to Ching. The murder weapons had been issued by the police department to Scanlan, who gave them to Ching knowing that they would be used in a killing, according to Ching.

"It didn't concern you that you were asking a person known to you as a police officer for weapons to kill someone else?" Deputy Prosecutor Michael McGuigan asked Ching.

"Not this police officer," Ching answered.

Scanlan's handgun—used by Naone to shoot Marsland—had earlier been reported stolen, Ching said. After the murder, the weapon was thrown into the Ala Wai Yacht Harbor on the edge of Waikiki, Ching told the jury.

When Marsland's body was discovered, HPD Chief Francis Keala himself went to the murder scene to identify the victim. Keala's son and Chuckers Marsland were friends and had been classmates at Punahou School, an elite Oahu private school. President Barack Obama graduated from Punahou five years after Keala and Marsland.

Some 12 hours after the homicide, friends and supporters of the victim's family gathered at the Marsland home in east Honolulu. Among the well-wishers was Eric Naone.

Naone said he paid his respects at the urging of the younger Marsland's girlfriend, who knew the two men were friends.

Chief Keala told Naone that he had to speak with the detective investigating the homicide, George Kruse, to tell what he knew about the victim. That's when Naone told his story of seeing the victim at the Infinity and then going to the Polynesian Palace to spend time with Ching, Mehau, Perry, and "Greg."

Another of the accused, Ray Scanlan, had regular contact with Chuck Marsland for years after Chuckers was murdered.

Chuck Marsland testified in the murder trial that he met numerous times with Scanlan and enlisted his help in finding his son's killers. Many of the meetings took place at the Punchbowl grave of Chuckers Marsland at the National Memorial Cemetery of the Pacific, the father said. In 1979, Marsland testified, Scanlan told him that the killers were Naone, Ching, and Nee.

Scanlan denied under oath that he had told Marsland that. He further denied giving Ching his police-issued handgun in 1975 to use in the murder. Scanlan admitted telling HPD in 1973 that the weapon, a .38-caliber Smith & Wesson revolver, had apparently been stolen from the glove compartment of his car. He said he filed the false police report because he "panicked" about the loss of the gun, which he later found behind the cushions of the sofa in his home.

By the time Scanlan said he found the gun, in November 1975, returning it to the police would have been a real problem. He had resigned from the force and was under indictment for heroin trafficking and illegal possession of a firearm. Federal drug agents had found a silencer-equipped .22-caliber gun in his car following the heroin bust, which occurred, ironically enough, at Punchbowl Cemetery.

One of Scanlan's codefendants in that heroin case, Leslie Kent, was a former local high school football standout associated with mob figures Henry Huihui and Alema Leota who had worked briefly as a guard in the Kuikui Plaza case. He initially escaped arrest in the heroin bust with a display of his broken-field running ability. Kent sprinted hell-for-leather down the slopes of Punchbowl, covered in thorny cactus plants and *kiawe* trees.

So Scanlan, stuck with his police handgun, turned for help to his cousin, police officer Clarence "Rags" Scanlan. Ray Scanlan said he gave the gun to his cousin "with the understanding that he would turn it in to the police department."

Then Rags Scanlan was called to the witness stand for the Perry Mason moment.

When his cousin later asked him what had become of the weapon, Rags said he couldn't remember but thought that he had mailed the gun anonymously to the police. Some six weeks before the Marsland murder trial started, Rags Scanlan said, he searched his home for the weapon but didn't find it.

Then, on the eve of the trial, he was cleaning his basement and found the gun in a manila envelope.

When Ray Scanlan's lawyer, James Koshiba, asked where the gun was now, Rags Scanlan said, "I've got it with me."[11]

The witness then pulled the gun, contained in a plastic bag, out of his jacket.

That pretty much sent the prosecution's case up in smoke.

The jury began deliberations shortly afterward and returned 13 hours later to acquit the three defendants of all charges. One juror told me the production of the handgun in court had a powerful influence on the panel's decision to acquit.

Defense lawyers said the big problem in the case was Ching himself. Much of his testimony was uncorroborated by other evidence, and he had a long history of lying. He admitted that history under cross-examination in the trial. "Being truthful is new," he testified.

He claimed that his conscience caused him to turn state's evidence. "Things were bothering me," he said. "I was having a hard time dealing with some of the crimes I committed, especially my crimes that were of violence," Ching told the jury.

He admitted that during his dealings with police and federal agents, he "gave them bits of truth and some lies." But after reaching his plea agreement with Marsland's office, he said, he had told the truth about the Marsland murder.

Then Ching was forced to acknowledge that after he signed the plea bargain, he "gave some false information" about the Kam murder, but later voluntarily recanted and "gave a true and accurate statement."

Just before the Marsland murder trial began in state court, federal prosecutors revealed that Ching had been deceptive in lie detector tests administered by federal agents.

The prosecutor's office labeled that disclosure, as well as other revelations about Ching from Honolulu police, as proof that competing law enforcement agencies had sabotaged Ching's credibility. The Justice Department and HPD denied those charges, saying they were legally obligated to release the information.

In mid-1985, Ching was sentenced to life in prison. He died 20 years later in his cell at Halawa Correctional Facility. Ching suffered from a variety of medical problems, including hepatitis C, related to his years of drug abuse.

Peter Carlisle, one of Marsland's deputies who went on to become chief prosecutor and later mayor of Honolulu, said that Ching "needed to die in prison."

Carlisle said he didn't know how many murders Ching committed. "We know he pleaded to four, but he'd given us information on eight to ten. There's lots of belief there were a number of other killings he was involved in," Carlisle told *Advertiser* reporter Will Hoover in 2005.

But that information was buried with Ching. Except for the Marsland case, the reasons for the murders Ching admitted committing were never made public.

HENRY HUIHUI

On May 9, 1984, syndicate figure Henry Huihui travelled with a posse of federal agents and police officers to three courts on two islands. At each stop, Huihui pleaded guilty to a menu of criminal offenses that included murder, racketeering, extortion, and gambling.

The U.S. Justice Department said Huihui had promised to cooperate in additional criminal cases, calling the arrangement a "significant breakthrough in the federal government's and local government's investigation into organized crime in Hawaii." Prosecutors said they believed Huihui would testify about "higher-ups" and "public corruption."

Those predictions were badly overblown. Huihui testified almost exclusively against underlings in his own organization.

Henry Huihui in state court. DAVID YAMADA, PHOTOGRAPHER; *HONOLULU STAR-ADVERTISER* COLLECTION; HAWAI'I STATE ARCHIVES.

Information he provided did lead to a murder indictment against former mob boss Nappy Pulawa and a self-described syndicate hit man named Royale Kamahoahoa. They were accused of killing a Windward Oahu gambling figure, Alexander Chong Kong, whose lifeless, bullet-riddled body was left in the Olomana Golf Course parking lot in 1974.

Those charges were dropped 10 months later after one of Huihui's plea deals, with Prosecutor Marsland, fell apart.

Huihui also gave authorities information about the 1970 murder of another Windward Oahu gambler, Francis Young. Authorities searched for Young's remains on the North Shore, near the earlier burial site of Lamont Nery and Fuzzy Iha, but found nothing. When syndicate snitch Roy Ryder testified in the first Nery-Iha murder trial, he said that Pulawa and Huihui had shot Young to death and buried him in a beachside grave near Dillingham Airfield.

Later, Nery and Iha were killed and buried in nearly the same location. According to Ryder's first version of that double murder, Pulawa ordered that the two men be buried in the same place as Young. "Put 'em where the pake stay," Ryder quoted Pulawa as saying. ("Pake," pronounced PAW-kay, is a pidgin term for Chinese.)

No trace of Young was ever found, and no one was charged with killing him.

Just two months after he disappeared, his family petitioned the courts to have Young declared dead. The court papers said Young had been "forcibly removed" from a Kailua bar called Biggie's Nut Shell by unknown persons on January 29, 1970.

"The circumstances and habits of said decedent indicate that he died on January 29, 1970," the petition said.

Ryder said nothing about Francis Young in the 1978 Nery-Iha retrial, which was my introduction to Chuck Marsland and the big players in Hawai'i's underworld, including Henry Huihui.

Huihui was a ruggedly good-looking man in those days, given to wearing tinted aviator-style glasses and carefully pressed denim jeans. (I once described him in a news story as "handsome in a pock-marked sort of way.")[12]

Huihui and his codefendants walked away unscathed from the Nery-Iha murder charges.

I wrote about his indirect connection to the Benny Madamba murder on the Big Island later in 1978. I also wrote several stories about him over the next couple of years that dealt with his activities as a union official. Huihui was a high school dropout who worked in his younger years as an electrician, eventually rising in the ranks of Local 1186 of the International Brotherhood of Electrical Workers. He grew close to 1186 boss Akito "Blackie" Fujikawa and was eventually named head of the local's Apprentice Training Division.

In 1979, the training division spent $1.2 million to acquire 69 acres of undeveloped real estate on Oahu's North Shore, christening the site "Uwila Ranch."

I got my hands on a brochure distributed by the union at a 1980 dedication ceremony at the property that explained *uwila*, the Hawaiian word for lightning, had also come to mean electricity. The property was intended to be used by the training division to "develop a variety of agricultural programs such as urban gardens" to allow union members and retirees "to get away from the city and learn to grow things," the brochure said. That didn't sound much like electrician training, and a U.S. Labor Department investigation later found exactly that, forcing Local 1186 to divest itself of the property.

I turned out other stories about questionable union financial deals, including leases of automobiles driven by Huihui and his associates.

I repeatedly heard that Huihui was using union underlings to run gambling and extortion enterprises on Oahu and the Big Island, but I couldn't fully nail down a story about it.

By then, Huihui was the focus of intense criminal investigations by the federal government and local law enforcement on Oahu and the Big Island. A Big Island grand jury first indicted Huihui and various followers on gambling and extortion charges.

The roof fell in on Huihui in early 1984. A federal grand jury indicted him and eight associates on a variety of charges, including racketeering, extortion, and criminal conspiracy.

Two murders were folded into the federal case as evidence of racketeering, but homicide is customarily not a federal offense, so the defendants were not specifically accused of the homicides.

Not long after the federal charges were laid, however, Huihui and four of his followers were charged with the murders in state court.

One of Huihui's codefendants in the federal case, Michael Patrick Ward, had cut a deal with investigators and was cooperating with both federal and state authorities. Huihui had initially pleaded not guilty to all the charges against him, but Ward's decision to cooperate led to a change of heart.

That produced Huihui's island-hopping sequential guilty pleas in May 1984. He admitted to ordering Ward to murder union rival Joe Lii and to personally shooting underling David Riveira.

Huihui told investigators that he had known Lii since he was a teenager and had once performed union strong-arm work for Lii.

Huihui claimed that he had joined organized crime in 1968 after a nephew, Moses Huihui Jr., was murdered. Huihui said he believed his nephew was killed in a syndicate "hit," and he wanted revenge.

He said that he and Joe Lii were once members of Nappy Pulawa's syndicate group, "The Company," which had planned in the early 1970s to take control of organized labor in Hawai'i. Those plans, which included murdering Teamsters boss Art Rutledge, were never carried out, but he and Lii continued their involvement in the labor movement.

Huihui testified that Lii and his henchmen were trying to move in on gambling and extortion rackets run by Huihui's group and had made threatening visits to IBEW job sites.

Blackie Fujikawa told Huihui that Lii had to be killed, so Huihui gave Michael Ward a gun and told him to commit the murder, Huihui told the FBI and police.

In court, Huihui delivered surprise testimony, saying that Larry Mehau had advance knowledge of the Lii hit.[13] During a visit to the Big Island, Huihui said, he encountered Mehau outside the Naniloa Surf Hotel in Hilo.

When the two men shook hands, Huihui testified, Mehau said, "You gonna take care of Joe?"

Huihui said he told Mehau yes, adding that he was "surprised he [Mehau] knew what was happening."

Mehau then "asked me if it was gonna be done quickly and I said yeah," Huihui told the court.

Huihui said when he returned to Oahu the following day, he summoned Ward to a meeting about the planned murder and told him "it had to be done that day."

"It was more important now than I ever thought it was," Huihui told Deputy Prosecutor Michael McGuigan.

"Why?" McGuigan asked.

"Because of that meeting with Larry," Huihui said.

Through his lawyer, David Schutter, Mehau denied that such a conversation ever took place. No one corroborated Huihui's story, and Mehau was never charged as a result of Huihui's testimony.

Huihui also told investigators that when he was still with The Company in 1978, Nappy Pulawa "made comments that Larry Mehau and Prosecuting Attorney Charles Marsland should be hit." Huihui claimed he and an unidentified man discussed the possibility of committing one of the murders when Mehau drove in or out of the state Capitol but took the idea no further.

Michael Ward shot Joe Lii multiple times outside the victim's office at the Inland Boatmen's Union.

Ward and another Huihui gang member, Jeffrey Kealoha, went to Lii's office on Alakea Street during the lunch hour on Friday, May 6, 1977. When the two men walked repeatedly past Lii's office, Lii became suspicious and left his office to confront the pair. He was shot dead in the hallway.

In Huihui's original statements to law enforcement, he said he told both Ward and Kealoha to murder Lii, adding that Kealoha later admitted to him that he abetted Ward in the homicide. But he backed away from directly implicating Kealoha when he testified at Kealoha's murder trial.

He claimed that Ward on his own had involved Kealoha and the alleged driver of the getaway car, Gilbert Madrid, in the murder. When confronted on the witness stand with his earlier story about Kealoha, Huihui testified, "I may have made some wrong statements." He said he had been "under a lot of stress" when he was first debriefed by federal and local law enforcement.

"After I thought about it, sitting in jail, I know I made an untrue statement," Huihui said on the witness stand. Huihui said virtually nothing incriminating on the witness stand against Madrid.

A state circuit court jury was unable to reach a unanimous verdict in the trial of Kealoha and Madrid. And the case was dropped after Marsland's office revoked its plea deal with Huihui.

Kealoha later pleaded guilty to helping murder Huihui gang member David Riveira.

Huihui also told differing versions of that crime, saying originally that Riveira was slain because he was a police informant. Later he said Riveira died because he had assaulted a member of Huihui's family.

The Riveira killing took place in the garage of an expensive home that associates in the IBEW had purchased for Huihui. The house, tucked on the edge of a forest reserve near the back of Nuuanu Valley, was the site of casino gambling games staged by the Huihui gang.

Riveira's hands were tied behind his back, and Huihui shot him in the head with a silenced handgun. Other gang members were then required to fire bullets into Riveira's body.

Huihui also told investigators that he paid Kealoha to kill Stanley Ota, a building contractor who was indicted in the infamous Punchbowl Cemetery heroin case. Ota was murdered while that case was pending. Kealoha was never charged in state court with the Ota homicide, but he pleaded guilty in federal court to racketeering offenses that included the Ota murder.

Apart from his uncorroborated allegations against Mehau, organized crime kingpin Henry Huihui ended up testifying in court—unsuccessfully for the most part—against his underlings.

When he was originally debriefed by the FBI and other agencies, Huihui claimed extensive knowledge of police and political corruption, such as that he had personally paid $50,000 to an official of Governor George Ariyoshi's political campaign. The cash was delivered, he said, during a meeting in the parking lot of a local high school.

Nothing ever came of that allegation.

In January 1985, while still in the middle of fulfilling his duties as a government witness, Huihui wrote a lengthy letter of complaint about his treatment by law enforcement.

"I would have been better off going to trial," he said.[14] "The relationship between the federal and the state prosecutor's offices continues to deteriorate. Plus, the professional jealousy that is evident through all your actions boggles my mind," Huihui wrote.

He laid the blame for the outcome of the Josiah Lii murder trial on Marsland's office. "My testimony at that trial was of no fault to me," he wrote.

"A noncompassionate and insensitive prosecutor will always result in the loss of cooperating witnesses, who from frustration and disgust, refuse to testify," the letter continued.

"I feel an urgent need to make a prediction here. My prediction is that all defendants will go free and only cooperating witnesses will go to jail," Huihui wrote.

But he also complimented Marsland for pursuing Larry Mehau.

"Thanks to Mr. Marsland and his efforts to keep things in the right perspective, Larry was never off the hook. I am the only person to defy Larry Mehau and the Pulawa mob," the letter said. Then he warned that "the leaders of organize[d] crime continue to function and go undetected."

He signed off the letter by combining the Hawaiian words for thanks and good-bye with a touch of American vernacular: "Mahalo, Aloha and Up Yours."

By the following year, Marsland's office had revoked its plea deal with Huihui, stating that he had provided lies and half-truths to investigators.

The U.S. Justice Department was satisfied with Huihui's performance and held to its commitment to seek a reduced prison term for him. That sentence was 22 years behind bars. In state court, prosecutors sought a life sentence with the possibility of parole. Huihui ultimately served some 26 years in prison before he was paroled in late 2010. He died in January 2015.

ROYALE KAMAHOAHOA

A final example of the perils of placing a mobster-turned-witness on the stand in court was provided by Royale Kamahoahoa, the self-described "hit man" accused by Huihui of murdering gambler Alexander Chong Kong in 1974.

In 1980, while serving a federal prison term for bank robbery, Kamahoahoa signed a sworn declaration that Art Rutledge had agreed to pay him $10,000 to murder gangland figure (and Rutledge union rival) William "Billy" Mookini in 1974. Kamahoahoa claimed that Josiah Lii had approached him about the deal on behalf of Rutledge.

Mookini, the target of the hit, was Kamahoahoa's cousin and had been identified by Huihui and others as a local syndicate member. Huihui told the FBI and police that Pulawa in the 1970s wanted Mookini to murder Rutledge as part of The Company's planned takeover of organized labor.

Kamahoahoa, whose glowering, wild-eyed stare certainly gave him the appearance of a dangerous man, said in the 1980 statement that he shot

Onetime Hawai'i organized crime leader Wilford "Nappy" Pulawa (center) surrounded by admitted hit man Royale Kamahoahoa (left) and defense attorney William Worthington (right). RON JETT, PHOTOGRAPHER; *HONOLULU STAR-ADVERTISER* COLLECTION; HAWAI'I STATE ARCHIVES.

Mookini in the head and body, firing rounds through the glass front door of a local eatery, the Beaver Grill.

Kamahoahoa said he was sure he had killed Mookini because he saw blood fountaining into the air from the victim's head wound. But Mookini survived the attack, although it left him with a limp and other serious medical problems.

Kamahoahoa originally denied involvement in the crime when he was tried on a charge of attempted murder. Kamahoahoa was acquitted in a jury trial conducted by hapless city prosecutor Maurice Sapienza—the same man who unsuccessfully prosecuted Aku Sakamoto and Fred Ruis for the 1970 assassination of Senator Larry Kuriyama and who investigated Kukui Plaza scandal figure Harry Chung after staying in lodgings arranged by Chung.

By 1980, Sapienza had entered private practice but wasn't finished with Kamahoahoa and Mookini. He was the man who travelled to McNeil Island federal penitentiary and took down Kamahoahoa's latest version of the crime. Sapienza then used the statement as the basis for a $160 million lawsuit filed by Mookini against Rutledge. Rutledge scoffed at the suit, calling it an attempt to stir up trouble for him when union leadership elections were pending.

Well before the case went to trial, Kamahoahoa reversed fields again, giving a new sworn statement in which he said he had never been hired by Rutledge and Lii to kill Mookini. That story, he said, was merely a lie meant to shake down Rutledge for money.

Unfazed by this turn of events, Sapienza and Mookini plowed ahead with their claims. When the case finally went to trial in 1984, Kamahoahoa took the stand and angrily denied shooting Mookini for money. He said the murder-for-hire story was a lie meant to squeeze money from Rutledge and damage his reputation as a labor leader.

Rutledge's lawyer told the jury that Kamahoahoa had shot Mookini, but the reason was jealousy. The two cousins were seeing the same woman, the lawyer said.

The jury wasted little time in finding for Rutledge.

The following year, based on Huihui's allegations, Kamahoahoa was indicted in the Kong murder case and held in jail for 10 months because he couldn't post $1 million bail. He was finally released after Huihui's plea deal dissolved.

A false arrest lawsuit Kamahoahoa filed went nowhere, but while it was pending, Kamahoahoa was himself sued in connection with his activities at a curious Zen Buddhism compound nestled in the heart of the Koolau mountain range that separates Honolulu from the windward side of Oahu.

Called the Chozen-ji International Zen Dojo, the facility was established by a former Honolulu high school band teacher named Stanley Tanouye. Devoting himself to the study of martial arts and the Rinzai form of Zen, Tanouye abandoned his band instructions and founded the Zen dojo at the very back of Kalihi Valley.

The facility and Tanouye began to attract a diverse variety of followers and visitors, including influential political and business leaders, as well as men of lower repute.

FBI agents following Charles Stevens, a notorious local organized crime figure, tailed him to the dojo. Another well-known criminal, Charles "Moose" Russell, became a devotee of the dojo, asserting that it had helped him overcome heart disease.

And Royale Kamahoahoa was also occasionally on the premises at the dojo.

According to the lawsuit, a well-connected local lawyer had taken a client to the dojo for spiritual and physical rehabilitation. The client, injured in a car accident, said he briefly met Tanouye and then was shown to another room where Kamahoahoa was introduced to him as "an admitted hit man," according to the suit.

Kamahoahoa applied overly vigorous physical therapy on the injured man, he complained in his suit. Kamahoahoa told the man to lie on his stomach and then "proceeded to step on my feet . . . and on my back," the plaintiff said.

"When I told him it hurt too much, to stop, he said, 'Praise the Lord! Release the pain from the body' and he continued to do it," the plaintiff said.

When asked why he didn't just leave, he said, "I was just afraid of that man."

The suit, in which the plaintiff claimed to have suffered a fractured lower back, was later settled under undisclosed terms.

CHAPTER NINE

Three Dogs and a Vet

One of the joys of reporting is its unpredictability: you're never quite sure what the day will bring or how a story will turn out. Frequently it's fun, sometimes it's funny, and every now and then the joke's on you.

Three examples come to mind, each of which involved a dog and its master.

DOG #1

While at KITV in 2000, I was spending time reviewing political finance records maintained by the state Campaign Spending Commission. The records, which hold details of the receipts and expenditures of campaigns for local and statewide political office, were always a reliable generator of stories.

In browsing through reports at the time, I wasn't looking for anything in particular but checking for unusual patterns or numbers. The gold-panning process: watching for glints of treasure amid piles of dross. This required regular and sometimes lengthy visits to the commission's office to pull and examine individual candidate reports.

With the advent of online posting of electronic campaign records, the work has become less tedious and time-consuming. But back then, much of the information that I found valuable, including places of employment and mailing addresses of donors, could only be found in the paper files.

I noticed that an unusual number of employees at a popular Chinese restaurant, Maple Garden, had donated significant sums of money to the campaigns of local politicians. Pulling out four years' worth of campaign reports for multiple officeholders and candidates, I found that Maple

Garden workers had given more than $25,000 to various Island political campaigns.

Large gifts had come from Maple Garden President Robert Hsu and his wife, whose combined donations totaled $7,800 to Mayor Jeremy Harris and others. That wasn't terribly surprising. Hsu was the proprietor of a popular restaurant where political fund-raisers were held with some regularity.

More surprising were $18,000 in donations from Maple Garden workers who were identified in the reports as waitresses, cooks, and kitchen helpers. Waitress Shirley Chew gave the most: $3,500 to the Harris campaign, $1,400 to Governor Ben Cayetano, $1,000 to Lieutenant Governor (and later U.S. Senator) Mazie Hirono, and $500 to Kauai County Mayor Maryanne Kusaka. A cook, Ding Jong Tong, hedged his political bets, giving $1,000 each to competing Honolulu mayoral candidates. Kitchen helper Wen Chang Chen gave $1,000 to one mayoral hopeful. Chen's address in the spending records was the same as cook Tong's, but when I called the home, the man who answered said he had never heard of Wen Chang Chen.

A couple of people familiar with the restaurant told me they had heard it was partly owned by officials of a large and successful engineering firm, R. M. Towill, that routinely landed no-bid consulting contracts from city and state government.

Officers and employees of R. M. Towill also donated handsomely to political campaigns, a routine practice in Honolulu's architecture and engineering community. The practice wasn't illegal, as long as the donations were within legal limits, weren't tied to contract awards, and were voluntarily made with personal funds.

It was illegal to make donations in another person's name, as it was to pay an employee a bonus on the understanding that the money would be used to make a political donation. And it was doubly illegal for that employer to then claim the bonus as a business expense.

I couldn't find any corporate paperwork that linked Towill to Maple Garden. Still, I wondered why restaurant workers would give so freely to political campaigns. It was true that some workers could have gained firsthand familiarity with candidates at fund-raisers, but the extent and variety of the donations were striking.

So I took a cameraman to Maple Garden for a lunch hour visit. Leaving my companion outside, I went into the restaurant and managed to speak briefly with Shirley Chew. She said she had no time to talk to me, was surprised by the figures I quoted to her, and then claimed that her command of English was limited.

I told her I would be happy to wait outside for a chance to speak with her in more detail, but she didn't respond. I went outside and told my cameraman what had happened and said we should wait until the restaurant closed after lunch to see if Chew might appear outside.

Eventually, she did walk out, and I approached her on the sidewalk with a microphone. When I began asking her questions, Chew said nothing but opened the large purse she was clutching to her stomach. A small dog surged out of the purse at me, snarling and snapping and struggling to get free of the purse and sink its little canines into me.

The sudden appearance of this belligerent little animal shocked me. It was like the creature bursting from John Hurt's chest in *Alien*. I reared away from Chew and her pet, which never actually made physical contact with me. I said something like "Thanks for your time" and quit the field in total defeat.

I did produce a story on the Maple Garden donations but left out the Towill angle because I couldn't confirm it.[1]

That simple story had a profound effect in later years on Island politics. Robert Watada, executive director of the Campaign Spending Commission, used the Maple Garden money as the starting point for a years-long investigation into what he termed the "pay to play" culture of Island political finance. I take no credit for the results of Watada's probe, which branched to a criminal investigation conducted by the Honolulu Police Department and Deputy Prosecutor Randy Lee.

Those probes netted nearly $2 million in fines and some 30 misdemeanor criminal convictions of officials and employees of top architectural and engineering firms.

R. M. Towill Chairman Donald Kim and President Russell Figueiroa entered no-contest pleas to arranging "false name" political contributions and were each fined $4,000. The charges were later erased after Kim and Figueiroa satisfactorily completed brief terms of court supervision. Additional charges against other Towill-connected donors were dismissed as part of a plea deal with prosecutors.

Watada told *Honolulu Star-Bulletin* reporter Rick Daysog that Kim and Figueiroa were "at the top of the pay-to-play food chain."[2]

Daysog, a bulldog on the campaign spending story, reported in 2001 on connections between the Towill company and the Maple Garden restaurant. Past company president Richard M. Towill once owned a piece of the restaurant, and Chairman Kim had been an officer of the Maple Garden corporation, Daysog found. And he reported "that notations on several of the Maple Garden checks used for political donations appear to link the donations to the Towill firm."[3]

I worked off and on for decades on stories that examined the nexus between such campaign donations and the selection of no-bid consultants, but it was virtually impossible to demonstrate an explicit quid pro quo relationship between the gifts and the contracts.

It was easy to show the *quid* part of the equation: the money. And the *quo* side, the contracts, was usually obvious. But the *pro* in the middle—an agreement that donations bought you contracts—was very elusive. The donors invariably said that they admired the politics of the candidates or that campaign gifts simply improved their chances of getting noticed, but you had to win the work on your own merits.

One series of stories exposed a variation on the pay-to-play scheme that could be described as "play then pay." Under that scheme, contractors selected for government consulting work kicked back a portion of their compensation to the campaign of the official who gave them the work.

Details of those and other stories I produced on this subject are covered in Chapter 11.

DOG #2

My second dog encounter came years later and also involved a sidewalk interview.

In 2012, I was working for the online news site *Hawaii Reporter*. The site's owner, publisher, editor, and principal reporter, Malia Zimmerman, had cultivated a source who claimed that an escort service called Volcano Girls was being operated out of the Waikiki apartment of University of Hawai'i Professor Lawrence "Bill" Boyd.

The Volcano Girls website certainly gave the appearance of a prostitution business, featuring nude and seminude photos of female escorts who were available to provide a "girlfriend experience" to interested customers. But the site was carefully constructed, mentioning no prices or explicit descriptions of the services provided by the "smoking hot" women shown on the site.

There was no way of connecting the site to Boyd or his apartment, except a contact telephone number.

When Malia and I reconnoitered Boyd's Ohua Street condominium building one day, we managed to get inside and walked down the first floor hallway to the door of Boyd's apartment. When we called the Volcano Girls' contact number, we could hear a phone ringing inside the apartment. We hung up and the ringing stopped; we called again and the ringing resumed.

We decided the story was a good candidate for some undercover work, so I made a series of calls to the Volcano Girls' phone number, presenting myself as a customer interested in securing the services of one of the escorts. I spoke first to a woman and then to a man, arranging an encounter with "a busty Caucasian" woman who called herself Kendra. I was instructed to go to the Ohua Street apartment for the meeting.

The man said the price of the meeting was "three" but wouldn't be more specific. Comments on the website said that meant $300. I was told to park my car in the lot of the nonprofit Waikiki Health Center and walk across Ohua Street to the apartment building. I was given the number and entry code for Boyd's apartment in the building.

Malia loaded me down with two hidden cameras, so I was shooting undercover video when I knocked on the door of Boyd's unit. A young woman opened the door and ushered me down a dark hallway to an equally dark bedroom. We introduced ourselves as Kendra and Jim, and I asked if the price was $300. She said the price was whatever had been agreed upon over the phone.

I nervously told her that I had changed my mind and wanted to cancel the appointment. By that point, I wasn't acting. I was extremely nervous and wanted nothing more than to get the hell out of there. I paid her a $50 "cancellation fee" and quickly left.

The undercover video turned out to be very murky and barely usable but good enough to justify an interview with Boyd.

Malia, our cameraman, and I confronted Boyd the following morning when he left the apartment building to walk his dog—just as Malia's impeccable source had said he would. The source also insisted that Honolulu police had made a prostitution bust several years earlier in Boyd's apartment, and we were in the process of running down that police report when I approached Boyd on the sidewalk.

He was friendly and accommodating, saying he knew nothing about a prostitution or escort business operating inside his apartment. When I told him I had been inside his apartment to meet with Kendra and had videotaped the encounter, he said he was "dumbfounded."

Boyd speculated that a woman named Lorraine Drake, who occupied a bedroom in the unit, might be responsible for the Volcano Girls' activities there. He said he and his wife were out of the apartment during daylight hours. I told him that the man who booked my appointment on the phone sounded just like him, but Boyd adamantly denied speaking to me.

When the interview began, Boyd's dog was on the ground at his feet, but as the exchange progressed, he picked up the animal and clutched it to his chest.

As the questioning grew more uncomfortable for him, he tightened his grip on the animal and held it higher on his chest. By the time we finished talking, he was nearly holding the dog directly in front of his face. The poor creature looked back and forth between Boyd and me and finally began trying to squirm its way out of Boyd's embrace.

I felt rather sorry for both dog and man by the time I stopped my questioning.

We did manage to get a copy of a May 2007 HPD report that related that an undercover cop had booked a $325 meeting in Boyd's apartment through the Volcano Girls' website. A 38-year-old woman was charged with prostitution after she promised to perform explicit sex acts with the officer, the report said.

I called Boyd and asked him about the report. He said he knew nothing about a prostitution arrest at his apartment. "In May of 2007, I think I was in San Francisco," Boyd told me.

We produced online video and print versions of the story for the *Hawaii Reporter* site,[4] and a version of the video story was also broadcast on the local Hawaii News Now television station.

We then got our hands on another report, written by the resident manager of the Ohua Street building about the 2007 prostitution arrest. The manager said that after the police left, "the owner of unit 1C approached me and said that the girl [referring to the prostitute] came in to change clothes and that he didn't know what was going on."[5]

The Volcano Girls stories were a source of great entertainment to morning radio show hosts Michael W. Perry and Larry Price, who dominated the AM radio waves during morning drive time and discussed the hidden camera investigation at great length. Some of my so-called friends were also vastly amused and took to referring to me as the man who pays women not to have sex with him.

DOG #3

The final dog tale began with a Japanese wedding business that was being operated on waterfront property of the Honolulu chapter of Disabled American Veterans, a national nonprofit advocacy group.

The phenomenon of Japanese couples travelling overseas for wedding ceremonies began in the mid-1990s and spread rapidly throughout Hawai'i.

Established churches found themselves doing land office business in conducting the ceremonies. Some churches hosted so many that it became a production-line affair. As limousines carrying one happy wedding party left the premises, more were arriving.

Companies eager to cash in on the business built their own chapels—as close to the ocean as possible to command the highest prices.

The odd aspect to the business was that virtually all of the ceremonies weren't really weddings at all. Most couples had been married in small private ceremonies at home, then travelled to Hawai'i or Australia for ersatz ceremonies attended by family members and close friends.

The driving force behind the phenomenon was money. It was actually a great deal cheaper and simpler to hold a small private wedding in Japan, followed by an overseas ceremony, than it was to hold a traditional grand ceremony in Japan.

The couples didn't acquire wedding licenses in Hawai'i because they were already married. The ceremonies were performed in English, and most churches that hosted the events dispensed with many of the normal religious aspects of the rites.

That raised interesting tax questions for the churches or nonprofit organizations like the DAV that were profiting from the business.

I had covered the subject in some detail before while at KITV, and state tax officials had told me that churches and nonprofit entities had to pay taxes on income generated by business activities like pretend weddings that were unrelated to their core activities.

After I returned to the *Advertiser* in 2002, I found another story in the making at the DAV property.

The land itself was on a dreary stretch of Nimitz Highway near Honolulu International Airport. Its one redeeming factor was that it fronted the ocean. The 11-acre property was owned by the state and leased free of charge to the DAV for development of a memorial to servicemen and women killed or disabled while in the armed forces.

A company specializing in Japanese weddings built two private chapels with windows that overlooked the Pacific and began booking hundreds of weddings at the venue. When the DAV signed a new contract with a competing company that offered more money, $300,000 per year, for the site, a lawsuit was filed that contained lots of interesting details about the business.

No building permits were obtained before the chapels, three "wedding pavilions," and other amenities were erected on the site. DAV officials called that an oversight that was being corrected. The company that paid for those improvements, La Mariage, Inc., claimed that it had also paid for a new entry gate and roadway at the property, naming the main thoroughfare after U.S. Senator Daniel Inouye. Inouye had come to the rescue of the DAV and a related nonprofit, Keehi Memorial Association, after complaints were lodged with the state that the weddings were an improper use of the memorial site.[6]

And La Mariage claimed that it had donated $140,000 to the two veterans groups and paid another $50,000 directly to officials of the organizations for construction, landscaping, and other services.

The DAV and the Memorial Association stoutly defended their use of the property. I knew there were critics but had some trouble finding anyone willing to go on the record with their complaints.

I finally found one in Roy Wiginton, a DAV vice commander, and needed to quickly arrange an interview and photograph of him because his availability was limited.

I called the photo desk, which dispatched staff photographer Rebecca Breyer to Wiginton's house. The written assignment given to her described Wiginton as a disabled vet.

I have observed over the years that many news photographers (as well as those operating television cameras) march to different drummers than the rest of us. Rebecca was no exception. She was a sweet, gregarious woman but a bit on the loopy side. She was crazy about animals and dolls. At one point, she assembled an elaborate, diorama-like display of dolls and action figures in a corner of the city room. The figures were meant to depict various employees of the newspaper. It grew to considerable size, and many staffers didn't quite know what to make of it. Eventually an editor ordered it dismantled.

When Rebecca returned from the Wiginton photo shoot, I asked to see her pictures. She happily complied, but I was disconcerted to see that every single one of the many shots she had taken included not just Wiginton but also his pet dog. Usually the dog was in a position of prominence.

Wiginton, wearing his DAV hat and seated in a wheelchair, had the dog in the middle of his lap, cradled in his arms or held out in front of him.

"These are great, Rebecca," I said. "But don't you have any without the dog?"

"Why would I?" she answered. "He's a vet so I had to include the dog."

It took me a beat or two to process this answer. I eventually explained that the man was a veteran, not a veterinarian.

She laughed merrily about the mix-up.

"You're going to be telling this story for a long time, aren't you?" she asked.

Yes, Rebecca, I am.

CHAPTER TEN

Pay to Play

A good portion of my professional career was spent at the junction of politics, money, and government contracts. It was hardly exhilarating work—analyzing campaign records, wrestling for access to contract files, researching corporate records, interviewing hostile and evasive officials.

Mostly this work resulted in straightforward reporting of who had gotten contract awards and how much they had paid in campaign donations. Once in a while, the stories prompted official investigations and reforms. The state senate cited my stories when it began a two-year series of hearings on the procurement code that ended with an overhaul of the system. Senators even unanimously passed a resolution honoring my reporting.

The resolution said I was "a consistently objective, tenacious and relentless researcher" and "a role model for all future journalists in Hawai'i." Several of the signatories later came to think less highly of me.

Pay-to-play stories I wrote also led to criminal investigations, indictments, and even some convictions and prison time. What follows is a representative sampling of some of those stories.

KUKUI PLAZA

The biggest and probably the best example was also the first. The Kukui Plaza scandal was textbook pay-to-play. Before and after receiving a $50 million city redevelopment contract, Oceanside Properties and its president, Hal Hansen, helped Honolulu Mayor Frank Fasi and his friends in myriad ways.

Although criminal charges against Fasi and fund-raiser Harry C. C. Chung were ultimately dismissed after Hansen refused to testify in open court, details of what he told the grand jury under oath and other evidence amassed against Fasi and Chung were made public during the trial, during the earlier city council hearings, and through independent research.

The indictment alleged that Fasi, Chung, and Hansen reached a "corrupt agreement" that required Hansen and Oceanside to reward Chung and Fasi for the Kukui Plaza contract. Some $65,000 in cash, campaign contributions, services, and other gratuities were paid, and much more was owed, prosecutors charged.

Hansen told the grand jury that he made eight cash payments totaling some $44,000 to Chung; $2,500 was given to Chung on the day Fasi picked Oceanside for the Kukui Plaza contract. Hansen gave seven personal checks totaling $3,050 to two Fasi campaign groups. One check was given just before the city stopped accepting development proposals for the Kukui project.

Hansen told the grand jury that the deal was reached during a "facts of life" meeting he had with Chung at Chung's 20th-Century Furniture office. In a very brief appearance on the witness stand during the trial, Hansen claimed he told special prosecutor Grant Cooper before his grand jury testimony that "I did not feel then and I do not feel now there ever was . . . a bribe agreement."

The day the indictment was unsealed, Fasi held a press conference in which he angrily and adamantly proclaimed his innocence, claiming that Governor George Ariyoshi and Cooper had targeted him in a political vendetta. With characteristic chutzpah, the mayor used the news conference to say that he would formally open his next gubernatorial campaign at an upcoming fund-raiser. He also solicited donations to a newly formed legal defense fund.

There was plenty to the Oceanside-Fasi-Chung relationship that was not included in the criminal case but fell under the pay-to-play umbrella:

- 20th-Century Furniture received the contract to supply carpeting, drapes, and other furnishings at Kukui Plaza.
- Another Chung company, Washerette Clinic, owned and maintained all the coin-operated washers and dryers in the 908-unit twin tower building.
- Oceanside picked Chung's son as insurance agent for Kukui Plaza.
- At Chung's request, Oceanside bought thousands of dollars' worth of stationery supplies for the Fasi campaign, storing the material

Mayor Fasi, lower right, at a 1976 fund-raiser. His bribery trial codefendant, Harry C. C. Chung, is at far left, leaning against the concrete pillar. BOB YOUNG, PHOTOGRAPHER; *HONOLULU STAR-ADVERTISER* COLLECTION; HAWAI'I STATE ARCHIVES.

at its company office until the campaign ran low. Televisions, adding machines, and calculators were also given to the campaign.

- The company bought a $7,000 movie camera that was used by Fasi's office to produce television ads and promotional films.
- Oceanside paid thousands more to air television commercials during prime-time hours that promoted mayoral programs.
- The company also prepared and published for Fasi a housing program that he presented as his own during his 1974 gubernatorial campaign. The program bore a striking similarity to another housing development proposal presented to the city four years earlier by one of Oceanside's competitors in the Kukui Plaza selection process.
- Oceanside even paid for carpeting installed at a hostess bar called Venus Lounge owned by the girlfriend of Matt Esposito, a longtime Fasi crony and city administration official.
- All the expenses incurred by Oceanside for these activities were charged by Oceanside to overhead spending for Kukui Plaza and

were used by the company to determine how much profit it could declare from the project.

- Friends of the mayor and Harry Chung were given preferential treatment in the purchase of specially priced moderate-income units at Kukui Plaza. Residents who had been displaced from their homes by construction of the project were supposed to have been given first claim on the special units, but many were not.[1]

$150,000=$51 MILLION

The early 1990s were taken up by multiple investigations of no-bid consulting contracts awarded by the state to companies that made regular donations to election campaigns and were manned by officials closely tied to the Democratic Party power structure of Hawai'i.

Using the state's open records law in 1992, I found an "open-ended" no-bid contract at the airport that lasted 11 years and grew from $150,000 to $51 million.[2]

The contract was held by M&E Pacific, an engineering firm whose principals included James Kumagai, a former state official and Democratic Party chairman. Various employees of the company had left government jobs to work for M&E. Some even went from M&E to the public payroll—the "revolving door" of consulting work that I found over and over again in my research.

The contractor was originally tasked with identifying necessary expansion projects at Honolulu International Airport. Then contract amendments were repeatedly added that gave M&E authority to plan and design the individual projects, including construction of an overseas terminal, new passenger concourses, and design of fire alarm, electronic security, flight information displays, and public address systems. As those work areas were identified, the contract was again expanded to require M&E to provide necessary "construction management services."

Not all of the $51 million was retained by M&E; much flowed through the company to well-connected subcontractors like Data House, Inc., a company founded by Daniel Arita, the former head of electronic data processing for state government. I wrote many other stories about no-bid public-sector work Data House had landed.

The company received three consecutive no-bid jobs worth almost $500,000 to computerize and automate Governor John Waihee's office. An audit found that the consultant contract had been improperly used to acquire computer equipment for the governor's office—acquisitions that should have been put out to bid. Data House president Arita and his wife donated generously to Waihee's campaign, and the company also supplied computer equipment to the campaign.[3]

This wasn't an entirely new situation: 10 years earlier, in 1982, I found the firm illegally occupying state-owned, low-cost waterfront warehouse space while simultaneously donating to, and working for, Governor George Ariyoshi's political campaign.[4]

MARVIN MIURA GOES TO PRISON

Marvin Miura's career in the public spotlight was short-lived but flamboyant. In 1989, Miura was a politically ambitious man stuck in a low-profile state job. He headed the Office of Environmental Quality Control (OEQC), an obscure agency that processed a great deal of paperwork.

He began making waves at the OEQC, expanding the work there into areas that arguably had environmental significance but were the responsibility of other government agencies. A short man with a big, bristling mustache, Miura cultivated a swashbuckling image—a sort of buccaneer-among-bureaucrats who had neither time nor patience for red tape or dithering. While laying the groundwork for a Maui County mayoral campaign, Miura began livening things up at OEQC, awarding a series of no-bid jobs to a small group of consultants.

OEQC employees, alarmed by Miura's activities, complained about him to the local FBI office but were unhappy about the apparent lack of response there. One of them tipped me to what was going on. I quickly peppered OEQC with records requests and found that Miura had awarded $365,000 in work to his cronies. Some $100,000 of the work was illegally divided into small increments worth less than $4,000. The practice, known as "parceling," allowed the direct award of work with minimal competition.[5]

The largest contract, for a $200,000 study of the need for a hazardous waste disposal facility in Hawai'i, was awarded without bid to the same group of Miura pals, none of whom had any expertise whatsoever in the field of hazardous waste.[6]

The cronies included a Democratic Party insider, Ko Hayashi, who was a longtime political backer of Governor John Waihee, as well as a University of Hawai'i business professor, Ross Prizzia.

I found political contributions from the OEQC consultants to Miura's nascent mayoral campaign and to Waihee's campaign committee.[7]

I also found paperwork that led from Miura directly to Waihee.[8]

After Miura sent a memo to the governor seeking approval to award the hazardous waste study, the governor received a detailed complaint letter

Marvin Miura. EDWIN TANJI, PHOTOGRAPHER; *HONOLULU STAR-ADVERTISER* COLLECTION; HAWAI'I STATE ARCHIVES.

about how Miura was manipulating the hazardous waste contract award.[9] The letter was written by a local attorney on behalf of a Mainland firm, Parametrix, Inc., that had helped Miura get the $200,000 in contract funds from the legislature and that wanted at least a chance at bidding for the contract.

"During the past legislative session, we were called on by Marvin Miura of the OEQC to prepare expert testimony for his use in support of the study," the letter, written by lawyer Lloyd Asato, said. "After the session, Parametrix was interested in being on a list to be considered for the study," the letter continued. "Marvin Miura told me this afternoon that the contract is let, that he cannot reveal the consultant and that it was a non-bid contract because the work is highly specialized," Asato wrote.

The lawyer asked for an investigation. "We request that you look into this situation, correct any irregularity and open this matter for competition."

None of that happened. Waihee approved the contract, telling me in an interview later that he approved the need for a study, not the contractor who would prepare it. He also told me that he knew no details of Miura's shenanigans at OEQC and "would have stopped" them if he had.

Asato's letter was sent by Waihee's office to the Health Department, which oversaw Miura and the OEQC. The Health Department then asked Miura to respond to Asato. Miura wrote a vaguely worded response that said state law allowed such a contract to be awarded without competitive bidding. The response, which said nothing about the request for an investigation, was sent back up the line to the governor's office and forwarded to Asato.

Miura acknowledged in an interview that his management style was "maybe unconventional" but was meant to break up what he called the "bureaucratic lump" of government. He denied behaving improperly in the selection of consultants and said the contractors he picked were qualified and professional.

"These guys were capable, so I said, 'Boom, let's do it,'" Miura told me.

But the hazardous waste study, when it was finally produced, was a toxic disaster. The deputy health director in charge of environmental issues said in an interview that the report's findings "appear to be partial, erroneous and misleading and they don't provide much evidence of original research." A top University of Hawai'i environmental scientist called the report "a waste of time."

When I was finishing up the first of what would be many Miura stories, I walked from the News Building to OEQC's office to retrieve additional records. I couldn't get through the door because the FBI was conducting a raid.

Miura, Hayashi, and Prizzia were later indicted on federal criminal charges, including fraud, kickbacks, money laundering, and tax evasion. Miura eventually pleaded guilty to demanding and receiving a $35,000 kickback from Prizzia and Hayashi. They also gave him a $1,800 trip to Thailand and paid Miura's son $15,000 for OEQC subcontract work. Hayashi and Prizzia pleaded guilty and received short prison sentences.

Prizzia, a tenured professor, lost his job at the University of Hawai'i but filed a successful grievance when he got out of prison and was restored to the faculty.

When Miura entered his guilty plea, his lawyer, Michael Weight, told reporters that his client had been unfairly targeted for conduct "that has been going on in Hawaii since time immemorial."[10] Weight said purchasing improprieties were widespread in state government. He quoted Frank Fasi's famous maxim: "All else being equal, you reward your friends and punish your enemies."

What Miura did "was not right," Weight said, "but if the government is going to pursue the likes of Marvin Miura, there are probably a number of other folks in town that had best be concerned."

KEN KIYABU REDECORATES

My contracting cronyism exposés in the early 1990s reached critical mass with a series of stories I wrote about numerous minicontracts awarded by the manager of Aloha Stadium.

Ken Kiyabu was a former legislator and Democratic Party stalwart who was given the stadium manager job in 1989. His professional background included work as a real estate agent and tour promoter. After serving in the legislature from 1975 to 1986, Kiyabu served a two-year stint as deputy state comptroller in the Department of Accounting and General Services,

Ken Kiyabu. *HONOLULU STAR-BULLETIN* PHOTO; *HONOLULU STAR-ADVERTISER* COLLECTION; HAWAI'I STATE ARCHIVES.

which oversaw most government contracting and purchasing activities, before transferring to the stadium job.

Aloha Stadium was a massive money pit of a structure that over the years produced a wealth of stories. The "weathered steel" used in its construction, meant to develop a protective "patina" of rust in the salty winds above Pearl Harbor, never worked quite as planned and led to tens of millions of dollars in repairs and legal claims. The stadium design, in which sections of stands could be rolled on concrete casters into football or baseball configurations, was equally defective, and eventually the stadium was locked into a football oval.

In late 1992, I took a look at stadium purchasing records and quickly noticed some obvious anomalies. A series of purchase orders for painting, carpeting, and drapery installation in the stadium executive offices were all written after the work had been performed. This was the reverse of the normal process: first you order the work, then it gets performed, then payment is made.

There was something even more suspicious about the paperwork. All the purchase orders, which totaled about $50,000, were for amounts under $4,000. It looked to me like clear-cut parceling, dicing a large job into small components to avoid putting the work out to competitive bid.[11]

Jobs under $4,000 were subject to much less formal purchasing rules, and that's what happened at Ken Kiyabu's office. The state comptroller's office—where Kiyabu used to work—had issued warnings to state procurement agents that parceling was illegal and could result in fines and termination.

The single largest purchase order I looked at, for $3,984, was issued to Jimmy Kitazaki. There was no indication what work Kitazaki provided, and his business address on the requisition order had been lined out and replaced with the address of another company involved in the stadium work, K&A Installers.

I found Kitazaki working at a retail furniture store that was conveniently within walking distance of my office. When I visited him in person, he readily said that he and Ken Kiyabu had been personal friends for 25 years, and he had voluntarily, and without pay, helped Kiyabu with his redecoration project. I asked about the $3,984 invoice, and he said that payment actually went to K&A for the purchase and installation of new carpeting at Kiyabu's office. The carpeting, called Karastani Tanipani, had a blue metallic threading because Kiyabu was "a blue man," Kitazaki said.

When I pressed him on why the bill wasn't sent directly to K&A, Kitazaki said "something was mentioned about bidding restrictions above $4,000."

The president of K&A, Alan Nakatsu, confirmed Kitazaki's account and added that two companies that also billed for services at the stadium hadn't done any work there at all. They allowed their company names to be used on invoices to keep each individual bill under $4,000, he explained.[12]

Kiyabu himself offered several explanations for what had happened. In late 1991, he said, word reached him that President George H. W. Bush would be visiting Aloha Stadium. So Kiyabu wanted to spruce up the place in advance of the visit. He also said that the reason the work was billed in small increments was because the stadium didn't have the budget for it, so it was performed over an extended period of time. The presidential visit was cancelled and lessened the need for immediate performance, Kiyabu told me.[13]

He confirmed his friendship with Kitazaki but said Kitazaki worked without pay. When asked why Kitazaki submitted a $3,984 bill to the state, Kiyabu said, "I thought he didn't bill us." Kiyabu signed Kitazaki's invoice on behalf of the stadium.

Kiyabu also said the contractors all performed fine work, and he asserted that it probably would have cost the state more if it had gone through the time-consuming and inefficient process of putting the work out to competitive bid.

As scandals go, this one was minor at best. A relatively small amount of money was involved when compared with other multimillion-dollar no-bid jobs I had covered. Nobody had paid to play. But the response to the Aloha Stadium stories was instantaneous public outrage. Readers called and wrote in with compliments and calls for more stories. Legislators demanded investigations and public hearings. The state announced a review of Aloha Stadium purchasing.

At the time, I liked to imagine that the sudden public umbrage had actually been accumulating over time, fed by my earlier stories. Maybe the stadium stories pushed this reservoir of resentment over the spillway.

In reality, though, I suspect there was a simpler explanation: carpets and drapes. People understood that stuff. A government official who cut corners to fancy up his office got people riled.

Within three weeks of the first story, the government's review was completed, and Ken Kiyabu had resigned.[14] The review found "glaring deficiencies" in how the stadium handled the refurbishment work. It also found "a fundamental weakness in the internal control system of the stadium in the procurement process."

Governor John Waihee and Attorney General Robert Marks said no further action would be taken against Kiyabu. "I agree that he violated the procurement process," Waihee said, adding that resignation was "a severe enough sanction" for Kiyabu.

Kiyabu said he had tried to perform his work as quickly and efficiently as possible but was thwarted by the state's "severely limiting" procurement code.

There had already been attempts to overhaul state procurement practices, centering on two tricky areas of government contracting: "sole-source" jobs, which were awarded directly to vendors, and "professional services" work. The latter involved services like architectural and engineering design that were awarded on criteria beyond simple price, including such things as past performance and professional capabilities of vendors.

Sole-source awards were justified by a variety of arguments. The most common was that only the selected contractor was qualified for the work—an argument that was sometimes true but too often accepted at face value. Another regular but dubious justification was the press of time—"we need this right away." A variation on this theme was "we already awarded it; please approve it retroactively because the contractor has started work." Perhaps the most common of all was "we've already used this contractor for similar work." A close relative of this last argument was "we used this contractor's proprietary software so we have to keep using him."

Unlike sole-source awards, hiring an architect or engineer usually included some semblance of competition. Prospective designers had to demonstrate that they were professionally qualified, that they had the requisite manpower, and, ideally, that they had previously completed similar work. It was the inclusion of these necessarily subjective criteria that opened the process to manipulation.

A 1990 study commissioned by the state comptroller found that Hawai'i's procurement system was chaotic, antiquated, and prone to abuse. It recommended adoption of a model procurement code developed by the American Bar Association. Pending that action, the consultant said, the state could still reduce the amount of no-bid and sole-source contracts it was awarding by 25 percent.

The following year, I found, the state actually increased those awards by 50 percent.[15]

A committee of procurement officials from around the state couldn't agree on whether adoption of the model code was a good idea. Against that backdrop came the parceling stories.

On the day Kiyabu resigned, the state senate announced creation of a special committee to investigate procurement issues and draft a new procurement code.

A reform bill the legislature passed in 1993 was vetoed by Governor Waihee. Reforms were enacted the following year, but I found soon enough that the new procedures, meant to seal consultant contracts from unfair influences, were far from watertight.

AIRPORT GAMES

In 1996, after I decamped from the *Advertiser* to television news, my first major project at KITV involved a hard look at Honolulu International Airport consulting contracts.

I had developed a very good source inside the airport bureaucracy. Airport officials, my source told me, were skirting provisions of the new procurement code and awarding consultant jobs to firms with political connections to the new governor, Ben Cayetano.

As proof, I was given an internal airport document that listed upcoming consultant jobs. Handwritten notes on the right margin of the list identified the firms that would be given the contracts. All the notes were written before the so-called new and evenhanded selection process had even begun, my source told me.

Some of the contracts had already been awarded by the time my source gave me the list. The names of the winners corresponded to the handwritten notes, but that didn't prove anything.

Without mentioning the handwritten list I had, I started asking for access to a large number of airport contract documents before the next job was awarded.

Some background information about how the new procurement system was supposed to work is necessary here.

Firms interested in architectural and engineering work had to first be prequalified by the state. As each new contract award approached, names of prequalified companies were submitted to small committees of state personnel, who graded the applicants according to predetermined criteria: professional achievements, past performance, familiarity with the type of work involved, that sort of thing.

The names of the best three applicants would then be given to a procurement officer in no particular order. The officer would then select a winner, negotiate the terms of the contract, and award the job. If the negotiations bogged down, they would be cancelled and begun again with another company on the list of finalists.

The fact that the list of finalists was unranked was supposed to give procurement officials room to maneuver: the same company wouldn't win all the time because there would be an ability to spread the work around among companies that had already been found best qualified for the jobs.

But my tipster said the system was being gamed. Screening committees were regularly submitting lists of finalists that contained names of companies friendly to the administration. And companies that were owned or otherwise connected to Dennis Mitsunaga, Governor Cayetano's personal friend and political fund-raiser, were landing an inordinate number of jobs, I was told.

The next contract on my list was a $600,000 job to plan improvements to the international arrivals terminal. The handwritten list said the job would go to a company called TM Designers. The list was right.

I started making phone calls to airport officials. My source told me that the handwriting on the list belonged to Ernest Kurosawa, a mid-level engineering official at the airport. When I reached Kurosawa on the phone, he said he thought the contract award process was manipulated for political reasons. But he wouldn't agree to an on-camera interview.

TM Designers had been in existence for only eight months, and a vice president of the company, Roy Iizaki, said the company was controlled by Dennis Mitsunaga. It was operating out of state-owned airport warehouse space that it shared with another Mitsunaga-controlled company. And Mitsunaga's main company, Mitsunaga & Associates, was a subcontractor on the international terminal job.

Mitsunaga refused to talk to me.

I lined up interviews with the head of the airports division, Jerry Matsuda, and his boss, Transportation Department Director Kazu Hayashida, the man who had formally picked TM Designers for the job.[16]

I told Hayashida I had a list written weeks before the pick that correctly said he would select TM Designers for the job. "I'm surprised that it was out," Hayashida said.

Asked if there were political aspects to the selection of TM Designers, Hayashida said, "I hope not. It should be more of a professional pick."

I interviewed Jerry Matsuda on camera and told him that Ernest Kurosawa said consultant awards were being politically manipulated. "He did?" Matsuda answered. "I'm not familiar with that."

I asked Matsuda if he had discussed with Kurosawa the companies that the administration preferred for consulting jobs. "No, not to my knowledge," he said. It was a very lukewarm denial.

I thought I was on my way to a career at *60 Minutes*. The men in these interviews were understandably nervous, but they also looked very shifty, something difficult to convey in newsprint.

Later in the interview, Matsuda collected himself and said flatly that there was nothing political about the selection process.

I also interviewed Governor Cayetano, who said, "There is no attempt to influence the way jobs are given out to consultant firms." He said Mitsunaga was a friend and political supporter who had been raising campaign money for him for 10 years. But he claimed that Mitsunaga wasn't getting much work from the state. "Maybe he hasn't had luck," Cayetano said. "If I were to manipulate the system, the man should be rolling in dough."

I followed up that first story with another the following day that showed the governor had personally manipulated the award of another pricey consulting job, for design improvements at one of the airport's busiest runways. The contract had gone to another Mitsunaga-connected company, Fujita & Associates. Mitsunaga was an original founder of that company, and his own firm was a subcontractor on the runway job. Score sheets prepared by the screening committee showed that Fujita had finished 10th of the 11 firms considered.[17]

But those scores were thrown out after the governor said he wanted the work to go to a local company. That whittled the list of competitors from 11 to 5 firms. Even then, Fujita finished fourth out of five applicants, according to the paperwork compiled under the new procurement law.

The new law said only the top three qualifiers could be considered for such a contract. But Hayashida ordered the list of finalists expanded to five firms. Then he gave the job to Fujita.

Cayetano's attorney general, Margery Bronster, sat for an interview and declared the selection process illegal. Limiting the qualified companies to only local firms was improper, Bronster said. And using a five-company list of finalists instead of three was legally questionable, she said: "The law is pretty clear that there is a list of three that is to be sent up to the procurement officer."

Hayashida said he picked Fujita because he was familiar with the company and knew it could do the job. He said he knew nothing about connections between Fujita and Mitsunaga. The governor relied on his earlier denial that there were no political considerations in the selection process.

The following week, the Fujita contract award was cancelled, and Cayetano said he was ordering an investigation of airport consulting jobs.

And Ernest Kurosawa, who had told me off camera the previous week that the process was subject to political manipulation, now was denying that he ever said such a thing. So I interviewed Kurosawa on camera, arming myself ahead of time with copies of his handwriting that matched the notes on the secret selection list.[18]

After he denied saying that contracts were politically influenced, I showed Kurosawa that handwritten list. "Do you recognize this?" I asked.

"Isn't that your handwriting on the right-hand edge of that?" Kurosawa was clearly rattled, and the state public relations officer who was present at the interview didn't step in to save him. She seemed as interested as I was in what he would say.

"I think this should be some other subject because I'm here just to clear the statement that you made," Kurosawa said.

"Doesn't this demonstrate that in fact the contractor selection . . . that contractors are preselected?" I asked.

"Not really," said Kurosawa.

I pressed on: "When did you write those names down?"

"I don't know if I did," he said.

"Isn't it your handwriting?"

"I don't know," he answered, studying the document.

I was in full *60 Minutes* mode now. "I brought another sample of your handwriting; we can compare them if you want."

He denied that the document showed manipulation of the process.

When I got back to the station and saw the raw footage of the interview, I realized my dreams of network stardom would have to wait. The longer the interview went, the higher my voice rose. By the time I produced the handwriting exemplar for Kurosawa, I was squeaking like an outraged mouse.

The next day, Cayetano blamed the problems in airport consulting on mid-level bureaucrats like Kurosawa. High-level officials like Hayashida would make the selections. "It's best to have this at a higher level where you folks, the press, can question people who are accountable, like me," Cayetano told me.

That was a truly silly solution, since Hayashida was already the Transportation Department's chief procurement officer and had final say on consultant selections. Plus Hayashida was a political appointee of the governor.

I pointed out that in the first year and a half on the job, Hayashida had repeatedly given consulting work worth millions of dollars to Mitsunaga-connected companies. On a $500,000 job at Lihue Airport on Kauai, Hayashida picked Mitsunaga for the work over two other companies that received higher marks from screeners.

"I've known Dennis for a long time. . . . Even before, when his father was a contractor," Hayashida said. "He has the necessary experience to do a lot of things."

Another Mitsunaga company, M&A, Inc., landed a $1 million job from Hayashida just weeks after the company was incorporated.[19]

The following week brought a look at the airport warehouse that several Mitsunaga-connected companies were using for their airport work.

The warehouse was leased by the state to Aloha Airlines, and there was no record in property files of any other tenants there. I found that four Mitsunaga-connected companies had been operating from that address for more than a year.

One was Blueline, Inc., a Mitsunaga venture that produced architectural drawings. Another was Punaluu Builders, a construction company. Mitsunaga & Associates called the warehouse its "branch office" in correspondence with the state. TM Designers also used the warehouse as its mailing address.

The state then cancelled Aloha's property permit because of the improper subleasing.[20]

Finally, 10 weeks after the governor announced that an investigation would be undertaken of the airport consulting contracts, I followed up with a story that there was no sign of an investigation.[21]

The attorney general's office was supposed to be looking into the matter, but I learned none of the staff investigators had received such an assignment. Hayashida said in an interview that no one had questioned him or anyone else in his department. But he did say that airport personnel like Kurosawa and Jerry Matsuda were no longer involved in consultant selections.

After Cayetano announced the investigation, Hayashida went ahead and picked Mitsunaga for the Lihue Airport job—just like Kurosawa's handwritten list said he would. "That was already in the process, we didn't want to delay the project. The main thing is that they were qualified for the work," said Hayashida.

I continued turning out stories about large consulting jobs landed by Mitsunaga during the Cayetano administration.

At the end of 1997, I produced a story about problems with a reroofing job at the lovely Korean Studies Center building on the University of Hawai'i campus. The construction specifications called for use of Japanese-made tiles for the job, a cultural gaffe that deeply offended the local Korean community with bitter memories of Japan's brutal occupation of their home country in World War II.

So the contract was withdrawn and rebid in such a way that only a Mitsunaga & Associates venture offered to do the work. The owner of a roofing company that wanted to bid went on camera to complain about the process.[22]

The report was finished in the middle of Christmas holidays, so KITV decided to hold it for a few days because it wasn't exactly a festive subject. Then it was unaccountably aired on Christmas night.

I was out at a party that evening and didn't know the story had run. When I got home, my loutish 21-year-old stepson told me that someone who sounded very angry had called me several times.

"Well, who was it?" I asked.

"I don't know" was the reply. "He said his name was Ben something . . . Ben Casanova? Something like that, I think."

On cue, the phone rang, and it was Governor Ben Cayetano.

He was furious about the story. It was unfair, it was a hit job, it wasn't right to run something like that on Christmas . . . he went on at some length. I told him I didn't even know the story had run, and there was really nothing I could do about it that night. We agreed to talk about it the next day, by which time he had calmed down and withdrawn his objections to the piece.

I continued turning out stories about Cayetano and Mitsunaga after I returned to the *Advertiser* in 2002, including a series about no-bid work given to Punaluu Builders by the state public housing agency. Those stories provoked federal housing officials to impose a complete overhaul of the state agency, which had been run by Mitsunaga's ex-wife.

The coverage made Cayetano so angry that he ordered all officials in his administration not to talk to me. "From now on, if Jim Dooley requests information, tell him to put it in writing and process his request as we would any other," Cayetano wrote in a memo. "As far as I am concerned, Dooley's story on HCDCH [the housing agency] was just another example of his unfairness," the memo continued.[23]

When I got my hands on the memo, I wanted to write a story about it. But the *Advertiser* editors refused. They said they preferred to handle the matter quietly by speaking directly to the governor. If that ever happened, I was never told about it.

At the end of Cayetano's administration, in 2002, came more stories about contracting subterfuge at the airport. Several airport officials and a group of construction contractors had been operating a bid-rigging scheme to corner the market on airport repair work.

The contractors, in collusion with airport supervisors, submitted phony and inflated bids for repair work worth less than $25,000. The long-running scheme bilked taxpayers out of more than $4 million. The contractors kicked back cash, gifts, and favors to the airport personnel.[24]

There was no proof that Cayetano or any of his political associates were aware of what was going on, but contractors who eventually pleaded guilty to criminal charges in state and federal court said they were regularly required to make cash payments of as much as $20,000 to a politically connected airport official, Richard Okada, who claimed the money was needed for "political contributions."

I looked hard but found scant evidence that the money ever found its way into Island political campaigns.

Okada was convicted in federal court and sentenced to five years in prison. His fellow airport supervisor, Dennis Hirokawa, drew a nine-year sentence. U.S. District Judge David Ezra said Hirokawa treated the airport like "his own personal piggy bank."[25]

Cayetano was succeeded as governor by Republican Linda Lingle, who, like many of her predecessors, promised to end cronyism in state contracting.

Lingle even ushered yet another procurement reform law through the legislature. The new law included requirements that members of consultant contract screening committees be "impartial and independent."

When Lingle signed the bill into law, she said it would "put to rest the appearance of impropriety in nonbid contracts."

The ink had barely dried on her signature when a politically connected company called Community Planning and Engineering, Inc., started landing multimillion-dollar no-bid consulting contracts at the state Department of Hawaiian Home Lands.

All three members of the department screening committee that picked Community Planning for its first five DHHL contracts had past connections to Community Planning. One, Joe Blevins, said he had been recruited by Community Planning President Joe Pickard to work at DHHL. Another, Larry Sumida, was recommended for his state job by Community Planning founder Bernard Kea. A third employee's connection was more remote: he had worked for the private company some seven years earlier.[26]

Blevins and Sumida had come from the private sector and were on their new state jobs for just a few weeks when they picked Community Planning as the best qualified firm for a no-bid $984,000 engineering consultant job.

Over the next three weeks, the same screening committee gave Community Planning four other no-bid jobs worth some $6.2 million.

Based in part on the experience gained from those first five jobs, Community Planning received six additional DHHL no-bid jobs worth $7.6 million over the following six months. The firm received the lion's share of all consulting work awarded by DHHL during the Lingle administration.

The company had received no DHHL work during the preceding 10 years. In fact, it had performed only a tiny amount of government work, preferring to stay in the private sector, where it had extensive experience in planning residential and commercial real estate developments.

Company President Pickard, who had purchased the firm just months before it started landing DHHL work, was a politically generous man. He made campaign donations to Democratic and Republican campaigns alike but tilted heavily to the GOP side of the ledger. In the previous five years, Pickard, his relatives, and his companies had donated more than $70,000 to the campaigns of Lingle; her lieutenant governor, James Aiona; and the Republican Party itself.

Micah Kane, the head of the Department of Hawaiian Home Lands, was a past chairman of the Hawai'i Republican Party.

In May 2004, after Pickard's company had received its first three DHHL consulting jobs, Pickard chaired a golf tournament fund-raiser for the GOP. He solicited "major sponsors" to donate anywhere from $500 to $5,000. "We have made progress by reforming the state's procurement system [and] bringing fiscal discipline in the way government spends taxpayer's hard-earned money," Pickard said in the solicitation.

Kane and Pickard defended the contract awards, saying political considerations had nothing to do with them, that they were based entirely on merit.

A final note on the pay-to-play issue: when I was working at the online news site *Hawaii Reporter* in 2012, Ben Cayetano came out of retirement and mounted a campaign to become mayor of Honolulu. Opponents used the state housing agency stories to depict Cayetano as a politician deeply involved in the pay-to-play system.

Luckily for him, my KITV airport stories were unavailable on the Internet and had largely been forgotten.

Cayetano lost the mayoral election.

CHAPTER ELEVEN

Pearl Harbor

Two days in college ROTC was my closest brush with military service. So I had a lot to learn when a source called from Pearl Harbor about contracting shenanigans at the shipyard.

A Boston-based consulting company called Harbridge House was getting a great deal of work from the Navy, my tipster said. Scuttlebutt had it that the shipyard deputy commander, Captain Paul A. Peterson, had steered a half-million-dollar contract to the company while investing in real estate with Harbridge House personnel.

The real estate angle was easily verified. My office was a five-minute walk from the state Bureau of Conveyances, an official records repository where copies of deeds, land sales, and other documents were recorded. I only had to go back a few years before I found the Peterson paperwork that listed all the partners in the deal.

I called back my source and read him the names. Nearly all worked for the consulting company, Harbridge House. One was the recently retired civilian chief planning officer at Pearl Harbor, Rudolph Krause, who had since begun work as manager of Harbridge House's Honolulu office.

I called Peterson for comment. I knew next to nothing about Harbridge House or the work it was doing for the Navy, but I wanted to get Peterson on the record before I started asking questions about the company. Maybe there was a reasonable explanation for the real estate deal, and I needed to find that out before committing more time to this. Also, I thought he might be more likely to talk to me before I started asking around about the consultant contract.

Peterson readily admitted the investment deal but said he had declared a conflict of interest and had no involvement in the award or administration of a $560,000 consulting contract then held by Harbridge House at Pearl Harbor. He complained that he and his partners had taken a bath on the condo purchase. "There was a guy selling quick profits, obviously with the risk involved in quick profits, so we got in on it," he said.

The investment was made while the condo project was in the development stage. By the time it was completed, the real estate market had soured, and the purchasers couldn't resell, Peterson told me. "We had expected to resell that condo under a much shorter period of time. I'm left with a deal, a holding, long after I had expected to," he said.

He insisted there was no connection between the investment and the Harbridge House contract, which involved planning a new computerized management information system for Pearl Harbor. The contract had been competitively bid, Peterson said, but Harbridge House was the only company that submitted a bid. As the chief planning officer for the shipyard, Peterson had written contract specifications that included strict experience requirements for prospective bidders. Harbridge House had very experienced personnel, Peterson said. "I cannot bring in Joe Amateur Home Computer Guy and put him on that," the captain said.

Sixty companies had expressed interest in bidding, but the only offer came from Harbridge House, Peterson acknowledged.

"There are some other damn good outfits around but I don't think they felt they could meet the requirements that we have in that [contract] for experience," said Peterson.[1]

Peterson's goose was basically cooked at that point. My original source and several others that I developed at the shipyard told me the captain's assertions that he had declared a conflict of interest and kept away from the contract award were disingenuous at best. Even taken at face value, the captain had engaged in a private business deal that disqualified him from an important piece of his shipyard responsibilities. And he had written contract specifications that appeared to directly benefit his partners in that private deal.

I needed to get a look at the contract paperwork. So I began what turned out to be a long and tortuous voyage through the murky seas of the federal Freedom of Information Act.

Any reporter or researcher familiar with the process will tell you that FOIA chews up time. And this was 1983—back when FOIA correspondence was still exchanged the old-fashioned way.

The first batch of documents produced by Pearl Harbor in response to my earliest FOIAs contained a wealth of eye-opening information about

Harbridge House. Library research and a helpful staffer at the *Boston Globe* newspaper provided more.

It was one of the oldest management consulting firms in the country, selling advice to government and industry. From its very beginning in 1950, Harbridge House enjoyed extremely close ties to the U.S. Navy. Its three founders were all Navy veterans, and one of them, Paul Ignatius, had served as secretary of the Navy. All three were graduates of the Harvard Business School in Cambridge, Massachusetts. The company's name was a combination of Harvard and Cambridge, and its first office, on Harvard Square, was opened at the start of the Korean War.

The Harbridge House material supplied by Pearl Harbor contained a good deal of promotional material about the firm's history and its activities around the country and internationally. When Harbridge House officials learned the extent of the Navy's disclosure to me, they were quite upset. A company attorney fired off (does anyone remember telexes?) an aggressively worded letter to the publisher of the *Advertiser.*

The Navy "violated federal law" when it "improperly released trade secrets and confidential business information" to me about Harbridge House, the letter said.[2] "Harbridge House directs that no use of this information be made and that it not be communicated to anyone outside the *Honolulu Advertiser.*" The company then said it needed a list of everyone who had seen the paperwork and "notarized statements" from them that promised the secrets would not be divulged.

Pushy telexes from important-sounding Washington, D.C., law firms were not an everyday occurrence at the *Advertiser,* particularly at the top-floor office of the publisher.

I had kept my editors in the loop about my activities, but it wasn't a big deal at the time and certainly wasn't anything that had been discussed with the publisher. So management summoned me to a meeting to discuss what I was up to.

I explained, and we looked at the Navy records and decided that they were interesting but did not seem to warrant the company's response. What were these guys so touchy about?

By the time that letter was written, Harbridge House had grown to multinational dimensions, with offices around the globe. It was owned by Allstate Insurance, which in turn was owned by retailing giant Sears Roebuck. There was plenty of horsepower behind the letter.

The attorney claimed that disclosure of the company's internal information would damage its competitive position in the marketplace. I was fairly early in my research but knew enough to find this assertion puzzling.

Virtually all of the company's Navy contracts were of the no-bid, sole-source variety that did not involve competition.

Jeff Portnoy, lawyer for the humble, locally owned *Honolulu Advertiser*, wrote a letter back to Harbridge House that essentially told the company to take its notarized statements and spin on them. Portnoy told the company that if it had a problem, it was with the Navy, not us.

The editors gave me the green light to continue.

I don't know if the outcome would have been different if the newspaper had been owned by Gannett. But I am certain that receipt of such a letter would have caused prolonged hand-wringing and second-guessing among the Gannett editors I have known. Nothing put the Big Fear into them like the prospect of getting sued. A death threat to a reporter wouldn't have nearly the impact of a threatened lawsuit. In fact, in my case, a death threat might have sounded like a good idea to some of them. But threaten a lawsuit, and watch the brakes start smoking.

In any event, I pressed ahead with my research. New documents received under FOIA led to additional requests. I was gradually learning the Navy and Defense Department procurement lingo and was able to refine later FOIA requests. I was also developing new sources who helped educate me about what additional records to ask for.

One anonymous tipster sent me letters postmarked in Washington, D.C. He or she—I never knew which—was obviously familiar with my FOIA campaign. "You're asking the wrong questions," the writer advised. "Ask for this. . . ." This was a strange and wonderful new development for me. I had a new source, 5,000 miles away, and I hadn't written a word yet.

Another prepublication result of my FOIA work was that the Navy began an internal audit of Harbridge House's contracts at Pearl Harbor. The Naval Investigative Service and the FBI also began nosing around.

All told, I wrote dozens of FOIA letters to a variety of agencies within the Navy and elsewhere in the Defense Department. All nine of the shipyards then in operation around the country received at least one FOIA request from me. Filing and reviewing all the paperwork I eventually amassed was a nightmare. I was never a particularly good record keeper. There are some reporters, and teams of reporters, who are masters at it: computerizing everything, cross-referencing, creating subfiles, suspense files, the whole schmear. One reporter I knew maintained magnificent files that documented his entire professional life: every story he'd ever researched, source files detailing every person he'd ever met, including people at gas stations and parties (regardless of their probable value as new sources). He spent so much time massaging all his data that he hardly ever wrote anything and had to become an editor.

Material began arriving at my office by the boxload. Newly received records raised new questions that provoked new FOIA requests. Some government offices responded quickly and in detail. Others balked, demanding advance payment of research fees. Others delayed. Some didn't respond at all.

Despite months of effort, I could never determine exactly how much work Harbridge House had received from the Navy and other parts of the Defense Department. Twice I was sent lists that purported to include all of the company's contracts awarded by federal agencies over a five-year period. The lists held $11 million worth of work, but they were glaringly incomplete. The first summary, sent to me by the Navy, didn't include the Pearl Harbor consulting contract, in force for three years. Another Harbridge House contract that I had obtained from the Long Beach Naval Shipyard was also missing from the list.

The woman who supplied the data to me worked at the Contracting Assistance and Control Division of the Naval Supply Systems Command. When I called her to complain about the omissions, she told me that if contracting agencies didn't submit the proper Defense Department "350 forms," the jobs wouldn't be entered in the federal database. When I asked how many other contracts might be missing from the files, she said, "We don't know. That's the bad part of the system."[3]

I talked to her boss, the head of the Contracting Assistance and Control Division, Frank Reich. He told me the system had been tightened up, but "there is a strong error rate in the data before 1981 or so. Before that, the people who filled out the forms didn't pay that much attention to what they were doing. Since 1981–82, the information tends to be more error-free than before," Reich assured me.

But the Pearl Harbor and Long Beach contracts were awarded in 1982, I pointed out. Why aren't they on your list? "I don't know," he said.

Three months later, the Defense Department sent me another list of Harbridge House contracts. Pearl Harbor and Long Beach were still missing.[4]

A striking fact about all the research I did on Navy consultant contracts was that the same irregularities and iniquities I had found at the state and county levels were all present in the federal system. Just on a grander scale.

CRONYISM

Auditors who examined the Harbridge House contracts as a result of my investigation found that Captain Peterson had initially tried to award the management information system contract directly to the company without any competitive bidding. When that effort was blocked by procurement personnel, Peterson wrote contract specs that were so restrictive only Harbridge House could meet them. "Placing such restrictions on [contract] solicitation is improper," the auditors found.[5]

All of that occurred when Peterson was doing personal business with the consultants.

The commanding officer at Pearl Harbor, Captain Thomas Marnane, also violated procurement regulations when he approved the sole-source purchase of a $131,000 training program from Harbridge House. The program required top shipyard personnel to spend two weekends at the luxury Kuilima Resort Hotel on Oahu's North Shore.

The president of Harbridge House, Harry Baker Ellis Jr., and a vice president of the company, Michael Farmer, invested in their own Honolulu real estate deal through Rudy Krause, then the top civilian planner at Pearl Harbor. While on the Navy payroll, Krause was involved in ordering $250,000 worth of work from Harbridge House.[6]

Krause and Farmer later were partners with Peterson in the Kauai real estate deal. Other Harbridge House personnel were coinvestors in that deal, along with Robert Gilmore, the head of data processing at the Long Beach Naval Shipyard, where Harbridge House had a $406,000 sole-source consulting contract. Farmer was also personal friends with a former commander at Pearl Harbor, John C. McArthur.

ONE JOB LEADS TO ANOTHER

A job at the Portsmouth, New Hampshire, Naval Shipyard brought Harbridge House to Pearl Harbor. The sole-source contract—to revise and update training materials related to the shipyard management information system—was supposed to cost $825,000 and last for a year. It eventually doubled in cost and duration.

A Navy audit of the Portsmouth contract, obtained under FOIA, said that the noncompetitive contract award appeared "unjustified, since extensive knowledge of the shipyard's management information system, the principal reason cited for the sole source action, was not required for most tasks ordered under the contract." More than 80 percent of the tasks, in fact, "were outside the scope" of the contract, the audit said.[7]

Some of those tasks required the consulting company to travel around the country and perform work at other shipyards, including Pearl Harbor. One, priced at $150,000, called for identification of health hazards at shipyards. One of the smaller tasks required Harbridge House to provide procurement training for Portsmouth personnel. The class was to cover "legal aspects of acquisition . . . to insure that system delays and pitfalls are well-recognized and avoided."

But the auditors found a problem: that training was already being provided by another contractor at Portsmouth at half the price charged by Harbridge House.

REVOLVING DOOR

When the top civilian employee at Pearl Harbor, Alfred "Blackie" Wong, retired after 42 years of federal service, he went straight to work for Harbridge House.[8] Wong was a defense contractor's dream employee. He was very good friends with U.S. Senator Daniel Inouye (and had even coinvested with Inouye in a couple of business ventures). He was an expert at lobbying Congress for military construction funds (known as MILCON in federal parlance). He retained close ties with powerful personages in Washington, including now-Admiral McArthur, an overseer of the entire naval shipyard empire.

And Wong knew more than any other man alive about how Pearl Harbor worked. The shipyard was the largest single industrial enterprise in the state, employed thousands of personnel, and wielded enormous economic and political influence in Hawai'i.

It was as if Wong never actually retired. His Cadillac sedan with the "100SP" personalized license plates (they stood for special assistant to the shipyard commander) still rolled daily though the main gate at Pearl. His new office was next door to his old one. And the work Wong performed for his new employer closely resembled his old duties: lobbying Congress for MILCON.

Like the Portsmouth contract before it, the Pearl Harbor contract contained tasks that appeared to be outside the scope of its stated purpose, including $99,000 in work assigned to Wong. Among those jobs: "Develop five-year MILCON project and work on additional funding for $27 million [in] utilities projects."

Tucked within Wong's work orders was another questionable item that skirted rules controlling the acquisition of computer hardware and software: the purchase of a $20,000 "printer plotter."

When I interviewed Wong, he said he had never heard of a printer plotter and had no idea one had been purchased in his name. He also said he quit working for Harbridge House after a dispute about money. The company was paying him $200 a day for his work but billing the Navy $600, he said.

After quitting the company, he stayed in his office at Pearl Harbor, working for the Pearl Harbor Association on another lobbying task—protecting and extending cost-of-living pay increases afforded to civilian federal employees in Hawai'i.

PARCELING

Harbridge House's Pearl Harbor consultant work was supposed to last a
year and cost $560,000. But the money was used up after six months, and
shipyard officials tried to double the price of the job.

Procurement personnel blocked that proposal. The extra work would
have to be put out to bid, they said. So Navy officials simply began ordering
the work in small increments—without telling the procurement watch-
dogs. It was precisely the same parceling maneuver Ken Kiyabu had used
to redecorate his office at Aloha Stadium. Just on a larger stage.

Navy officials "effectively masked the extension of work from the contracting officer's review . . . after previous attempts to extend the [contract]
ceiling were disapproved," Navy auditors later found.[9]

When the ceiling on such small purchases was $10,000, the bills consis-
tently came in at $9,700 to $10,000, according to paperwork I obtained under
FOIA.

When the limit was raised to $25,000, the Navy began ordering work
valued at $24,800 to $25,000, the paperwork showed.

Even the less formal purchase orders were supposed to be accomplished
with some attempt at competition—calling other vendors and getting price
quotes over the phone, for instance. But Navy auditors found little to no
evidence of competition. "It appears that aggressive attempts to find new
sources were not made," the auditors reported.

I found almost $200,000 in parceled purchases in the Harbridge House
contract papers obtained under FOIA from the Navy.

The Harbridge House series of stories was written in eight installments
that took seven months to research and write.

Publication was supposed to start on a Sunday in mid-July. But when
I called the city desk the night before to check on the last-minute status,
I was told the stories had been held up by the executive editor. It wasn't
running.

I was already pretty wrought up before I made the call. I always got jit-
tery in the days and hours before the deadline of a major new story. The
longer I worked on something, the more nervous I got before publication.

The guy on the desk didn't know why the stories had been held. I made
a frantic series of calls to the homes of various editors but couldn't reach
anyone. Editor-in-Chief George Chaplin was out of town and unreachable.
But Executive Editor Buck Buchwach lived three blocks away from me,
so I decided to walk over there. My wife at the time, newscaster Leslie
Wilcox, told me not to make a fool of myself, but I needed to know what
was going on.

Buchwach's house was dark, and no one answered the door when I banged on it like a SWAT officer. Leslie had made the walk with me and was highly amused by my antics. "Maybe he's inside, hiding in the dark," she said. She was trying to shame me, but it only wound me up more. She had a real talent for that.

I finally gave up and left a note on his front door.

Buck eventually called me back at home and said something about problems with the graphics illustrating the series that I didn't understand. Maybe I wasn't in a state to understand. But I think he was just antsy about running the stories on his watch and wanted to wait until Chaplin returned. The weeklong delay turned out to be fortuitous, though, because I received a new FOIA release about the Portsmouth part of Harbridge House's work that made a valuable addition to the series.

I followed the series with several other stories. The three-star admiral in charge of the Navy Sea Systems Command had ordered a halt to Harbridge House contracts, citing "real or perceived favoritism" in the award of the work.[10] "I do not want the practice of sole source awards to Harbridge House, Inc., to continue," Admiral Earl Fowler said in a memo sent to all shipyards. He rescinded that directive a month later "following a review of all existing Harbridge House contracts."

But the second memo "re-emphasized the need to acquire [consultant] services on a competitive basis unless compelling reasons dictate otherwise," Fowler's office told me.

I followed those stories with another about a $2.2 million sole-source contract Fowler himself had awarded to a consulting firm called Anadac, Inc. The new company had never received a Navy contract before but had worked as a subcontractor on Navy no-bid jobs awarded to Harbridge House. Anadac was founded by a former assistant secretary of the Navy.[11]

There was one last postscript story written late in the year. I finally figured out who Robert J. Gilmore was. He was the sole partner in Paul Peterson's condo investment partnership whom I hadn't been able to identify.[12] Gilmore was the civilian administrator of a $460,000 no-bid contract awarded to Harbridge House at the Navy's Long Beach shipyard.

I kicked myself for not finding that out sooner.

CHAPTER TWELVE

Huis

In *Chinatown,* the film noir classic starring Jack Nicholson, there's an act of wanton callousness that appalls me every time I see it. Not the famous "my sister, my daughter" slapping scene. That's horrifying enough, but the one that really makes my skin crawl occurs when Nicholson's character, Jake Gittes, looks up property records in giant plat books at the Los Angeles Hall of Records and then cavalierly rips out the page of owners he's interested in.

That's just disgusting behavior.

I have lugged similar oversized volumes down from the shelves at the Hawai'i Bureau of Conveyances to read their sometimes precious contents. It's awful to think that someone before me could have torn out a page I needed.

The availability and integrity of such records helped me author a series of articles that revealed the existence of secret real estate partnerships, called *huis,* which for decades had bought, sold, and developed raw land in Hawai'i and made millions of dollars in profits for judges, politicians, mobsters, government officials, and ordinary citizens.[1]

Some of this work was later used by authors George Cooper and Gavan Daws to produce *Land and Power,* a penetrating and exhaustive analysis of the fundamental redistribution of wealth and political influence in post–World War II Hawai'i. Talk about bamboo forests, hidden connections, and a complex array of names and histories: try *Land and Power* on for size sometime.[2]

Reviewing the *hui* stories now and remembering the work that went into them brought several striking realizations.

One was how naive and fortunate I was when I first began blundering around in real estate and probate court records. I literally had no idea what I was doing or where I was going.

Another was how tedious, time-consuming, and unattractive this sort of work could be. I cumulatively spent weeks of my time in public records archives and rarely encountered other reporters doing the same sort of work. The editors I worked for then indulged me, and I worked hard to reward their confidence in me. (One of them, Thomas Brislin, once memorably likened reporters to family pets. Some are like dogs, he said: you tell them to fetch something, and they'll happily chase around until they find it. Others are like cats, Brislin continued: you let them out the door in the morning, and eventually they'll come back to drop something surprising at your feet. I like to think I fell into the cat category.)

My review of the *hui* stories also brought a renewed respect for the power of public documentary records and their singular importance in lighting the gloomy corners of society.

The author reviews election return printout in the newsroom. Capitol Bureau Chief Jerry Burris is in the background. GREGORY YAMAMOTO, PHOTOGRAPHER; *HONOLULU ADVERTISER*.

The *hui* research began in early 1980 when I was living in Niu Valley, one of a string of residential communities tucked into the folds of the Koolau mountain range on the eastern edge of Oahu. I noticed a great deal of construction activity coming from the next community along the coast in Kuliouou Valley. I asked around a bit and found that a new public housing project was under development in the back of the valley. I was vaguely aware that this project had been kicking around the Hawai'i Housing Authority for quite a while, and now it was under way. There hadn't been any coverage of the project, so I thought it might be worth a look.

I visited the Hawai'i Housing Authority offices, took a look at the files, and learned that the developer of the project was Kikuo Yanagi. He turned out to be a stockbroker, not a housing developer, and I was curious about how he became involved in a multimillion-dollar construction deal with the state. So I did some standard background research on Yanagi.

I checked our library at the newspaper, the so-called morgue, and pulled whatever stories had been written about him. I went to Oahu's circuit court to look up his name in the indexes of court cases at the clerk's office. I reviewed corporate records at the Department of Commerce and Consumer Affairs. And I stopped by the Bureau of Conveyances to research real estate transactions involving Yanagi. The bureau contains a wealth of other information beyond title transfers, including state and federal tax liens, powers of attorney, and mortgage loan recordings. I eventually wrote a pair of nuts-and-bolts stories about the history and ever-increasing costs of the Kuliouou Valley project, as well as a sidebar about Kikuo Yanagi.[3]

In the course of researching Kikuo Yanagi, I became interested in another man, Wallace Yanagi, an investor in the housing development. Our newspaper files told me that he was the administrator of Maui Memorial Hospital—a state job—and real estate records told me he was also heavily involved in real estate deals around the state, including development of Manoa Valley Market Place, a small but busy shopping center behind the Oahu campus of the University of Hawai'i.

I wondered how a man running a hospital on Maui had the time to do all this, so I began looking at him in more detail. He certainly wasn't doing anything wrong, but he was *interesting*. I was prospecting at this point, panning the stream, looking for indications of gold. If I didn't find anything, I'd drop it and prospect elsewhere.

And it wasn't like I was devoting my life to this research. I was churning out plenty of copy on a wide and eclectic range of other subjects during this period. In the two months before I wrote the Kuliouou Valley stories, I also wrote about serious problems in the Maui coroner's office,[4] an international law enforcement conference on the yakuza,[5] personal favors performed for local mob boss Charley Stevens by U.S. Marshal Ed Keliikoa (who resigned after the stories ran),[6] Charles Marsland's decision to enter the Honolulu prosecutor's election,[7] exiled Philippines President Ferdinand Marcos' $800,000 Hawai'i house purchase,[8] and a new conjugal visits program at a state prison.[9]

While examining Wallace Yanagi's real estate deals, I found that he had regularly partnered with a Maui businessman named Masaru "Pundy" Yokouchi. I recognized Yokouchi's name but wasn't sure why. So I went back to our newspaper's library and learned that Yokouchi was a Maui real estate broker and developer who had some very good political connections with the state administration. He was also the president of a company called Valley Isle Realty.

Yokouchi's family ran a Maui bakery, and his nickname came from his childhood mispronunciation of *pao duce*, Portuguese sweet bread.

He had been part of the so-called Democratic revolution in state politics in 1954 and had been a good friend of the late governor, Jack Burns. Yokouchi was a political operative for Burns on Maui for a number of years. He did not make a secret of that—he was widely known to be the political patronage chairman on Maui under Burns. A giant photo of Jack Burns hung on one wall in Yokouchi's Valley Isle Realty office.

So I decided to look a little further into Yanagi and Yokouchi, who also happened to be partners in the Manoa Valley Market Place on Oahu and other projects elsewhere in the state.

At the Bureau of Conveyances, I found a land transaction in the Kula area of Maui that referenced a probate court file in Honolulu.

I have found probate court to be a wonderful source of information. Probate cases are generated at the death of an individual who owns land or who dies intestate—without a will. Probate court oversees the administration and dissolution of estates, and you can find things there that just can't be found anywhere else. It's a little crass to say, but when people die suddenly, secrets that they have labored all their lives to keep get revealed in probate files. There's no longer any way to hide real estate investments that you may not have wanted to be publicly known.

I looked at the probate file that was referenced in the Bureau of Conveyances and found that it involved the estate of Sajiro Matsui. I vaguely remembered that name as someone I'd come across in work on organized crime. His nickname was Sambo, and he'd been murdered several years earlier.

I pulled the news clippings on Sambo Matsui. He had been the owner of a vending machine company and had disappeared while shopping at a market near Diamond Head. He left a basket of groceries at the checkout register, and his car was in the parking lot with the keys still in it. The day after Matsui disappeared, organized crime figure Alvin Kaohu showed up at the market, identified himself as a friend of Matsui's, and asked questions about the missing man.[10]

A year or so later, Matsui's bones were discovered on the North Shore. He had been shot in the head. Matsui's family then filed the probate case, which listed partial ownership of property in the Kula area of Maui.

The court records revealed that a number of other people held interests with Matsui in the Kula property. I was puzzled to see that few of the names of the Kula landowners listed in the probate file appeared in real estate records filed at the Bureau of Conveyances. I didn't realize it at the time, but I had found my first *hui*.

Three names that turned up in my research of Matsui and his real estate deals were Yoshikazu "Zuke" Matsui (brother of the dead man), Stanley "Banjo" Tamura, and James Izumi.

All three, I quickly determined, were, or had been, important public officials on Maui. Zuke Matsui was the former longtime head of the Maui Planning Commission and at the time was the deputy director of the Maui Department of Planning. James Izumi was the long-serving head of the Maui County Personnel Department. Banjo Tamura had been the chief teller for Maui County until he was stabbed to death in another unsolved organized crime "hit."[11] Zuke Matsui and James Izumi had also been longtime officers or directors of Valley Isle Realty with Pundy Yokouchi.

I wondered if there was a chance that the personal financial affairs of these men had overlapped with their duties in public office. Had they disclosed them? Had they declared conflicts of interest? I also learned that there was a probate file generated after the death of Banjo Tamura, but I would have to go to Maui to see it. I talked these matters over with my editors and our Maui-based reporter, Edwin Tanji, and we all decided it would be a good idea for me to go to the Valley Isle.

The Tamura probate was a jewel box. He had been involved in 12 *huis*. After he died, two organized crime figures, Takeo "Maui Take" Yamauchi and Yujiro "Tani" Matsuoka, had filed legal claims on portions of the Tamura estate.[12]

Yamauchi was familiar to me. He had been one of the local criminal figures cited by Nevada gaming regulators who tried to deny Ash Resnick his casino operator's license in Las Vegas. A year before my trip to Maui, Yamauchi had been tried but acquitted in federal court of extortion charges brought by the Organized Crime Strike Force.

In that trial, Yamauchi testified that although he was no longer involved in illegal gambling, he had once helped run large-scale illicit bookie operations with Banjo Tamura.

Yamauchi also admitted to FBI agents a past involvement with Tani Matsuoka—a coclaimant to assets in the Tamura estate—in illegal gambling operations.

Tani Matsuoka had been murdered gangland style three years after Tamura was rubbed out. Matsuoka's late-model Cadillac was abandoned at the Maui Beach Hotel, and three weeks later his body was found in a sugarcane field. He had been shot to death.

After that murder, Yamauchi expressed a fear to FBI agents that "I'm next."

I pulled out Matsuoka's probate file. He had been a member of five investment *huis.*

During my Maui trip, Ed Tanji and I arranged an interview with Wallace Yanagi at Maui Memorial Hospital. His involvement in the Oahu public housing venture near my house had first started me on the *hui* hunt.

In analyzing real estate records and probate files, I had come across references to what appeared to be another *hui* called Waipao Joint Venture. It had purchased and sold land in a then-pristine coastal area of Maui called Makena. There was a good deal of public controversy under way at the time about plans to develop this site as a resort condominium called the Makena Surf. The records I had found indicated that Yanagi was part of Waipao Joint Venture.

We talked about how it was possible for a hospital administrator to be involved in so many different business ventures: housing and shopping center developments on Oahu, real estate deals at Valley Isle Realty, and so on. He said his outside activities were secondary to his hospital job, where he averaged 10 hours of work a day. The rest, he said, was mostly processing paperwork.

He became very uncomfortable when I asked about what involvement he might have in the Makena Surf property. "I have nothing to do with that" was his first answer.

When I asked about his involvement in Waipao Joint Venture, he said, "Why are you asking me all these questions? You guys are going to get me in trouble. Not all the *huis* in this state are registered, you know."[13] More questioning followed. Yanagi reluctantly explained that he was one of six principals involved in the venture. Five of the six, including Yanagi, actually headed separate sub-*huis* of their own. He claimed he couldn't remember the names of individual investors. "A lot of small people," Yanagi said.

All the records were at Valley Isle Realty, he said.

In preparation for a talk with Pundy Yokouchi at Valley Isle, I had spent a good deal of time poring over county records of real estate developments the company and its principals had been involved in. I found that over the previous 20 years, there had always been a Valley Isle Realty official or employee serving on the Maui Planning Commission or Maui County Council. During most years, there was a Valley Isle name on both the commission and council.[14] I found that Zuke Matsui had apparently committed ethical violations when he acted on public planning issues without disclosing personal financial connections to some of them.[15]

He denied acting improperly, saying that any official acts he had taken were ministerial and pro forma. In one case, Matsui handled paperwork for an application to the Maui Planning Department from the Maui Beach Hotel for construction of a 449-room addition. Matsui was deputy director of the department. He was also listed as vice president of Maui Beach Hotel and a director of, and stockholder in, the company. Matsui said he did nothing more than handle paperwork and was not involved in any way in the decision to approve the application.

"There was no decision making, no nothing," he told me.

But Matsui's boss, Maui Planning Director Toshio Ishikawa, said Matsui's job required him to be deeply involved in reviewing the application. If he had personal conflicts of interest with the applicant, he should have disclosed them but did not, Ishikawa said.

Matsui never disclosed his ties to the hotel, and he was ethically required to do so, the director said.

"I believe department personnel should have enough intelligence and propriety to be aware of any areas of sensitivity that may affect him personally or affect the development of projects," Ishikawa said.[16]

The same situation applied with the Makena Surf development application. Matsui had invested in one of the sub-*huis* of investors who had sold the land to the condo developer. He claimed he took no part in reviewing the development application at the Planning Department.

Ishikawa said Matsui should have been involved and should have disclosed his financial ties to the developer. "If he didn't, he wouldn't have been doing his job," Ishikawa said.

Matsui resigned from the department shortly before I interviewed him. He went back to work selling real estate at Valley Isle Realty with his pal Pundy.

I interviewed Yokouchi several times and found him to be an affable, charming, and cultured man. Over the course of our conversations, he asked me several times, "Why are you doing this? Who put you up to it?"

He was never satisfied when I told him no one was behind it, that it was a simple reporter's curiosity about how things worked.

The way Yokouchi and others told it, the *huis* were a product of simpler days, when young men and women raised in plantation-era circumstances pooled together what little money they had to invest for the future.

There was never any thought given to registering the partnerships with the state. That was an unforeseen complication that arose in later years and simply wasn't addressed, they said. The *huis* filed all necessary forms with tax authorities and paid all taxes due, said Yokouchi.

As Yokouchi and his friends emerged from plantation housing and took part in the Democratic Party postwar political revolution in Hawai'i, Yokouchi said, some gained success in business, others in politics and business, and others in crime.

It wasn't a nefarious plot, he said. It just happened. Maui was a small place, everybody knew everybody else, family and personal connections were deep and complicated, and why do I have to explain all this to you—who's really behind all these questions?

He complained that having Valley Isle personnel serving in public office was a hindrance, not a help to the company. Every time an issue involving the company came before them in their official capacities, they had to declare a conflict of interest and abstain from acting or voting. There were two salespeople on his staff then serving on the county council, and those abstentions counted as no votes, he said.

"If I'm so devious and powerful, why wouldn't I get people appointed to the council who obviously don't work for me?" he said.[17]

Okay, I said, tell me about Waipao Joint Venture. Who are the investors?

There were 86 of them, and some individuals might represent even more people in sub-sub-*huis* that he didn't even know about, Yokouchi told me. He declined to give me names. Most wouldn't mind if their identities were made public, but some would; he didn't know for sure and thus couldn't name anyone. But there was nobody political involved, he insisted.

In the meantime, I had been pressing the state official responsible for enforcing state business registration laws, Russel Nagata, on the question of whether *huis* should formally file paperwork with his department as limited partnerships. I thought they looked and acted like limited partnerships: groups of passive investors who entrusted their money to general partners who made all the financial decisions for the group. But I wasn't a lawyer, and it wasn't a clear-cut, easy question to answer. There would be political repercussions whichever way Nagata ruled. Ultimately, Nagata said he believed that *huis* of unrelated persons who buy property as an investment should register with the state.

"There is a gray area in the law about whether family *huis* are partnerships," Nagata said in an interview. But when *hui* members were not related to each other by blood, the intent of the law was clear, Nagata said: "They should register."

He acknowledged that there were a great many such investment *huis* that should be registered but were not. "What this means," I wrote in a Sunday front-page story, "is that there are a great many secret landowners in Hawaii who shouldn't be secret at all."[18]

Nagata later rolled back on his registration opinion in an interview with the *Land and Power* authors. *Huis* that engaged in passive ownership of land were under no obligation to register, he said. They had to take some action, "like attempting to rezone the land they owned, before qualifying as a partnership in the eyes of Hawaii law," Cooper and Daws quoted Nagata as saying.[19]

Nagata said he suggested otherwise to me because of "the adverse publicity" that my stories had generated, Daws and Cooper wrote.

I found another gigantic *hui* called Landco that met all of Nagata's criteria for registration . . . and then some. Landco had been formed in the early 1960s and had developed a large Maui residential community called Pukalani.

Landco was still going strong when I researched and wrote my stories in 1980. Landco was listed in the Maui telephone directory, but there wasn't a whiff of it in business registration records.

The attorney for Landco, former state legislator Meyer Ueoka, said the business had begun as a joint venture meant to complete a single project, but it just "kept going."[20]

I managed to ferret out the names of politicians, government officials, bankers, developers, and even a state supreme court justice who were members of Landco.

Pundy Yokouchi, of course, was part of the *hui*. He told me that he held a one-thirteenth share of Landco but was actually acting as a trustee for 10 other people he declined to name.

One of the founders and managers of Landco, Donald Tokunaga, told me that ownership shares had been so fractionalized that he had no idea how many people held a piece of the business. People occasionally told him they were shareholders, "and it's a surprise to me," he said.

I turned out maybe a dozen *hui* stories and sidebars in the first half of 1980. The coverage concentrated on Maui. The interlocking *hui* relationships and deals connected Pundy Yokouchi to virtually every significant political, business, and labor leader in the county. Just the ties between Yokouchi and longtime Maui Mayor Elmer Cravalho made my head spin.

(There used to be a saying on Maui: Pundy has the land, Elmer has the water.) Not much real estate got developed on the Valley Isle without the direct or indirect involvement of both men.

All those early *hui* stories were preludes to the big one later in the year, which centered on the hidden ownership history of a beachfront parcel of property on Kauai called Nukolii. Like the Makena Surf project on Maui, proposed construction of a resort hotel at the Nukolii site had inflamed antidevelopment passions on Kauai. Feelings were so high that a referendum vote was scheduled later in the year on whether the project should be allowed to go forward.

I kept hearing whispers that there was a hidden *hui* in the Nukolii background and that Pundy Yokouchi had organized it. One convincing caller said I should check out a Kauai property purchase by Walter Shimoda, Yokouchi's regular attorney, in 1974.

It took me a while to find it because it was recorded in 1977: the deal was a $1.2 million agreement-of-sale purchase that was signed in 1974 but wasn't publicly recorded until 1977. Some 60 acres of shoreline land owned by the largest corporation in the state, Amfac, Inc., was sold to Walter Shimoda. The property was a site commonly known as Nukolii.

A year later, Shimoda resold the land for $5.25 million to a large Mainland company, Pacific Standard Life Insurance.

I called Shimoda and Yokouchi to ask if this was a *hui* deal. They wouldn't talk to me. I called everybody I could think of to ask the same question: Amfac, Pacific Standard Life, others I had dealt with in my months of *hui* research. Many of the people I spoke to confirmed that Shimoda was representing a *hui*. One individual claimed knowledge of the *hui* members and encouraged me to keep digging. "You'll be surprised by the names," this source said.

At the same time, I was researching the history of the property to find an explanation for the $4 million increase in sale price in just over a year.

Amfac was perhaps the most sophisticated player in the Hawai'i real estate market, and I couldn't understand why the company would sell seemingly prime waterfront property for such a low price. Then I found that, until recently, the land hadn't been prime at all—it had been zoned by the state as agricultural property unavailable for urban development.

But the state Land Use Commission then reclassified the property for resort development. I became very interested in when and why that happened.

Commission files and hearing transcripts showed that Amfac had sought and received rezoning slightly before the sale to Shimoda was signed and long before the deal was publicly recorded.

And I knew the name of the Amfac executive, C. Earl Stoner Jr., who represented the company before the LUC. Stoner was a Maui guy, and I had seen his name in other Valley Isle real estate deals connected to Pundy Yokouchi. Stoner testified before the LUC that not only did Amfac still own the land but also it planned to build a hotel and luxury housing there.

Almost simultaneously, my inquiries about the underlying *hui* finally paid off. An impeccable source gave me a list of the 46 Nukolii *hui* members. It included the names of some very important people in Hawai'i, plus the usual suspects from Maui. And there was a new name: Earl Stoner. My tipster's information was very specific: Stoner's interest was held in trust for him by a Maui contractor, Daniel P. S. Fong.

When I called Stoner, he had left Amfac and was doing real estate deals on Maui. He denied being a member of Shimoda's *hui* and said he didn't even know such a *hui* existed.

"I am not a member of Walter Shimoda's *hui*. I never was a member of Walter Shimoda's *hui*. I don't even know that Walter Shimoda has a *hui*," Stoner told me. Others continued to tell me that Stoner was part of the group. He continued to deny it but then admitted that he knew there was a *hui*.

"I know there's a *hui*, but I'm not in it," he said the second time I talked to him.

Finally, I reached Yokouchi and got him to intercede with Stoner for me. Stoner was travelling on the Mainland when I reached him for our third interview. "I am involved in the thing through my partner Danny Fong," he said.

But he maintained that he didn't invest until 1975, after he testified at the LUC about Nukolii in 1974 and after he went into business for himself in 1975.

He said he knew that the *hui* had bought the land from Amfac when he testified before the LUC, but he didn't know that the group had resold for a $4 million profit to Pacific Standard.

Because the original purchase was on an agreement-of-sale basis, title to the land hadn't formally transferred to the *hui*, and that was why he told the commission that Amfac owned the land and intended to develop it. "I know the thing looks god-awful, but I don't know what else to say," Stoner told me.[21]

He later asserted to Cooper and Daws that I had initially confused him because I was asking about the Shimoda *hui*. Once he realized I was talking about Pundy Yokouchi's *hui*, he admitted that he was an investor, according to *Land and Power*.[22]

But it was always clear that we were talking about the Nukolii *hui*, so his protestations on that point ring hollow.

Further, despite Stoner's claims to me that he had only invested after he left Amfac, he and Yokouchi told Daws and Cooper that Stoner held a share in the *hui* when he told the LUC that Amfac owned the land and intended to develop it.

Other members of the secret Nukolii *hui* who chopped up a $4 million profit included:

- The son and daughter of former governor Jack Burns. The son, James Burns, was a judge on the state intermediate court of appeals.
- Hawai'i Supreme Court Justice Edward Nakamura.
- Hawai'i District Court Judge Edwin Honda.
- Maui Circuit Judge Kase Higa.
- Pundy Yokouchi and a cohort of his pals, including past and present Maui County officials Zuke Matsui, Lanny Morisaki, Wallace Yanagi, and Charles Ota.
- Thomas Yagi, head of the influential ILWU union on Maui and member of the state Board of Land and Natural Resources.
- University of Hawai'i Regent Harriet Mizuguchi, wife of state senate president Norman Mizuguchi.
- Mieko Yoshinaga, wife of Nadao Yoshinaga, longtime chairman of the Senate Ways and Means Committee and a very powerful behind-the-scenes force in Democratic Party politics.
- John E. S. Kim, a convicted federal felon who entered a guilty plea in an income tax evasion case at the same time the Nukolii *hui* was organized.[23]

I singled out Kim and Judge Edwin Honda for special attention in my Nukolii story.

Kim's tax case grew from a fraudulent personal land deal he orchestrated in the late 1960s when he was affiliated with Amfac. A good source of mine with long ties to Amfac told me that Kim had worked for Amfac's chief executive "in the political arena."

Kim's Amfac duties included working as an unofficial lobbyist for the company before government agencies and at the legislature, my source told me.

Honda, before becoming a judge, had served as director of the state Department of Regulatory Agencies, the agency responsible for enforcing partnership registration laws. He held that post when the Nukolii *hui* was formed.

I asked Honda if the *hui* should have been registered when he ran the department. "I was never actually called upon to make any sort of determination," Honda told me. When I asked for his opinion now, he said, "I've never confronted that. I would rather not have to say."

I had rushed to get the Nukolii story in print before the referendum vote on Kauai. It was published eight days before the vote and caused a big stink on the island. By a 2–1 margin, voters passed the referendum, which blocked the resort development.

County Mayor Eduardo Malapit and his administration then held that the developer—by then Japanese corporate giant Hasegawa Komuten—had established vested rights to develop the property and was allowed to proceed. Opponents in the antidevelopment group Committee to Save Nukolii sued the county but lost in circuit court. They appealed, and the Hawai'i Supreme Court, in a remarkable decision that caught the attention of land use experts around the country, reversed the lower court ruling and voided the county's action.

The developers had plowed ahead with construction after the original county go-ahead and howled that they had sunk tens of millions of dollars into the project. The resort condo part of the project was complete, but the hotel was 70 percent unfinished. All work was halted.

Pro-development forces tried an appeal to the U.S. Supreme Court, which declined to hear the case. The developers and their supporters then found a novel new tactic: they mounted a successful petition drive that would place a new referendum for Kauai voters in a special 1984 election. Hasegawa Komuten footed the bill for the expenses of the balloting and for much of the prevote, pro-development electioneering. Perhaps unsurprisingly, pro-development votes carried the day by a 52–48 percent margin.

The vote was counted nearly five years after I first noticed those big trucks rolling in and out of Kuliouou Valley.

Another five years after that, in 1989, a new bamboo shoot that had tendrils connecting back to the original Nukolii and pay-to-play forests popped up in federal bankruptcy court, of all places.

John Kim, the lobbyist-fixer who played an important behind-the-scenes role in the Nukolii development, had played a similar role in the planned development of a huge waterfront residential and commercial project on Oahu called Ewa Marina, court records showed.[24] The original Ewa Marina developer, MSM and Associates, Inc., had lent Kim more than $500,000 "for the purpose of making secret illegal payments to government and other officials," a group of MSM stockholders alleged after MSM went bankrupt.

"Kim has stated on a number of occasions that the funds loaned to him and (to his company, J.K. Enterprises) were utilized for the benefit of MSM and for that reason he should not be required to repay these obligations," the stockholders alleged.

Kim was also a secret stockholder in MSM, with his shares held in trust for him by his son-in-law, the records showed. He was also paid a $5,000-a-month salary by the company.

I couldn't reach Kim for comment, but in a deposition taken in the case, he said he did little more for the company than make occasional phone calls "to influential people."

The bankruptcy records showed that while MSM suffered severe and chronic cash shortages, officials there spent lavishly to entertain government officials and potential business partners. The firm hired the former director of the city Department of Land Utilization, Tyrone Kusao, who "acted as principal liaison between MSM and Associates and the city administration and City Council in obtaining permits required for the project," Kusao said in a court affidavit.

City ordinances banned former officials from performing certain services within a year of leaving the public payroll. When I called Kusao about his MSM work, he claimed he worked as an "inside man for the company" and did not violate the ban.

Kusao also worked as a lobbyist for MSM at the city but never registered as such. MSM President Walter Tagawa, a retired U.S. Army general, acted as company lobbyist but never bothered to register that activity with the city. An MSM internal memo said the duties of Kusao and Tagawa were "responsible for the political aspects" of zoning and water usage issues.

Tagawa acknowledged to me that MSM spent generously in the political arena, including campaign donations, despite its severe money problems. "I guess we were trying to seek support from all of them. Not to buy their votes, but it's the traditional way of supporting a political candidate," Tagawa said.[25]

CHAPTER THIRTEEN

Death and Taxes

It's called the death care industry: processing and disposal of human ca-
davers. Like virtually every other human endeavor, there's money to be
made if you put your mind to it. Sometimes lots of money.

Three times in my career, I made lengthy visits to the death care industry. The first, in 1980, concerned the primitive coroner's system on the
Neighbor Islands. The next two, in 1990 and 2007, focused on "pre-need"
funeral plans and brought me into contact with future and former governors of Hawai'i.

A coroner is a government official responsible for certifying the death
of an individual. In cases of unattended or violent death, the coroner must
determine the causes, usually through autopsies conducted by qualified
experts.

Problems with this system were particularly acute in Maui County,
which included, besides Maui, the islands of Molokai and Lanai.

"Sometimes I think it's just not a good idea to die over here," Kenneth
Ongais, the owner of a Maui mortuary, told me.[1]

Ongais recounted the story of a man found dead on Molokai whose
remains were kept in cold storage for months before anyone got around
to x-raying him to determine a possible cause of death.

The chairman of the University of Hawai'i's pathology department
remembered the case of a man found hanged on Lanai who was buried
before anyone thought to determine the actual cause of death.

The county police chief served as Maui coroner, and police officers were
deputy coroners. When called to an unattended or violent death, the offi-

cers would notify mortuary workers to retrieve the corpse and transport it to a mortuary embalming room, where an autopsy was performed.

Three mortuaries competed for the pickups, which were supposed to be performed on a rotating basis. The mortuaries were also supposed to charge the county a flat fee for the service.

That wasn't happening. Patrol officers had favorite mortuaries. Sometimes the families of the decedents, not the county, were charged the removal fee, which varied in size, depending on the vendor.

Although there was a state-of-the-art underutilized morgue at the state-run hospital on Maui, official autopsies were still performed in embalming rooms by a family physician who had no training as a pathologist and described his autopsy work as "a hobby."[2] The physician, Dr. Kenneth Haling, readily acknowledged to me that he "could use some help in the job, particularly in the pathology end of it."

I found an autopsy report written by Haling after he examined the body of a young man killed in a fiery car crash. On the autopsy report, Haling described the condition of the deceased as "well-cooked."

The Maui police chief–coroner said he didn't know about the availability of the hospital morgue and was unaware of the removal fee anomalies.

There were also several disturbing complaints about the business practices of one Maui mortuary owner, Joseph Bulgo. He tried to charge the parents of a young woman who had been violently murdered a "storage fee" for keeping her partial remains in a freezer for 15 months while police and prosecutors investigated the homicide. Bulgo said his electricity bill for the service was $150 per month and he wanted $2,250 from the distraught parents of the victim.[3]

After the remains were transferred to Ongais' mortuary, he said his expenses for the storage service were $3 a month and he had no intention of charging family members a dime.

The family of a Colorado tourist who died on a Maui vacation complained to state and county officials that Bulgo tried to overcharge them more than $1,000 for handling the remains of the woman and shipping them home.

Bulgo and the general manager of his mortuary, who was a part-time minister, denied the allegations and were very angry with me when I questioned them about the dispute. "I give you God's word that if you print any of these lies about me I will pursue you to the end of the earth to win a libel suit," said the minister.

Bulgo warned me of a different sort of doom. "I will have you disinfected," he said ominously. When I asked what that meant, he answered,

"It's a mortuary term. It means you'll be *pau*" (the Hawaiian word for over and done with). It was like back-to-back threats from God and the devil.

I quoted both men in the story but heard no more from them.

My forays into the stygian realm of cemeteries and mortuaries involved millions of dollars held in trust for buyers of pre-need funeral plans.

Under the pre-need system, funeral-burial plan sellers convince customers to pay in advance for future services. Most of the money is held in interest-earning trust accounts. But in Hawai'i, 30 percent is taken off the top to pay the sales commissions and administrative expenses of the seller. It's like paying the sales commission on a car purchase but waiting decades for delivery of the vehicle.

The 30 percent rake-off has come under harsh criticism in various quarters of the national death care industry but is still in full force in Hawai'i. Two well-regarded organizations, the Funeral Consumers Alliance and the National Funeral Directors Association, have regularly recommended elimination of the practice and enactment of laws requiring "100 percent trusting" of pre-need funds.

Thirty-two states had "100 percent trusting" laws. Of the remainder, only Hawai'i and Florida allowed the 30 percent rake-off. Alabama law was silent on the subject.[4]

"One hundred percent of the monies placed in a prefunded funeral account should be used for the purpose intended and funeral homes should not be able to legally use any percentage of that fund until it provides the at-need service," John J. Hogan Jr., president of the National Funeral Directors Association, told me.

Bills to change the Hawai'i law were regularly shot down at the Hawai'i legislature, where industry officials and their lobbyists worked hard to protect the status quo.

The head of the state office that regulated the industry did not speak with critics before advocating retention of the 30/70 percent trusting system.

Government officials "typically will consult with industry representatives" on proposed legislation, "but it is not standard practice to roundtable it, to get feedback from everybody ahead of time," the regulator, Joanne Uchida, said in an interview.

Then there were the trust funds themselves, which bulged with tens of millions of dollars of customers' money and over the course of three decades attracted an array of sharp operators and outright scoundrels who hated to see good money lying fallow.

In the 1980s, all three cemeteries on the Big Island collapsed financially, and state regulators charged with overseeing them found large deficiencies in their trust funds.

One operation had been run by a lawyer with a history of mental illness until he sold out to a pair of itinerant casket salesmen from Florida. One of the pair, Mark Fellman, began selling pre-need funeral plans and somehow gained access to the company's trust funds.

Fellman disappeared after helping himself to $385,000. A theft indictment was returned against him in 1986 but was never executed. Plot holders and pre-need customers who had paid into the trust funds pushed the company into bankruptcy and sued Fellman, the state, and other parties for $1 million. Eventually the plaintiffs managed to collect $30,000.[5]

On Oahu, problems cropped up at a small cemetery operation called Greenhaven, which in 1990 had foundered in foreclosure and bankruptcy proceedings. The memorial park was being run by a former lawyer from the Pacific Northwest, Carl Martin Brandenfels, who said the business records were in disarray when he arrived on the scene.

Brandenfels had been convicted of federal securities violations in Seattle and had been accused in bankruptcy court in Honolulu of running a related company with "incompetence, mismanagement, fraud and/or dishonesty."

When I asked him about his history, Brandenfels said, "I've done a lot of things in my life, made a lot of mistakes, but I don't think it's fair to bring up that stuff from my past."[6]

One of the largest cemetery and funeral operations in the state was run in 1990 by John Henry Felix, a very successful businessman who also dabbled in politics.

His competitors at one time accused Felix of improperly removing cash from trust funds and replacing it with real estate assets. He angrily said the transactions had been approved by the state and the trust fund's third-party trustee. In any event, he said, real estate had been replaced with cash to allay concerns about the health of the trust funds.[7]

Felix at the time was a member of the Honolulu City Council, and I discovered that he and fellow councilman Neil Abercrombie, who had previously served a brief stint as a U.S. congressman, had partnered in a plan to start a mortuary sciences program at a local college.

I found that Felix had allowed Abercrombie campaign workers to use phone banks at one of his funeral company's sales offices, which should have been reported as an in-kind campaign contribution but was not. Abercrombie's wife also worked for Felix's company and for his political campaign, but the nearly $10,000 in income she received was not reported on financial disclosure forms the couple had to file with the city clerk.

Abercrombie acknowledged the oversights and filed amendments to the forms.[8]

A mortuary worker slipped me paperwork about a nonprofit company formed by Abercrombie and Felix, the Institute for Life Sciences, which was intended to study aging and death issues, as well as sponsor the mortuary college plan.

Felix's funeral services company also planned at one time to use the institute to conduct telephone surveys that would develop "leads" for the sale of pre-need funeral plans, according to the paperwork. "Leads from this survey can be 'sold' to our Memorial Estate Planning Division," the paperwork said. "Leads are the lifeline of a sales person."

Abercrombie and Felix said the mortuary sciences idea failed, and the telephone survey plan was never put into effect.[9]

Abercrombie was voted back to Congress in 1991 and served nine terms there, then served a single term as Hawai'i governor before losing his reelection bid in 2014.

In the mid-2000s, I found myself once again writing about missing pre-need trust funds.

The death care industry by then had undergone a nationwide consolidation, with large operators gobbling up smaller mom-and-pop companies around the country. One of those carnivores, a Canadian-based company called the Loewen Group, had amassed ownership of a large number of mortuaries and cemeteries in Hawai'i before eventually filing for bankruptcy.

A Texas couple, John Dooley (no relation) and Katheryn Hoover, along with a California associate, Richard Bricka, decided in 2002 to enter the death care industry in a big way by acquiring the Loewen Group's Hawai'i assets from bankruptcy court.

The partners had a problem, though. The company they formed, Right-Star, had no money. But Dooley and his associates had a plan: they would finance their purchase by using the $60 million held in trust for Loewen's 40,000 Hawai'i customers.[10]

As later detailed in court suits, a criminal prosecution, and other proceedings, RightStar set out to find a lender willing to front them $30 million to buy the Loewen assets, then use the trust funds to pay back the loan.

RightStar claimed to have "discovered a secret: the trusts were overfunded by $30 million," a hearing panel of the National Association of Securities Dealers later determined. "RightStar believed that once it concluded the acquisition, the trust could provide the surplus trust funds to RightStar, which could then use those funds to pay for the acquisition."[11] It was a dubious plan at best, but Dooley found a securities dealer, Lance C. Newby, who bought into it. Newby was working in the Hawai'i office of

Raymond James Financial Services, Inc., and he pitched the idea to his bosses.

They refused to approve it, but Newby went ahead and issued a $30 million loan commitment letter without the knowledge of his bosses, the NASD later ruled when it stripped Newby of his securities license. When Raymond James found out about the letter, they disavowed it and Newby was "permitted to resign," according to the NASD.

Newby then assisted RightStar in securing financial backing from a Las Vegas "hard money lender," Vestin Group Inc., that offered high-interest-rate loans for high-risk ventures customarily secured by real estate.

Newby was subsequently banned for life from the securities industry and moved to Costa Rica. He filed personal bankruptcy papers in Florida that listed $23.8 million in liabilities, the largest of which was a $22 million debt claimed by the state of Hawai'i for his RightStar activities. Newby denied owing that money and denied any RightStar wrongdoing.

After using Vestin funds to buy various cemetery, mortuary, and funeral businesses in Hawai'i, the RightStar principals set about obtaining licenses to operate the businesses from regulators at the state Department of Commerce and Consumer Affairs.

RightStar hired former governor John Waihee, an attorney in private practice, to assist them. He was later retained as one of four trustees responsible for oversight of the RightStar trust funds. According to court records, the trustees were paid an "inception fee" of $200,000 plus monthly compensation of $5,000 to $10,000.

It didn't take long for RightStar to unravel. Vestin filed a mortgage foreclosure suit against RightStar in 2004, touching off a tornado of lawsuits and investigations that raged for 10 years.

State Attorney General Mark Bennett (later the private attorney for police detective Ken Kamakana) likewise sued RightStar, its principals, and trustees for fraud.

Waihee and his fellow trustees steadfastly claimed that they did no wrong and in fact tried repeatedly to alert regulators to problems inside the company. Bennett alleged that they had illegally helped to divert $30 million from funeral and burial trust funds.

In April 2012, Waihee and his fellow trustees agreed to pay $1.3 million to settle the claims against them, but admitted no wrongdoing.

Deputy Attorney General C. Bryan Fitzgerald, who helped pursue the state cases for a decade, said, "I guess you could say all of this is ending with a whimper instead of a bang." But he noted that the company, which had emerged from court-supervised receivership, had been taken over by a new owner, and all customer contracts had been honored.

The local attorney for Vestin, Paul Alston, claimed that the company "lost north of $30 million" in the RightStar debacle. "We were taken advantage of by a group of con artists and we paid a high price," he said.

RightStar founder John Dooley was the only person prosecuted in the aftermath of RightStar's collapse. He eventually pleaded no contest to charges of stealing $50,000 and served a five-year probation sentence. In 2014, Dooley and Hoover agreed to settlement terms with the state in the final remaining piece of RightStar litigation.

TAXING SITUATIONS

Computer-assisted reporting (known in the journalism biz as CAR) involves accessing and analyzing large amounts of electronic data and turning it into news stories. I tried my hand at it many times over the years, usually with less than satisfactory results. The keys to success, I learned, were obtaining the data in usable form and getting help from technical experts who knew what they were doing.

My first attempt at CAR was by far the most successful. In 1992, I wanted to take a long, hard look at the state Tax Department, with emphasis on tax delinquencies.

To that end, I asked the state for electronic records of delinquent taxpayers. At the time, the state was in the throes of one of its periodic budget crunches, so I knew that stories about uncollected taxes would guarantee high readership. The problem was getting the information and understanding it. State law, I found, said that tax delinquencies were public records, so I cited those statutes when I first approached the department about accessing the records. No one had asked before, so there was a great deal of back-and-forth about what was public and what was not, what form the records should take, how I could access them, and so forth.

Officials eventually said they would give me access to a hard-copy, computer-generated list of delinquencies that was, as I recall, nearly a foot thick.

Following advice from experts at Investigative Reporters and Editors (IRE), a great nonprofit supporter of journalism that hosted conferences and seminars around the country about the nuts and bolts of reporting, I asked the tax authorities for an electronic copy of this list, stored in government mainframe computers on what were known as nine-track magnetic tapes.

The *Advertiser* had a mainframe computer of its own, so I simultaneously sought in-house help on accessing our own hardware to read and analyze the government data.

One of the things the IRE experts had warned about CAR work was what they called the "holy shit" moment: that instant when you finally have all the data, hardware, and software synchronized and your computer spits out its results. If those results cause you to shout, "Holy shit! What a great story!" you have probably done something wrong, the geeks warned.

I had one of those moments. Tax delinquencies, the computer told me, totaled $100 million. And that number could easily double if it included unpaid penalties and interest. Accounts that had been written off as uncollectible would further inflate the total. That amounted to 10 percent of the state budget at a time when spending was frozen.

In backtracking and double-checking the data, we could find no flaws in our methodology, but officials from the Tax Department had bad news. Their own data were corrupt: lists of delinquent taxpayers were replete with errors and duplications. As a result, the department couldn't release the lists for public consumption because that would mean falsely identifying some individuals and business as tax deadbeats.

Generally speaking, the total numbers were correct, but there were devils in the details.

Tax Director Richard Kahle said, "My personal preference is you publish the list. But you know and I know that the list is not clean enough to publish. For that, I apologize, but it is a resource allocation problem. We do not have the resources to clean up the list as opposed to collecting the delinquencies."[12]

I was able to identify some of the largest delinquents, verify the amounts owed, and write a story about them.

I was also able to report that the governor, John Waihee, had been identified by tax collectors as a delinquent. Waihee and his wife had failed to pay general excise taxes on rental income generated by an apartment they owned.

I checked with the governor's press secretary, Carolyn Tanaka, who blamed the matter on an "oversight" by the first couple's accountant.

The Waihees had properly obtained a tax license for the rental business income, but the accountant forgot to pay the tax bill. No one would say how much was owed, but it wasn't a big chunk of money. The excise tax was 4 percent, so even if the Waihees had been able to rent their apartment for $1,000 a month, the annual tax owed would have been $480.

Then I found another oversight: the Waihees had failed to disclose their rental income on personal financial disclosure forms filed with the state Ethics Commission. Waihee filed an amendment to his form after I questioned Tanaka about it. "Thank you for keeping us honest," she said.

The disclosure rules only required filers to reveal a range of income received rather than a specific amount. The amendment filed by Waihee said the apartment rental generated between $1,000 and $10,000 per year, so taxes owed would have run from $40 to $400.

The total delinquencies were just a small part of the stories I turned out that year about the Tax Department.

During the course of the research, I found that a company that called itself Regal Travel had amassed a huge tax delinquency that the state later wrote off as uncollectible. I was confused because I knew there was a large and apparently quite successful company of the same name that was still in business and had transportation services contracts in force with the state.

That led to Part 2 of the series on the Tax Department. Here's the top of that story:

"After a company calling itself Regal Travel built up some $221,000 in delinquent state taxes in 1995, it was shut down and a new company called Regal Travel, Inc. appeared in its place.

"The new Regal Travel was very similar to the old: same owner, same offices, same phone numbers, same activities. But there was one very important difference: the old Regal Travel owed the taxes; the new one did not.

"The state Tax Department halted all efforts to collect those delinquent taxes in July 1990, two months after Regal Travel, Inc. [the new company] landed a state contract to arrange travel for the University of Hawaii athletic department. Regal Travel, Inc. was paid $850,000 under that contract last year."[13]

A sidebar reported that Tax Director Kahle had ordered an investigation into the Regal Travel tax arrearages. "I must say, and admit to some embarrassment, that you found a relationship between two corporations that we did not."[14]

Regal Travel owner Raymond Miyashiro referred questions about the matter to his attorney, who said he was unfamiliar with the business histories of the two Regal Travel companies but said the tax delinquencies had not necessarily flowed from one company to the other.

Miyashiro owned another company, Trans Hawaiian Services, which had rented buses to the political campaign of Governor Waihee and parked its bus fleet on valuable vacant property owned by the state.[15]

The following year, the state collected $300,000 from Miyashiro to settle the delinquency. The 1994 resolution was accelerated, oddly enough, by Mayor Frank Fasi, then embarked on his fourth, and final, unsuccessful campaign for the governor's office. The mayor hosted a morning radio show and regularly used it to harpoon the state administration for its handling of tax delinquencies. Kahle told me that his office was swamped with calls and letters from Fasi listeners every time the mayor railed on the Regal Travel issue. Kahle pointedly announced that the settlement had been finalized just before the October primary election.[16]

At about this same time, the mayor was using his radio show to call me a "whore" and a "journalistic prostitute" after I helped cover the prosecution of a city official in a minor pay-to-play kickback case. The name-calling became so commonplace that I finally wrote a response that was published in the opinion section of the newspaper. "I think he's being a bit harsh," I wrote of Fasi. "I could live with 'stooge,' I suppose, or maybe even 'bimbo.' But I draw the line at 'whore.' "[17]

I noted that the mayor had made bales of political hay from other pay-to-play scandals I had uncovered in the state administration but never mentioned where those stories came from. "Frank's been taking advantage of me for years and I never charged him a dime," I wrote.

Part 3 of the series concerned the contents of a wonderful whistle-blower lawsuit filed against the Tax Department by a longtime employee who was shunned as a pariah after she reported widespread questionable activities by her colleagues.[18]

Among the revelations of the lawsuit:

- A high-ranking official of the department had been improperly granting tax clearances to "raunchy" hostess bars so that they could stay open for business. The official, Lawrence Nakano, said when I first interviewed him about the allegation that it had only happened once as a favor to a bar owner who "promised me that the amount [owed] would be cleared up." Nakano later admitted granting more clearances to other bars but said he didn't know how many. He acknowledged that he had no authority to grant the certificates. Nakano was allowed to transfer to another state department after his activities became known.
- An auditor who investigated the tax clearance issue later determined that 63 bars had received clearances when they did not deserve them. The auditor said he initially began to review all liquor-dispenser tax clearances but found the task "boring" and performed "random checks" of liquor dispensers that had received tax clearances.
- The same auditor turned up evidence that department personnel had been illegally and arbitrarily waiving penalty and interest payments owed by tax delinquents. The auditor said he dropped that investigation because "it was real difficult questioning fellow employees about wrongdoing."

- A department employee was running an illegal sports betting operation from his office desk. The man's supervisor admitted in court papers that he had admonished the worker about this behavior and advised him to operate his bookmaking business from the departmental men's room. The employee, who was later promoted, denied taking bets at work but did claim to have helped his supervisor place a few wagers with an outside party.
- The worker who filed the whistle-blower lawsuit said she did so only after her supervisors failed to act when she reported workplace shenanigans to them. She was then treated as a "rat" and an "informer" and was denied promotions she had earned, the suit alleged. The state later paid the whistle-blower an undisclosed sum to settle her claims.

The tax series also dealt with the sorry state of computerization in the department, a subject that rose again and again in later years. Kahle admitted that new computer systems the department installed to track different sources of revenue—income, excise, tobacco, hotel, and other taxes—couldn't "talk" to each other, forcing personnel to perform calculations and reconciliations by hand.[19]

Computerized audits and examinations had increased, but Kahle couldn't say how much money audits produced annually for the state. The department was badly short of human auditors because the pay was too low for experienced professionals, forcing the department to hire "kids out of college and train them," said Kahle. As soon as those workers completed journeyman-level training and gained expertise, they departed for the private sector, said Kahle's audit division chief, Richard Chiogioji.[20]

The department rarely resorted to hardened collection techniques used by the Internal Revenue Service, like seizure of assets or real estate foreclosure, and tax crimes were almost never prosecuted because nearly all were misdemeanor offenses, Kahle said.

LEO OHAI

Any discussion of death and taxes in Hawai'i must include the story of Leo Ohai, a remarkable commercial fisherman who regularly survived brushes with death at sea and spent decades on land holding government debt collectors at bay.

Here's the start of a Leo Ohai profile I wrote in 2007: "Benjamin Franklin said the only certainties in life are death and taxes—but he never met Leo Ohai."[21]

The part-Hawaiian Ohai was going strong at 82 when I met him, skippering a commercial fishing boat and spending his downtime pursuing a 20-year dream of building a specially designed, state-of-the-art vessel that could perform a variety of fishing: longlining, netfishing, trapfishing, and *akule* (a tropical ocean fish) or lobster fishing.

Advertiser news archives and Ohai's son Nephi told the stories of his adventures at sea.

While skin-diving off Kona on the Big Island in 1963, Ohai suffered a case of the bends and needed life-saving treatment at the U.S. Navy's recompression chamber at Pearl Harbor.

Ohai could pilot an aircraft and decided to fly himself back to Oahu. He kept losing consciousness during the two-hour flight, and the 24-year-old woman who accompanied him, Virginia King, wasn't a pilot.

King kept reviving him. "He'd check the instruments and get us straightened out, then we'd be all right for a bit before he began blacking out again," King told reporters. "It was like that the whole time."

The landing, King said, "wasn't the smoothest but it was good enough for us."

Ohai had pioneered the use of aircraft for fish-spotting in the 1950s, logging thousands of hours of flight time when his fishing business was based on Kauai.

Fishing boat skippers from California tried to lure Ohai to the docks at San Pedro, but he decided to stay at home, Nephi Ohai told me.

In 1967, Ohai's plane crashed and sank in Molokai's channel. Ohai escaped the wreck and floated in a life vest for 20 hours, carried by tides and currents halfway to Oahu, then halfway to Lanai. He finally bodysurfed ashore, naked and barefoot, to a remote Molokai headland and then had to walk another six hours to find help.

The next year, Ohai landed his malfunctioning Piper aircraft on the Ala Wai golf course near Waikiki beach, coasting to a stop on the 12th green.

Ohai survived a shark attack off Molokai in 1981. His right hand, "hanging by strings," was surgically reattached by doctors at the Queen's Medical Center, Nephi said. "He's got some numbness because of nerve damage, but basically it's OK."

Onshore, Ohai's attempts at boatbuilding brought him a world of difficulties. His family company borrowed $560,000 in 1982 from a state loan program meant to help revitalize the local fishing industry. The program made a second loan of $166,000 in 1986 to the Ohais.

When the state closed the boat loan program not long after that, the Ohais' long crusade to build their boat and repay the state loans was just beginning. Waves of tax liens from federal, state, and local government were filed against them.

The state threatened foreclosure on the boat loans and dunned the family for unpaid wharfage and related waterfront debts. Still they carried on, eventually filing a suit against the state that alleged delays in loan disbursements caused construction costs to spiral upward. By 2002, the state said the Ohais owed $1.24 million in unpaid principal and interest.[22]

The Ohais lost that suit in 2007 when a state judge ruled that the debts, since grown to $1.6 million, had to be repaid. But the Ohais filed new legal claims against the state that were still pending as of this writing. Settlement talks were said to be nearing fruition.

The Ohais' legal fight with the state stretched over 14 years, beating the RightStar litigation by a good 24 months.

Ted Hong, an attorney who represented the Ohais free of charge in some of their legal travails, said, "The Ohais are great fishermen, but there's room for improvement as businessmen."[23]

CHAPTER FOURTEEN

Teamsters

The long, sorry history of organized crime and the International Brotherhood of Teamsters union stretches back decades, with unionized mobsters repeatedly committing vicious crimes, including murder, arson, drug trafficking, assault, and much more.

That's just in Hawai'i.

On the national stage, the picture is even uglier. The story of the unholy partnership between Teamsters boss Jimmy Hoffa and the mob has been chronicled in detail through congressional hearings and criminal prosecutions, as well as in groundbreaking investigative works by Walter Sheridan, Wallace Turner, Dan Moldea, Steven Brill, Gus Russo, and many others.

The mob-Teamsters ties did not die with the disappearance and death of Hoffa in 1975.

So thorough and durable has been the syndicate's hold on the Teamsters that the U.S. Justice Department forced the union in 1989 to accept continuous, close oversight of its activities through what is called the Independent Review Board, a body created by the U.S. District Court in New York.

As of this writing, the IRB and its oversight are still in place, despite periodic attempts by the Teamsters to dissolve them. The IRB enforces a permanent court injunction that forbids Teamsters from "racketeering activities" and knowing associations with members or associates of the five New York Mafia families "or any other criminal group."[1]

After cataloguing ties between local organized crime and Hawai'i Teamsters in the "production unit" of the union that supplies drivers to film, television, and commercial productions in the Islands, I tried a couple of times to see if the IRB had any interest in looking into the matter.

It did not. An IRB investigator told me privately that the organization largely limited itself to Mafia associations, and I had to agree that there did not appear to be any of those in Hawai'i. But members of the local syndicate had been turning up as Hawai'i Teamsters Union production unit drivers ever since union patriarch Arthur Rutledge founded the unit in the 1960s.

ERIC NAONE AND HERSHEY ENTIN

My interest in the Teamsters began in 1978, when production unit driver Tramp Kawakami was identified by Honolulu and Nevada law enforcement authorities as a Hawai'i organized crime figure.

Then came the first Ronnie Ching stories in the early 1980s: a heroin-addicted professional killer was working as a Teamsters driver on the *Magnum, P.I.* television series.

I spent a lot of time researching the production unit in those years. I found that the roster of drivers included men like Ray Scanlan and Eric Naone, two organized crime figures with felony records who had hung out in Don Ho's dressing room and were acquitted in the Chuckers Marsland murder trial.

Naone first made news in 1975, when he worked briefly as a business agent–bodyguard for Art Rutledge. In a federal court hearing that concerned a dispute over the election of Teamsters officers, Rutledge testified that organized crime was trying to muscle its way into the union. Two business agents had quit after telling Rutledge "they'd like to live instead of die," Rutledge testified.

The agents had been told "by certain powerful people . . . that the boys are taking over," Rutledge said in the hearing, which was covered by *Advertiser* labor reporter Charles Turner.[2]

Rutledge didn't say more, but then Eric Naone took the stand and indicated that the takeover was being directed by syndicate figure Alema Leota. Naone said that former Teamsters organizer Josiah Lii had invoked Leota's name during a conversation with Naone.[3]

Lii and Leota were syndicate associates of Nappy Pulawa in the early 1970s, when the mob had designs on taking direct control of the Teamsters. According to mobster-turned-witness Henry Huihui, they discussed, but never followed through on, plans to murder Rutledge. Huihui later pleaded guilty to ordering the murder of Lii.

As for Eric Naone, his stint as a Teamsters business agent was brief. Within a few months of his federal court testimony for Rutledge, Naone had been questioned by police about the Chuckers Marsland murder and then was involved in a bizarre and inept kidnap-for-ransom case in Los Angeles.[4]

Naone and another man, Hershey Entin, were arrested following the gunpoint abduction of a former Las Vegas showgirl and *Playboy* centerfold, Corinne Heffron, from her Bel Air home. Two masked men took cash and a handgun from her well-to-do husband, Robert Heffron, tied him up, and demanded a $300,000 ransom payment from him before fleeing with the woman locked in the trunk of their car. But Robert Heffron quickly freed himself and called the police, giving them the license number of the getaway car. Within minutes, a patrol car stopped the vehicle and freed Corinne Heffron from the trunk.

Art Rutledge told Chuck Turner of the *Advertiser* that he was "shocked" by the news of Naone's Los Angeles escapade. Then he said Naone had been only a temporary Teamsters hire, working for the union for just three months.

Investigative reporter Gene Hunter of the *Advertiser* produced a story several days later that revealed that both Hershey Entin and Eric Naone were frequently seen backstage at Don Ho's show.[5]

Entin had been in Hawai'i for five years, working as an unpaid gofer for Don Ho and as a bookkeeper for Larry Mehau's security guard company, and then Mehau fired him for undisclosed reasons, Hunter reported.

Ho expressed amazement at Entin's arrest. "He's been a good boy all his life," Ho told Hunter. "It's a shock to me. It's inconceivable to me for the guy to do something like that."

Hunter's story said Entin had recently left Hawai'i for California, telling friends that he had inherited $1 million from his grandfather's estate. Charges against Entin were ultimately dismissed. Naone was convicted of robbery and sentenced to 10 years in prison.

While the California charges were pending, Naone was arrested in Hawai'i for another peculiar crime. After purchasing gun ammunition and holsters at a retail store, Naone was charged with being a felon in possession of ammunition. He told authorities that he was doing a favor for a friend. The ammo and holsters were supposed to be sent to the Philippines for a high-ranking general in that country's military, Naone claimed.[6]

Federal prosecutors mocked that story as "preposterous," and Naone was convicted and sentenced to 18 months behind bars.[7]

Naone and Entin ended up as Teamsters movie drivers. Naone worked for years in the Hawai'i production unit, and Entin drove vehicles in Southern California and elsewhere on the Mainland as a member of the Hollywood-based Local 399.

THE MILLION-DOLLAR MOVIE FUND

After establishing the production unit in the 1960s and populating it with a rogue's gallery of felons and head-breakers, Art Rutledge began assessing its members extra dues and funneling that money into accounts controlled by Unity House. The crafty Rutledge had created Unity House in the 1950s as a buffer to protect assets of the Teamsters and the hotel-restaurant workers union locals from outside predations by government agencies, as well as higher-ups in his own unions.

Rutledge wisely invested Unity House funds in Waikiki real estate, where the assets regularly redoubled in value. He explained more than once that the independent setup of Unity House protected its assets from raids by national union officials who looked for excuses to place the Hawai'i locals into trusteeship as a means of getting their hands on all that cash.

The nature of Unity House also protected it from oversight by federal agencies. An investigation of Unity House mounted by the U.S. General Accounting Office for a U.S. Senate committee concluded that Unity House was immune from the oversight and reporting requirements imposed on unions by the U.S. Department of Labor. The U.S. Justice Department and Hawai'i Department of Labor investigated Unity House and Rutledge on multiple occasions, including probes begun in the late 1970s that focused on whether the extra dues assessed on production unit drivers were a form of illegal kickbacks extracted from film and television producers as a cost of doing business in the Islands.

In 1981, I found that Rutledge had established a nonprofit called the Hawai'i Pacific Cinema Development Foundation and that he intended to finance it with $1 million amassed over the years from production unit drivers.[8]

The leadership of the foundation made for interesting reading. Rutledge was president. Tramp Kawakami—the local organized crime figure who had worked in the production unit for years, driving on such shows as the original *Hawaii Five-0*—was sergeant-at-arms of the foundation. Serving as vice president was Ed Brennan, the Republican Party National Committee member from Hawai'i. And the foundation secretary was Linda Lingle, then a member of the Maui County Council. In 1998, Lingle became the first woman governor of Hawai'i and the first Republican to hold that office since 1962.

Lingle, who had worked briefly for the Teamsters before going into politics, hastily told me that she was in the process of resigning from the foundation board because of her workload in county office. The resignation paperwork hadn't been finalized, she said. Lingle also said she didn't know Kawakami and was unaware of his reputation in law enforcement.[9]

Kawakami wouldn't talk to me, and Brennan was unreachable.

Rutledge said he was aware of, but gave no credence to, Kawakami's reputation. He said he doubted if Kawakami had ever spent any time in jail and was on the foundation board because of his knowledge of film and television productions. Rutledge claimed that he had stopped accepting "voluntary contributions" from production unit drivers a year earlier after the "special fund" where the money was held at Unity House reached $1 million.[10]

The foundation intended to use the money to foster development of "film and video arts," including, Rutledge said, construction of a "first-class" production studio on Oahu. He told me that the site of the women's state prison on the windward side of the island would make an ideal location for the studio if the state would make the land available. Some 20 or 30 acres could be spared because the state no longer needed all that land, Rutledge said. "Good girls do what bad girls used to do," said Rutledge.

The idea never took root. Unity House and the foundation would later put their production unit money to some extremely dubious uses.

More information about production unit finances emerged in subsequent years after friction between Los Angeles—and Hawai'i-based Teamsters flared up on movie and television productions in the Islands. Problems began brewing after Leo Reed, a former Hawai'i football star, police officer, and Art Rutledge protégé, was elected head of Teamsters Local 399 in Los Angeles. In the late 1980s, Reed began asserting contractual authority over Teamsters who drove equipment shipped to Hawai'i for use on shoots in Hawai'i.

A master contract signed by Hollywood studios and producers with Local 399 gave Reed control over who drove Hollywood-owned equipment in western states, including Hawai'i, but the agreement had been loosely enforced before Reed came into power. Animosity between the two groups of drivers began roiling the atmosphere on production sets, even shutting down shows for brief periods.

Then a group of Hawai'i-based production unit drivers who had aligned themselves with Reed complained to the FBI and to me about Rutledge's management of the unit.

Among the complainants was Ray Scanlan, convicted heroin trafficker and accused but acquitted killer.[11] Scanlan and others said Rutledge had been assessing production unit drivers between 3 and 15 percent of their gross pay for decades, but they had nothing to show for it. The only time the tithing stopped was during an FBI criminal investigation of the practice in the late 1970s and early 1980s, but the assessments resumed when the federal agents went away, the drivers said. Scanlan said he and other drivers had lied to the FBI but now wanted to tell the truth.

"We stood up and said, 'We like to pay,'" Scanlan told me. "But that wasn't true. The truth is, we don't want to pay the money, but if you don't pay, you don't work."

Rutledge scoffed at the dissidents, calling them "childish" and saying the production unit funds were intact and still earning interest in the Cinema Development Foundation account. "You can rest assured that whatever assets we've got, we still have," Rutledge said in one of his typically Delphic quotes.

Production unit drivers were still being assessed 3 percent of their pay, but the money was going to Teamsters coffers and not the foundation, he said.

Tony Rutledge, Art's son and heir apparent in union affairs, said the cinema development fund was untouched and, with interest, had grown to $1.7 million.

The war of words increased. Art Rutledge called Leo Reed "a local boy gone nutty with power" who was scheming to take over the Hawai'i Teamsters local.[12] Reed and his brothers were involved in "a nefarious plot . . . to establish themselves as the czars of the movie production business in Hawai'i," Rutledge said in an interview.

Reed fired back by phone from Hollywood. "This is 1989, not 1932. The Old Man, his problem is he's been around too long, a decade too long," Reed said.

Rutledge required film and television producers to hire many more drivers than were necessary and insisted on personal control of who worked and who didn't, Reed said. "I'll tell you something: if the Old Man would only ease up and treat those producers right, just have the necessary drivers, in my opinion, there would be 10 times more shows produced in Hawai'i," said Reed.

His brother Leroy, a 399 member who regularly worked in Hawai'i, agreed. When the movie *Uncommon Valor* was filmed on Kauai, producers had to hire 75 drivers, he said.[13] "I did *Beverly Hills Cop II* [filmed in Los Angeles], the most drivers I had was 32, but only 25 full-time. Seventy-five drivers, that's ridiculous," Reed said.

Tom Selleck, star and coproducer of the immensely popular *Magnum, P.I.* television series, tactfully agreed with the Reeds. He said the show had to hire twice as many drivers in Hawai'i as it did in Los Angeles. "Hiring and firing is also very difficult," Selleck said.

"Unions here practically insist on placing whoever they want on the payroll. I'm a union member and I believe in seniority, but I also believe in hiring on the basis of ability," he said.[14]

Rutledge said the number and names of drivers hired were determined by contract language and by his "powers as a negotiator."

The Los Angeles and Hawai'i drivers continued to butt heads on production sets, threatening each other and distressing cast and crew members. Ray Scanlan warned that there was a real possibility of physical violence but said the pro-Reed drivers didn't want anyone to get hurt. "We are not contemplating violence. We don't want it. All we want is to clean house and invite other production companies to come to Hawai'i and work with a clean union," he said.

Tony Rutledge told me that he believed Larry Mehau was providing background assistance to the pro-Reed, anti-Rutledge drivers. He claimed that Mehau had supported a Rutledge opponent in a recent union election and had two "good friends" who were allied with the Reeds. Those friends were Ray Scanlan and Cyril Kahale, Rutledge said. Kahale was a Teamster with Reed's 399 local.[15]

Mehau had no comment, but an associate of his said that while Mehau was friendly with men on both sides of the dispute, he had not involved himself in it. Leo Reed acknowledged knowing Mehau but said he had no role in the jurisdictional fight. Art Rutledge added his own cryptic point of view: "I know Larry, he's on a friendly basis with everyone. I've known him for years. He has, up until now, respected my jurisdiction, and I respect his, whatever it may be."

On the set of the *Jake and the Fat Man* television series, problems boiled over after Hawai'i drivers didn't appear for work because they had been called to a "special meeting" by Art Rutledge.[16]

Leroy Reed, the transportation coordinator on the show, told me a few days later that he had used "guys off the street, friends of mine" to fill in for the absent Hawai'i drivers. That brought an infuriated Art Rutledge to the set, where he saw the nonunion drivers.

"Art came over there and saw them and he went crazy," Reed said.

"He says, 'You get those guys out of here,' screaming," Reed recounted.

"Then he goes screaming to the producers and the producers said, 'Please, Leroy, get rid of them so Art won't go nuts,'" Reed continued.

Rutledge was "running around the parking lot and trying to get his guys, the drivers, all stirred up," Reed said, so he got rid of the "off-the-street" drivers. Things calmed down after that, but, Reed said, "We still got the intimidation, daily intimidation. Those other guys look at you, you hear bad things are coming up, you better watch yourself."

The problems became so acute that union higher-ups called Rutledge and Leo Reed to a sit-down in Scottsdale, Arizona. Although both men said after that meeting that they had buried the hatchet and resolved their differences, problems continued to simmer.[17]

Hostilities were reopened on the set of a television production called *Island Son* being filmed on Oahu.[18]

Another of Rutledge's sons, Arthur Jr., was driving on the show but was fired after a dispute with the Los Angeles–based transportation coordinator. Rutledge Jr. had asked for a day off to attend to personal business, but the coordinator refused. When Rutledge didn't appear for work that day, he was fired. That brought Tony Rutledge to the set. He told the Hawai'i 996 drivers to walk off the jobsite.

But some of the drivers were part of the anti-Rutledge, pro-Reed faction inside the Hawai'i local, and they refused to walk.

One, a hulking man named Masa Niko, gave his account of what happened next. "I told him I'm not going to walk because I have a job to do. Tony questioned me about which side I was on and I said no side, I was hired to do a job and that's what I'm going to do," said Niko.

"He told everybody to get in their trucks and leave. People started to leave but the police stopped them," Niko continued.

That brought Art Rutledge and Leroy Reed to the set. The two men conferred briefly, and peace was eventually restored. Tony Rutledge later blamed the show's producer for the problems. Art Rutledge blamed "the asshole in charge of the drivers."

Reynold Kamekona, a 996 driver on the show and member of the pro-Reed group, blamed Art Rutledge. "It's a power thing. The Old Man wants to run everything his way, for his family and friends, and the hell with everybody else," Kamekona told me. "If you complain, you're out of a job."

ARSON, MURDER, AND MORE

Four violent events that made major news in the 1990s and early 2000s featured direct or indirect involvement of production unit drivers.

The first occurred in 1991 when Teamsters George Cambra and Joseph "Joe Boy" Tavares torched movie production trucks owned by competitors of George Cambra Movie Production Trucks, Inc. Tavares was the half-brother of professional murderer and Teamster driver Ronald Ching. The fires forced two companies out of business and left Cambra as the major vehicle supplier to the film and television industries in Hawai'i.

The second was the 1992 murder of David Walden, an executive of Star Suites, Inc., a Missouri firm that had begun shipping its own production vehicles to Hawai'i to compete with Cambra's company.

The third was the daylight murder of two men at a Windward Oahu public golf course. A third man was shot in the face but survived. The violence was part of an underworld struggle to control illegal gambling operations.

The fourth was the horrifying murder of a two-year-child, Cyrus Belt, tossed from a freeway overpass into oncoming traffic below.

Cambra and Tavares

On different nights in 1991, intentionally set fires engulfed and destroyed expensive movie production vehicles owned by two Hawai'i firms, Auto Mastics, Inc., and Mokulua Consultants, Inc.

The crimes were unsolved for years and might have always remained so. But in 1992, David Walden was murdered at Pier 24 on the Honolulu waterfront, an event that sent tremors of anxiety through the local and national film industries and provoked closer attention to the truck fires. Eight years after the truck fires, federal authorities brought an arson conspiracy case against Cambra and Tavares.

The arson case was buttressed when another Local 996 production unit driver, Reynold Kamekona, agreed to testify as a prosecution witness against Tavares and Cambra. Kamekona—the same man I had interviewed on the set of *Island Son*—said he had helped Tavares torch the trucks, using a mixture of diesel fuel and gasoline provided by Cambra.

Kamekona's cooperation was part of an unusual two-pronged deal reached with the U.S. Attorney's office. In return for his testimony, Kamekona would not be charged, and federal authorities would also lighten the prospective sentence then looming over Kamekona's brother, Harlan "Bruce" Kamekona.[19]

Bruce Kamekona, also a Teamster movie driver, had been caught by the feds in a large-scale drug-trafficking case that involved shipment of pound quantities of "ice" from Hawai'i to Guam.

The feds were also pressuring Cambra, Tavares, and the Kamekona brothers to tell what they knew about the Walden murder. Cambra and Tavares each claimed that the other man was responsible for the slaying but provided unconvincing and insufficient details to support their allegations.

Bruce and Reynold Kamekona knew a great deal about the murder but said they did not know who had actually committed it. They told investigators that Cambra had been at odds with Walden over the movie trucks Walden's company had brought to Hawai'i and initially leased to Cambra. They described shouting matches they witnessed between Cambra and Walden and said Cambra had been physically threatening Walden in the days before the murder.

They knew that on the morning of the killing, Walden was due to arrive at Pier 24 on the Honolulu waterfront with at least one of his vehicles that had been used for a production being filmed on Maui. The Kamekona brothers and Tavares were supposed to meet Walden at the dock and take possession of the Walden vehicle that was to be used on another shoot on Oahu, Bruce Kamekona told authorities.[20]

Bruce said he told Cambra about the meeting with Walden the day before it was scheduled to occur. On the morning of the murder, Bruce said, his brother Reynold was supposed to call him when the equipment arrived, and Bruce would then drive to the dock to help move it. When Reynold did call, he was in a "hysterical" state and said that Walden had been shot, Bruce told investigators.

Bruce then drove from the windward side of Oahu to the dock, he said. On the way, he said, he saw fellow movie driver Jon "Sudee" Dahl driving in the opposite direction on Old Pali Road, a secondary road paralleling the main Pali Highway that linked the Honolulu and windward sides of Oahu.

Witnesses at the murder scene said that two helmeted men astride a motorcycle had driven up to Walden at the dock. The passenger on the vehicle, whom they could not identify, had shot Walden to death, they said. The driver of the motorcycle was also unidentified.

Dahl, Cambra, and many other Teamsters interviewed by police and federal agents all denied involvement in, or knowledge of, the homicide.

A month after the murder, Cambra was involved in a violent encounter with fellow Teamster Eric Naone that left Cambra badly beaten and with a bloody hole in one of his hands.[21] The beating occurred at a meeting of Teamster movie drivers, including Cambra, Tavares, Bruce Kamekona, Naone, Blaine Kaakimaka, and Stan Mataele.[22]

The meeting was held at a Kewalo Basin business that supplied ice to fishing and pleasure boats berthed in the adjacent harbor. Cambra told federal investigators that the other Teamsters at the meeting, led by Tavares, were trying to force him to transfer ownership of a movie truck to them. That claim was the basis for an extortion charge added by the U.S. Attorney's office to the arson indictment of Tavares.[23]

Bruce Kamekona, Eric Naone, and Tavares, however, told different stories about the ice house violence.

In papers filed in the arson-extortion case, Tavares and his attorneys said Naone told HPD Major Louis Souza after the beating that Naone called the meeting because "Cambra was spreading rumors that Naone and his associates had murdered Walden."[24]

Tavares said the beating occurred after "Cambra admitted to soliciting the murder of Walden." The Tavares court papers also asserted that Cambra initially told HPD Detective Joseph Ryan "his beating was related to the Walden murder and that it was done by the Walden murderers." Cambra also told Ryan that he believed there was an "80 percent chance" that he would be murdered for "saying anything like this," according to a partial transcript of the Ryan-Cambra interview attached to the court filing.

Bruce Kamekona told a third, slightly different version of the beating. In a 1998 debriefing with federal agents and police after his arrest in the meth-trafficking case, Kamekona said the ice house meeting was called because Cambra was "telling everyone they would get hurt" if they continued using Star Suites equipment.

"During this meeting, Cambra told Naone that the old man, in reference to Larry Mehau, had told Cambra that he had to do what he had to do in reference to controlling the movie industry," Kamekona told investigators.[25] "Naone told Cambra that he should not drop names."

There was no corroborating testimony from anyone else about Cambra's allegations concerning Mehau.

Cambra was beaten by Naone, suffering a broken jaw. He was also stabbed through the hand with a fishing spear.

Cambra said nothing about the Walden murder when he testified at the arson-extortion trial of Tavares. After reaching a plea deal with the government, Cambra took the witness stand and said the ice house assault occurred because Tavares was trying to force Cambra to transfer ownership of movie vehicles to Tavares. The federal court jury that heard the case in 1999 acquitted Tavares of the beating-related charges but convicted him of arson conspiracy.

While Tavares and Cambra were awaiting sentencing in that case, a federal grand jury met to hear evidence in the Walden murder investigation.

Various drivers from the production unit were called to testify. I covered the event with a KITV cameraman outside the federal courthouse, but none of the drivers had anything substantive to say when they completed their testimony.[26]

Driver Sudee Dahl was accompanied by attorney Stacy Moniz, but neither man would talk about the grand jury session. Moniz was a well-known Honolulu lawyer who had helped represent Larry Mehau in the "godfather of organized crime" lawsuit Mehau had filed against Rick Reed, an aide in the Honolulu prosecuting attorney's office.

Moniz had also successfully defended former Hawai'i prison guard and current Teamsters production unit driver Blaine Kaakimaka from a murder conspiracy charge in the Eric Kamanu slaying.

Moniz was a longtime board member of the Hawai'i Pacific Cinema Development Foundation, the nonprofit founded by Art Rutledge that controlled a million-dollar treasure chest of fees collected from movie drivers.

When Moniz appeared with Dahl and other drivers called to testify before the grand jury, he was in serious legal difficulties of his own. Under indictment for federal tax offenses, Moniz had initially agreed to plead guilty in that case but then changed his mind and withdrew the plea.

Larry Mehau and Stacy Moniz, center, meet with attorney David Schutter. RICHARD AMBO, PHOTOGRAPHER; *HONOLULU STAR-ADVERTISER* COLLECTION; HAWAI'I STATE ARCHIVES.

To defend himself, Moniz then argued in court papers that authorities had illegally seized records from his office as part of a long-running investigation into his personal ties to organized crime. The office records had been removed from Moniz's law office without a search warrant by a former law partner and an off-duty HPD officer who was married to a secretary in the office. Moniz argued that the seizure was illegally orchestrated by investigators bent on proving his ties to the mob.

In one pretrial hearing, HPD Detective Ken Kamakana testified that Moniz was not a mobster but had clients, friends, and associates who were organized crime members,[27] including Teamster movie drivers Kaakimaka, Bruce Perry, and Lyle Yasuhara. Kaakimaka was a Moniz business associate and legal client, Kamakana said on the stand, before the presiding judge, Alan Kay, stopped the detective from saying more.

Bruce Perry was the son of longtime Larry Mehau close associate George Perry Jr. Bruce was a former longshoreman who had occasionally worked as a movie driver. The younger Perry had been tried twice in an assault case that left a fellow stevedore, Quentin "Rocky" Tahara, blinded in one eye. Both trials ended in hung juries, but Tahara later won a million-dollar judgment against Perry in civil court.

Yasuhara, the son of a former HPD officer, had been arrested the previous year in a gambling case on the Big Island. That prosecution was later dismissed because of a faulty search warrant. At the time of the Moniz trial, Yasuhara was a Teamster driver on the Hawai'i version of the *Baywatch* television series.

Moniz later filed more documents in his criminal case that were intended to buttress his illegal search argument but also portrayed him in a far from flattering light. Moniz obtained sworn affidavits from police officers who said they had attended law enforcement conferences in which Moniz's name appeared in Hawai'i organized crime "link charts" that depicted the hierarchy of the local mob.[28]

One affidavit, from a recently retired HPD officer, Wayne Chun-Fat, said Moniz had been identified as an organized crime figure in a 1995 briefing conducted by HPD's Criminal Intelligence Unit, where Kamakana worked.[29]

Chun-Fat said Moniz was connected in a link chart to Blaine Kaakimaka and George Perry Jr., both of whom were identified as mob members in the 1995 briefing, according to Chun-Fat's affidavit. "During this briefing, Moniz was described as a lawyer and associate of Kaakimaka and Perry," Chun-Fat's affidavit said. "Moniz was presented as being as much of an organized crime figure as Perry and Kaakimaka."

Another affidavit, from Kauai Police Department Officer Jerald Kim, said Moniz had been "targeted, profiled, put under surveillance, photographed and criminally investigated" by the HPD CIU from 1993 through at least 1998.

In a 1996 statewide criminal intelligence conference that Kim attended, Moniz was again linked to Perry and Kaakimaka, as well as to the 1994 murder of David Walden and to Teamster truck driver and owner George Cambra, Kim said in his affidavit.

In the end, Moniz's self-inflicted besmirching failed to sway the court, and he was convicted of federal tax crimes. Judge Kay sentenced him to 27 months in prison for "pervasive attempts to obstruct justice." Facing disbarment proceedings, Moniz surrendered his license to practice law.

The grand jury's investigation of the Walden murder was closed, and no one was charged in the case. Honolulu police later mounted a cold case investigation of the homicide, conducting DNA testing of a cigarette butt recovered from the murder scene. But the only DNA found belonged to the victim.

On the 20th anniversary of the killing, Walden's daughter, Angela Whitford, convinced Honolulu police and Hawai'i news outlets to publicize the unsolved case and seek public assistance in solving it.

The murder case is still open.

Murder at the Pali

The Pali Golf Course at midday in January 2004 was a very pleasant place to spend an afternoon. Built in the 1950s at the windward base of the magisterial Koolau mountain range, the course was owned by the city and attracted a mixture of tourists and local residents who appreciated the cheap greens fees and overlooked threadbare conditions on some greens and fairways. The views were spectacular: in one direction, the azure waters of Kaneohe and Kailua Bays glittered in the sunlight; in the other, the deeply fissured perpendicular mountain walls were robed in green and crowned with clouds.

The surrounding countryside was undeveloped and bucolic. Visitors usually heard birdcalls and occasional shouts of "Fore!" in the background. But on January 4, a fusillade of gunfire echoed around the course after two underworld factions warring for control of illegal gambling protection money rendezvoused in the Pali parking lot.

The meeting was supposed to be a peaceful one where differences could be discussed and perhaps resolved. The various parties had first encountered each other that morning at the funeral of a mutual acquaintance and arranged to meet again at the golf course.

Shortly after the two groups met, men from one faction—Rodney Joseph Jr., Ethan "Malu" Motta, and Kevin "Pancho" Gonsalves—took out handguns and began shooting.

Two of their rivals were killed, and a third, although shot in the face by Motta with a .22-caliber gun, survived.

One of the victims, Lepo Utu Taliese, was fatally injured but survived long enough to run through the parking lot and clubhouse as more gunfire rang out around him. One .380-caliber round pierced the window of the golf course pro shop.

Taliese stumbled past the 18th green and down the fairway, eventually collapsing in the rough as shocked golfers and maintenance workers looked on, then rushed to attend him. In a dying declaration, Taliese said Motta and Joseph had killed him.

Motta and Joseph were arrested before nightfall. Motta was detained at the airport, waiting for a flight back to his home in Hilo on the Big Island. Joseph self-surrendered to police.

Other reporters were covering the main story, with Peter Boylan of the *Advertiser* quickly detailing background information about events that led up to the killings and arrests.

I knew a bit about Rodney Joseph and his family's long history of connections to local organized crime. I was struck by the similarity of the killings to the old days of open mob warfare and suggested a sidebar story to that effect.

I got the go-ahead, wrote the piece, and turned it in.
Here it is:

To old-time law enforcement officers here, the story of Tuesday's bloody mayhem at the Pali golf course sounded eerily like headlines from the heyday of Honolulu organized crime turf wars in the late 1960s and early 1970s involving control of illegal gambling games.

And the family name of one man arrested by police in the Pali case, Rodney Joseph Jr., brought back a lot of memories for retired cops and prosecutors who worked cases 30 years ago.

Rodney Joseph Jr.'s father first made the news here in the early 1970s when he and his brother Terrance "Tony" Joseph were arrested for allegedly beating a Honolulu police officer.

The brothers hired an up-and-coming Honolulu defense lawyer, David Schutter, who argued that the altercation was really a contest between a martial arts instructor (the police officer) and his pupil (Rodney Joseph Sr.). The pupil won, argued Schutter. The Joseph brothers were acquitted. Schutter went on to great success in the local defense bar, representing some of the biggest names in the local criminal syndicate.

Another brother of Rodney Sr. and Tony Joseph, Jeffrey, is now serving time in federal prison for drug offenses.

Rodney Joseph Sr. and brother Tony married sisters Vanessa and Aletha "None" Orso. Their mother, Leimomi Catherine "Momi" Kau, worked in a laundry in Chinatown that was known as a gathering place for syndicate figures in the 60s and early 70s.

Local syndicate lieutenant Francis Burke was shot to death in the street near the laundry entrance one October afternoon in 1970. He died in the gutter with a five-dollar bill clutched in his hand. Across the street was an illegal gambling operation run by Walter "Hotcha" Hong.

Originally arrested for murder in the Burke case was John Freeman "John John" Orso, a cousin of the Orso sisters, whose life was the stuff of pulp fiction. He had been a decorated war hero, a conscientious objector, a heroin addict, and a burglar. Charges against Orso in the Burke murder were later dropped. He successfully sued the city for false arrest.

None Joseph, Rodney Jr.'s auntie, later married Honolulu organized crime boss Charles Stevens. Their daughter married convicted organized crime hit man Wallace "Ditto" Rodrigues, called the "most dangerous man in Hawai'i" by prosecutors in 1999. Rodrigues is now serving a 100-year prison term for multiple homicide and manslaughter convictions.

Another auntie of Rodney Jr., Marion Orso, married one-time local organized crime figure Charles "Moose" Russell, who told the *Advertiser* in 1996 that he continued to be friends with criminal figures but had been a legitimate businessman since being released from prison in 1982.

Rodney Joseph Jr. was convicted here in 1989 of burglary and terroristic threatening charges with his cousin Jonnaven Monalim and another man. An amateur boxer, Monalim was later convicted of assaulting a minor in Makaha in 1998 while serving probation for the earlier felony charges. The 1998 case stirred considerable controversy after a circuit court judge, over the strenuous objections of the city prosecutor's office, delayed the start of Monalim's 10-year prison term so he could spend time with his newborn child.

Like his father and his cousin, Rodney Joseph Jr. is accomplished in the martial arts. He was a heavyweight kickboxer and has been active in Leeward Coast boxing circles.

His great-uncle, Carl "Bobo" Olson, was a world-class boxer, at one time holding the middleweight championship.

The story never ran. Editor Mark Platte didn't like it, so it was consigned to the "Splatte File." As the case against the three Pali shooters later unfolded in federal court, the story turned out to be unwittingly prescient in several ways.

The Stevens family tree was a unifying theme in the prosecution's case against the killers. I didn't know when I wrote the story that Ethan Motta, a codefendant in the Pali case, was a cousin of Rodney Joseph Jr. and was considered a part of the Charley Stevens family. Various witnesses testified in the ensuing trial that Motta became involved in the gambling business because he intended to rebuild the criminal organization once run by his "uncle" Charley Stevens.

And Jonnaven Monalim, another Joseph cousin, turned out to be an FBI informant who delivered crucial testimony for the prosecution in the Pali murder trial.

Nearly a month after I wrote my story, the rival *Honolulu Star-Bulletin* published one by reporter Sally Apgar that covered many of the familial connections that ran through the murder case.[30] It was a fine story that centered on Charley Stevens and included an overview of the history of modern-day Hawai'i organized crime.

But Apgar also missed Motta's ties to the Stevens and Joseph families. And she made no mention at all of Jonnaven Monalim.

I had given Monalim considerable publicity in March 2004—two months after the Pali shootings but years before his involvement in the case became public—when I found him in business with an influential state law enforcement officer, Hawai'i Sheriff John Souza.[31]

A former Honolulu police officer, Souza was engaged to (and would later marry) then state senate president and future U.S. congresswoman Colleen Hanabusa.

Monalim had purchased real estate from Souza (which the sheriff had earlier bought from Hanabusa's family) and was making monthly payments to Souza when the story was published.

Organized crime figure
Charley Stevens.
*HONOLULU STAR-
ADVERTISER* COLLECTION;
HAWAI'I STATE ARCHIVES.

Souza said the sale occurred well before he took the sheriff's job. He told me he knew Monalim's reputation but was motivated to sell what he called a "dead dog of a property."

"I would never have done that after I took office," Souza told me. "I know who this guy is and what his reputation is. When I dealt with this guy, he looked totally clean. He was preaching that had had done his time and learned his lesson."

The only problem with that position, my story disclosed, was that FBI agents and police had executed a search warrant at Monalim's house less than a week earlier. That search turned out to be the start of Monalim's career as a government informant, which ended when he took the witness stand in the Pali murder trial.

Souza resigned as sheriff because of what he called the "bad appearance" of the Monalim deal and because he said he didn't want his personal business activities to detract from Hanabusa's political future.

The Souza-Hanabusa-Monalim-Pali connections illustrate the organic nature of reporting in the Islands. One family of bamboo trees—Jonnaven

Monalim, Rodney Joseph, and Ethan Motta—stands alone but is connected to a myriad of other bamboo stands.

Off in one direction are John Souza and Colleen Hanabusa. In another is real estate developer Jeff Stone, a strong political backer of Hanabusa and business associate of John Souza. Over yonder is the Bishop Estate with strong subterranean connections to Stone. Then there is the Teamsters bamboo patch, with a root system solidly tied to the Pali murders.

The second prosecution witness to testify in the federal court racketeering trial was George Cambra Jr., son of the convicted arsonist and movie truck owner. Cambra Jr. was a member in his own right of the Teamsters movie driving clan.

Cambra Jr. told the jury that he was working at his family's truck yard the afternoon of the Pali murders when his friend Rodney Joseph paid a visit.

Joseph gave Cambra three handguns and asked him to destroy them. If Cambra was surprised or disturbed by this request, he said nothing about it on the witness stand. He told the jury he broke up the weapons into "bird seed"–sized pieces and threw them into a stream.[32]

Ammunition given to Cambra was discarded into a storm grate. Police later recovered the bullets but found no trace of the guns.

The trial was a fascinating affair, featuring an appearance by a well-known New York criminal defense attorney, Charles Carnesi, who took time off from representing John Gotti Jr., son of the notorious Gambino crime family boss, to represent Motta, the would-be successor to Hawai'i mob boss Charley Stevens.[33]

Motta's exact kinship to Stevens was mysterious. Motta's mother insisted that there was no blood relationship. Stevens' obituary, written by his family after Stevens died in federal prison, listed Motta as the *hanai* son of Stevens—the informal adoption practice common in Hawaiian society. Motta called Stevens his uncle and said Rodney Joseph—Stevens' nephew—was his cousin.[34]

Motta was a college graduate and had been the president of the student body while attending the University of Hawai'i at Hilo on the Big Island.

Soft-spoken and articulate, Motta presented himself during the trial as a hardworking, dedicated family man who was bemused by the authorities' efforts to portray him as a murderous mobster.

On the witness stand, Motta said he worked as a family therapist, dabbled in politics, and was a business entrepreneur. He said that before he was arrested, he was trying to find financial backers for a device he had invented called "Baby Cry No More," which simulated a mother's heartbeat to calm restive infants.[35]

An acquaintance and fellow inventor, Raymond Gomes, called Motta on the Big Island and asked him to help mediate a dispute between rival criminal groups that were protecting illegal gambling games, Motta testified. No explanation was given in the trial as to why Motta would be able to provide such a service.

Gomes invoked the Fifth Amendment when called to testify.

Motta said when he went with Joseph to the golf course parking lot meeting, his cousin gave him a handgun and told him to "be careful." He became alarmed when one of the men they met, Taliese, started shouting, and a truck carrying "a bunch of guys" approached.

He pulled his gun and shot one of victims, Tinoimalo Sao, because he was frightened for his life, Motta told the jury. "I fired twice. I didn't know at the time that I had hit anyone," Motta said.

"I never intended to shoot anybody. I was scared," he said.

The final witness in the trial was Jonnaven Monalim, who had worn a hidden FBI microphone to a meeting with Motta several months after the murders. Monalim said he agreed to wear the wire after the 2004 raid of his house by police and FBI agents. He cooperated because authorities said they had evidence tying him to drug trafficking and money laundering.

Motta was free on $1 million bail, and the meeting with Monalim took place at a fund-raiser organized on the Big Island by Motta's family and friends to help pay for his legal expenses. Big Island Mayor William "Billy" Kenoi, a rising star in the Hawai'i Democratic Party, spoke at the fund-raiser.[36]

Monalim testified that Motta told him he "had a mission in mind, to take over [illegal gambling] completely."[37]

According to Monalim, Motta said the murders were a "blood on the table" statement to underworld rivals. Motta bragged that he had "a judge in his pocket" and planned to win the criminal case when it was initially scheduled to be prosecuted in state court.

Motta said that "if he gets through this [murder case], he's gonna be bigger than his uncle," Monalim said. (The case was ultimately transferred to federal court, and there was never any evidence presented to support Motta's "judge in his pocket" claim.)

The parallels between Motta and Charley Stevens were striking. The racketeering prosecution of Stevens 20 years earlier had been the last major organized crime case mounted by federal authorities in Hawai'i.

Stevens pleaded guilty to drug- and gun-trafficking offenses and also admitted that he had earlier bribed a state judge to overturn a double murder conviction. He was sentenced to 20 years in prison.

Motta and Joseph were convicted in a jury trial and are now serving life-without-parole sentences in federal prison. Codefendant Kevin Gonsalves pleaded guilty and was sentenced to 27½ years behind bars.

Drugs, Guns, Cash, and a Cop

In 2005, production unit drivers were travelling to and from federal prison with regularity.[38] Brothers Randolph and Audwin Aiwohi were busted in May in a big federal drug-trafficking and firearms case.

"Randy" Aiwohi was held without bail pending trial after the U.S. Attorney's office called him a "danger to the community."[39] Aiwohi said in court papers that he had been making $10,000 a month as a movie driver earlier in the year.

The search of a Big Island ranch owned by Audwin Aiwohi yielded $240,000 worth of crystal methamphetamine, $192,523 in cash, 17 firearms, and nearly 900 rounds of ammunition, according to court records. The raid was part of a federal Organized Crime Drug Enforcement Task Force investigation in Honolulu, according to papers filed in the case by Steven Marceleno, an agent with Immigration and Customs Enforcement.[40]

A stolen, loaded handgun was found beside Randy Aiwohi's bed, Assistant U.S. Attorney Chris Thomas said in court. The raid was the result of an "eight-month investigation" that included use of federal wiretaps, Thomas said.

Audwin Aiwohi was also ordered held without bail by U.S. Magistrate Judge Kevin Chang.

The Aiwohi brothers eventually pleaded guilty to federal drug charges. Randolph got a five-year prison term and Audwin 10 years.[41]

Audwin Aiwohi and three other Teamsters movie drivers had previously been charged with conspiracy to commit murder in the 1989 slaying of Windward Oahu bodybuilder Eric Kamanu. Those charges were later dismissed because of statute of limitation problems. One of the original defendants in the Kamanu murder conspiracy case, movie driver John Joseph "Joe" Griffiths, later pleaded guilty to "recklessly causing the death" of Kamanu. Griffiths also pleaded guilty to federal drug-trafficking offenses and was sentenced to a 10-year prison term.[42]

Griffiths kept his Teamsters Union membership dues current while he was in prison, Mel Kahele, head of Teamsters Local 996, told me in 2005.[43] Kahele acknowledged that men with serious criminal records had been in the production unit for decades. He said the union was cleaning itself up, but it was a slow process.

I found that almost half of all 71 drivers then on the production unit membership list had criminal records. "I don't know what the reason is,"

Kahele told me. "I think it must be the money. Drivers make so much money and the work is not that hard."[44]

I found that other Hawai'i-based movie drivers, Douglas "Hollywood" Farias and Douglas Paahao, had recently begun federal prison terms for drug crimes. Another, Stan Mataele, was about to begin an eight-month federal sentence for a drug offense.[45]

None of the charges were tied to the work the men performed on movie and television productions, although Farias claimed that some of the $66,200 in cash seized from him by federal agents was actually money earned from the sale of T-shirts on movie sets. Farias pleaded guilty in the case and was sentenced to 10 years behind bars.

Paahao drew a five-year sentence after pleading guilty to trafficking in crystal methamphetamine.

Although he lived in Hawai'i, Paahao was a member of Teamsters Union Local 399 in Los Angeles and drove trucks and other vehicles shipped to Hawai'i by movie and television productions that shoot on location here.

All Hawai'i drivers at one time were members of Local 399, but the head of that union local, Leo Reed, had transferred jurisdiction of the Hawai'i drivers to another Southern California local and eventually to Local 996.

"I don't want to have nothing to do with Hawai'i [Teamsters] no more," Reed said in a 2002 interview. "There are some good drivers in Hawai'i. They're great Teamsters and it's a shame they have to suffer . . . because of a few individuals."

Mataele, also a member of Local 399, was Leo Reed's in-law. While awaiting trial in his drug case, Mataele was twice allowed to travel to the Mainland to drive trucks for Local 399 on two major Hollywood productions, *Friday Night Lights* and *National Treasure*, that were shot in Texas and on the East Coast, respectively, according to court papers.

While some Teamster movie drivers were heading off to prison in mid-2005, others were returning to Hawai'i after completing lengthy stays behind bars for felony offenses.

Driver Harlan Bruce Kamekona was in a halfway house following his release from prison for a 1997 drug-trafficking conviction.

Driver Joseph "Joe Boy" Tavares—the half-brother of hit man Ronald Ching—was in a halfway house in San Francisco, following his release from federal prison for the 1998 arson conviction. Tavares was originally sentenced to 15 years in prison, but federal authorities later agreed to cut that sentence in half for undisclosed reasons.

George Cambra, who was convicted of criminal conspiracy in the same case, was released from federal prison in 2004. His lawyer, Brook Hart, called Cambra "a reformed man."

I also found that a Honolulu police officer, William Duarte, was working days as a production unit driver and nights as a cop. Duarte had been fired from the force after committing two on-duty crimes but had been re-hired after successfully grieving the termination.[46] He had spent time in federal prison after he was convicted of helping to cover up the beating of a prisoner in the police cellblock. He was also convicted of assaulting a man during a traffic stop.

After his return to the force, Duarte's police wages were garnished to pay down a $32,000 civil judgment incurred after he and two other men assaulted a customer in the House of Blues nightclub in Las Vegas. Duarte's codefendants in that case were another Honolulu police officer and a fellow production unit driver.[47]

I checked with the Teamsters Independent Review Board in New York City to ask if they had any interest in Teamsters or organized crime activities in the Islands. An official there declined comment but did say that the IRB had brought charges against Teamsters members for illegal activities connected to movie and television productions in Orlando, Miami, and Chicago.

Death and Ice

The last time I had seen Teamster movie driver Lilo Asiata was outside the federal grand jury investigating the murder of David Walden.

Now Asiata was in the news again, explaining that he had been asleep in his apartment when a crazed meth addict got hold of Asiata's 23-month-old grandson, Cyrus Belt, and threw the toddler from a freeway overpass into midday traffic 30 feet below.

Asiata was not implicated in the horrific crime, except perhaps as a neglectful caregiver who should have been keeping a closer eye on the little boy.

One thing was clear, however: Asiata's Iolani Avenue apartment on the slopes of Punchbowl was ground zero for ice addicts. Nancy Chanco, Asiata's daughter and the mother of Cyrus, wasn't home when her son was murdered. She was smoking ice at a downtown gambling den and would spend the rest of the day shoplifting at Ala Moana Center.[48]

Her boyfriend and fellow ice addict, Shane Mizusawa, had been with Cyrus earlier in the day. The boy had been found by an off-duty police officer sitting in the middle of Iolani Avenue while Mizusawa unloaded his car nearby.

Mizusawa told the officer that Cyrus had briefly wandered away. Mizusawa angrily berated a neighbor, Matthew Higa, who had watched but done nothing when the toddler walked into the busy thoroughfare. The officer gave Cyrus back to Mizusawa. Matthew Higa was the man who later tossed little Cyrus from the overpass.

Mizusawa, Chanco, and Higa had smoked ice together in the past, sometimes with Higa's meth-addicted father, Shelton Higa.[49] In fact, Mizusawa and Chanco had recommended their apartment building as a place for the Higas to live. The Higas moved into an upstairs apartment above the unit occupied by Chanco, Mizusawa, Asiata, and Cyrus.

The child's biological father, David Belt, was in prison for drug offenses. The boy's uncle, Teamster movie driver Philip Asiata, had a terrible drug addiction problem.[50]

Chanco had been investigated previously by child welfare authorities. A state worker was scheduled to check on the welfare of the little boy, but he died before that visit occurred.

Witnesses saw Higa throw Cyrus off a pedestrian overpass and then watched him saunter back toward Punchbowl, where he was sitting beside a bush and smoking a cigarette when he was arrested by police.

Higa had a history of psychiatric problems. He told police that a woman had given him a bag containing the little boy and told him to throw it off the bridge.

Prosecutor Peter Carlisle said in his final argument that Cyrus "lived in a world of ice," surrounded by adults addicted to the drug. The supervision of the toddler was deplorable, Carlisle said, but Higa alone was guilty of murder. Higa "killed that small child" because he was high on ice, the prosecutor said.[51]

At the funeral for Cyrus, the presiding minister turned out to be an ex-convict named Claudio Borge Jr. I had written a story about Borge more than 20 years earlier that quoted federal prosecutors as saying he was a "major organized crime figure" who had trafficked in narcotics and admitted participating in three grisly mob murders.[52]

After serving time for drug crimes (the murder claims were never proved), Borge became a spiritual leader whose work included ministering to prison inmates.

SEX, DRUGS, AND *LOST*

On the same day in 2010, two Teamster drivers who had worked on the hit ABC television series *Lost* appeared in different courts to answer new criminal charges against them.

Reynold Kamekona, who witnessed the Walden murder at Pier 24, was arrested after soliciting an undercover police officer for oral sex. A bag of crystal meth was discovered in his pocket. Kamekona pleaded guilty and was sentenced to five years of probation. The crimes were appended to a criminal record that included felony convictions for auto theft and criminal property damage.[53]

Two hours after Kamekona entered his plea, Philip Asiata—son of Lilo, brother of Nancy Chanco, and uncle of Cyrus Belt—was in another court for new drug offenses.

Asiata's record listed more than 125 arrests and 52 convictions. A psychiatric expert who had examined Asiata said he was unfit for trial because of "polysubstance abuse" and an organic brain injury suffered in a 1995 accident. Dr. Martin Blinder said Asiata told him that "before the accident I was a heroin addict and used crack but I don't do drugs any more. I'm a Teamster."[54]

Blinder reported that Asiata began drinking heavily after "his driver's license was recently taken from him because of purported deficits in his driving ability."

Asiata was in the Teamsters production unit and driving vehicles on *Lost* when he lost his license. Asiata was referred for evaluation to the state-run psychiatric facility, Hawai'i State Hospital. He was eventually pronounced fit for trial, pleaded guilty, and was sentenced to a new five-year term of probation.

TWO MORE VIOLENT DEATHS

Bruce Kamekona—brother of Reynold, past production unit driver, and convicted meth trafficker—killed himself after attacking a former girlfriend with a gun and a knife at a Windward Oahu bowling alley in 2010. The woman was critically injured but survived several stab wounds. Kamekona succumbed to self-inflicted stab wounds.

Two years after Kamekona died, Aaron Torres, a Teamsters production unit official working on the new *Hawaii Five-0* television series, died in a violent struggle with police at his home.[55] Torres was in a cocaine-induced delirium when he died, according to the Honolulu medical examiner. He was asphyxiated by police trying to subdue him. He had a minor criminal record, and the autopsy of his body showed a "history of cocaine abuse."

Torres was working as a Teamsters captain on the *Hawaii Five-0* production, overseeing the drivers and vehicles used to move people and equipment on the show.

Property owned by Torres and his family had been used by George Cambra Movie Production Trucks, Inc., as a vehicle storage site until city inspectors cited the family for violating agricultural zoning restrictions on the property.

Torres' family won a $1.4 million judgment against the police following the killing, according to a 2014 television report.[56]

George Cambra Jr. also worked on the *Hawaii Five-0* show in 2011 but was sidelined by serious drug problems and criminal charges.[57] Cambra forged checks and stole money from the family company, admitting that he used the cash to buy drugs.

George Cambra Sr. told authorities that his son's drug problems were so acute that the younger man believed his dogs were talking to him and that he heard voices emanating up to him from the ground. Cambra Jr. signed a plea agreement and was sentenced to probation.[58]

He continued to work as a Teamsters movie driver on *Hawaii Five-0*, even after he violated the terms of probation on multiple occasions. In October 2013, Cambra stopped meeting his probation officer altogether. An arrest warrant was issued under the state's strict HOPE probation program but went unserved for four months. HOPE—the acronym stands for Hawai'i's Opportunity for Probation with Enforcement—promises immediate arrest and punishment for probation violations. But Cambra was at large, and his drug use continued.

Finally, in February 2014, police stopped Cambra when he was riding a bicycle at night without a light. He gave them a false name, then admitted his identity, and told the officers a HOPE warrant was out for his arrest. A search of his backpack turned up two ice pipes and a small quantity of methamphetamine.

Cambra was charged with new drug offenses—promotion of a dangerous drug and possession of drug paraphernalia. In a new plea deal with prosecutors, Cambra pleaded guilty in both criminal cases and was sentenced to another HOPE five-year probation term.[59]

CHAPTER FIFTEEN

Larry Mehau

Thirty years after Larry Ehukai Mehau was first alleged to be the godfather of organized crime in Hawai'i, the FBI and Honolulu police officers were still identifying him as a mobster.

Through all those years, Mehau was never charged with a crime and remained a friend and political backer of the most powerful people in Hawai'i, with U.S. Senator Daniel Inouye and two governors at the top of the list.

It's an amazing story and an abiding mystery. Is he or isn't he? I don't know the answer. I do know that sworn testimony from numerous Honolulu police officers naming Mehau as a mobster was suppressed by the *Honolulu Advertiser* after the newspaper became part of the Gannett news conglomerate.

I wrote my first investigative Mehau story in 1979, when I found that his security guard company, Hawai'i Protective Association, had hired 12 special deputies to beef up its forces at a Hawaiian-rights demonstration at Hilo Airport on the Big Island of Hawai'i.[1]

Among the group were Cyril Kahale Jr. and two other convicted felons, Gabriel Aio and George Perry Jr., who were close Mehau associates and who would figure in other stories I would write in later years.

State officials said only one of the special guards had the requisite training and licensing to provide security at such a highly charged, potentially violent event. And the exception, former Honolulu police officer Francis Borges, had been fired from HPD for using excessive force against civilians.

Larry Mehau.
GREGORY YAMAMOTO,
PHOTOGRAPHER;
*HONOLULU STAR-
ADVERTISER* COLLECTION;
HAWAI'I STATE ARCHIVES.

A Big Island police official said officers there didn't know who the special guards were. The Hilo cops had concerns about the security detail because they had the look of "street fighters," Deputy Chief Martin Kaaua told me.

"It was kind of a hairy deal for us," Kaaua said. The police identified the men by checking their hotel registrations.

Mehau himself was a former HPD officer who maintained close ties to the department throughout his life. While on the force, Mehau made a name for himself as a no-nonsense cop who specialized in vice busts, particularly gambling offenses, and was an accomplished martial arts expert. And he made important friends while working as a cop, including Dan Inouye and future governors John Burns and George Ariyoshi.

Mehau once testified in court that he had worked on Burns' political campaigns, describing his activities as "just helping." Police officials had ordered officers "not to be involved in politics," Mehau said, but he and his friends did it anyway. They "used to do a lot of background things, tear down old buildings, make signs, things like that. That's when we were on the vice squad, we did a lot of that," he said.

Mehau and Inouye first met when Inouye was a deputy prosecutor and Mehau was a vice officer. Mehau said he worked on Inouye's first political campaign after Inouye "came to the vice office and told us he wanted to enter politics and we helped him."

Mehau was born in Hilo on December 10, 1929.

He attended grammar school on the Big Island, then high school at Kamehameha Schools in Honolulu, where a fellow student was Don Ho.

Mehau graduated in 1948 and attended the University of Hawai'i for two years without graduating. He moved back to the Big Island and was hired as an officer with the police department there.

In early 1953, Mehau moved back to Oahu and applied for a job as an officer at HPD. On his employment application, Mehau said he had been raised on his father's ranch and had worked as a salesman, rancher, and police officer.[2]

Asked if he had ever been convicted of a crime, Mehau said yes—for a "traffic accident" that resulted in a suspended sentence. Asked why he wanted to work for the Honolulu police, Mehau said he had always planned to make his home in Honolulu.

Then, prophetically, Mehau wrote: "Having formally being [sic] employed by the Hawaii Police department, thought it wise and profitable to apply for appointment into this one."

The grammar may have been fractured, but the planning and foresight of the young man were impeccable.

The precise nature of Mehau's earliest work as an HPD officer is unknown, but like other recruits who are unknown to the underworld—and to other officers—he was asked to perform undercover work.

In May 1954, HPD Assistant Chief Arthur Tarbell wrote a report on Mehau's first-year probationary period.[3]

"The subject officer has been assigned exclusively to undercover and investigative work since his entry into the Department," he wrote.

"His background as a uniformed police officer in foot and motor patrol assignments with the Hilo Police Department had early reflected here an established knowledge, ability and self-confidence," the memo continued.

"The subject officer is intelligent and reflects a healthy curiosity and thirst for further police knowledge which has already made him of more than average value in his service with this Department.

"He presents a fine appearance and stands out among his fellow officers in strength, prowess and physical conditioning," the memo continued.

"Most important of all, the subject officer's character and integrity have been rather severely tested and found wholesome. By nature of certain of his investigative assignments, some personnel of the Department, having apparent cause for concern, have sought to intimidate, reflect upon and ultimately dissuade him from an honest performance of his assignments," Tarbell wrote.

"In this process, he has endured jibes and innuendo threatening unpopularity and desertion by fellow officers in times of distress. The loyalty of this officer, therefore, has been made quite apparent and has been demonstrated at no little cost to his personal feelings. His acceptance among the rank and file and superiors, nevertheless, has become manifest, especially among those officers who respect efficient performance of duty in keeping with instructions issued by superiors," Tarbell wrote.

"The subject officer is highly recommended for retention in service," the memo concluded.

By 1954, Mehau was assigned to HPD's Vice Division and also began making a name for himself as a martial arts expert.

In a 1957 demonstration staged for a national police chiefs' convention held at the Royal Hawaiian Hotel, Sergeant Mehau broke single bricks in half with bare-handed karate chops. He then moved on to double-stacked bricks, but they crumbled instead of breaking cleanly. Mehau, described in an *Advertiser* news story as "a determined man," kept whacking new pairs of bricks until "stomachs began turning" in the audience.

Arthur Tarbell, who hosted the event and had since been promoted to deputy chief, finally had to stop Mehau. The sergeant then suspended himself between two chairs as three other officers placed a 300-pound rock on his stomach and bashed it with a nine-pound sledgehammer.

"Sergeant Mehau didn't even grunt," the story said.[4]

Mehau also made news as an amateur sumo wrestler, winning a Hawai'i championship in 1957 and later winning five of six tournaments in Japan.

In 1958, Mehau's work in vice landed him in public trouble. He was suspended for 10 days and demoted to patrolman for using what police officials termed "irregular but not illegal procedures." It was called the "sweetening case" because vice officers were paying informants cash to come up with tips about illegal activities. The money came from a police evidence fund and was used to "induce informants to bring cases in," a police investigation found.[5]

The practice was known as "sweetening the bird," and Mehau told superiors that he had come up with the idea in 1954, according to police records.

Eleven other officers in the gambling detail were involved, but only Mehau was both suspended and demoted.

Mehau had a "close association with a man who has an extensive criminal record" and was taking the man with him on vice raids, news accounts said at the time.

Tarbell announced the personnel action against Mehau but described him as an "outstanding" vice officer. "His principal faults were indiscretion and poor judgment developing from his zealous efforts to achieve new heights in vice arrests," Tarbell said.[6]

The *Honolulu Star-Bulletin* reported at the time that in a year as head of the morals squad, Mehau "made 224 arrests, charged 199 persons and brought in $11,134 in revenue from bond and bail money." And in 11 months as gambling squad sergeant, Mehau "raided 485 gambling games, arrested 4,126 persons and brought in $62,933.90 in revenue," the newspaper reported.

If those numbers are accurate, Mehau was averaging one and a half raids every single day of those 11 months. Even if the numbers are inflated, Honolulu was plainly a wide-open town back in those days.

It turned out that Mehau's demotion never actually took place. Tarbell said later that the plan was to demote him for six months and then restore him to his sergeant's rank, but such a move was impossible under civil service rules. So the demotion was cancelled.[7]

Mehau's informant in the sweetening case was a known police character named Antone N. Texeira. Mehau acknowledged taking Texeira along with him during vice raids—a violation of police procedures—and admitted that during one raid of a cockfight, Texeira got "carried away" and personally placed one of the gamblers under arrest. "He was cautioned often about staying clear of any action that might take place," Mehau said of Texeira.[8]

While the sweetening case was under investigation by police, Texeira was arrested on a charge of forcing an 18-year-old woman into prostitution. HPD Assistant Chief Leon Straus said that when Texeira was arrested, he bragged to the arresting officers that he was "a big-time gambling operator."[9]

The procuring charge against Texeira was later dropped for lack of evidence.

While at HPD, Mehau also worked in what was called the Metro Squad, which *Advertiser* columnist Eddie Sherman said was a "special trouble-shooting unit" of the department. Metro Squad members wore street clothes, drove unmarked cars, and "looked for trouble," Sherman wrote, adding that he rode with the officers on almost a weekly basis for years and became good friends with Mehau.

Among Mehau's other duties on the force, Sherman wrote, was providing personal security to VIPs and visiting dignitaries. Marlon Brando prowled around Honolulu with Mehau, as did another actor, Robert Conrad, star of the television series *Hawaiian Eye*. Dignitaries protected by

Mehau included President Dwight Eisenhower, Vice President Richard Nixon, the kings of Nepal and Thailand, German Chancellor Konrad Adenauer, and President Sukarno of Indonesia.

In 1962, Mehau was awarded a lease to ranch land in the spectacular Kamuela area on the slopes of the Mauna Kea volcano on the Big Island. The lease came from the Department of Hawaiian Home Lands, a state agency that holds former Hawaiian crown land in trust for native Hawaiians.

Mehau said in a memo to Chief Dan Liu—routed first to Deputy Chief Tarbell—that he "had been at the head of the list of applicants [for Big Island pastoral land] for many years and was informed February 19, 1962 that three lots would be available."[10]

He said he planned to move to the Big Island in about a year, giving him enough time to "complete whatever is needed before a family could move onto the lot."

Then Mehau made an odd request. He was working in vice but asked to be transferred to another post.

"The undersigned has always enjoyed the work of the viceman but feels that for the department's good he should be transferred out," Mehau wrote. "This would not give anyone an opening to comment on the possibilities the undersigned would have while spending his last year with the Vice Division," he said.[11]

Mehau's meaning was obviously clear to his superiors, who assigned him in June 1962 to be the sergeant in charge of the HPD canine unit.

That assignment did not stop Sergeant Mehau from continuing to associate with underworld characters, police records show. In a February 19, 1963, memo, Assistant Chief Dewey Mookini wrote that on a visit the previous day to the police pistol range, where police dogs were trained, he discovered Mehau with gambler Walter W. C. "Hotcha" Hong. (Hong was later the lead defendant in the ill-fated 1971 federal crackdown on illegal Hawai'i gambling.)

Mookini reported that Hong's personal dog was being trained by HPD personnel: "I asked 'Hotcha' if his dog is being trained regularly, and he said, well, off-and-on."

"Having a known gambler with his dog at the Pistol Range where our Canine Corps and instructors are being trained is not the proper thing," Mookini said.

"This is a violation of the instructions issued to him [Mehau] sometime ago in not allowing gamblers there to be trained because the Department does not wish to be criticized by people," Mookini wrote.[12]

Mehau was then transferred out of the canine unit and assigned to the Traffic Accident Investigation Bureau.

He resigned from HPD April 15, 1964, collecting disability benefits because of a service-related injury.

Mehau's friend Hotcha Hong was no run-of-the-mill gambler. By the time of the dog-training incident, he already had a lengthy arrest record for gambling offenses. One of the earliest stories in news files about Hong, in 1950, said he had been charged with running an illegal casino on Nuuanu Avenue in downtown Honolulu.

The charge was dismissed, on a motion by prosecutor Kazuo Oyama, after Wong's defense lawyer argued that the search warrant used by police in the raid of Hong's game was defective. When Hong was arrested again on gambling promotion charges the following year, his new defense lawyer, former prosecutor Kazuo Oyama, successfully disputed the legality of the new search warrant.

When syndicate warfare in Honolulu erupted in paroxysms of violence in the late 1960s and early 1970s, Mehau was splitting time between his Big Island ranch and building his Honolulu-based security guard company into a major statewide business force.

Mehau first invested in Hawai'i Protective Association after it was founded by former HPD officers Thomas and Gerald Freeman; later, he took a controlling interest in the firm.

Mehau was also making a name for himself in politics and government. In 1970, Governor John Burns, a close Mehau friend who also happened to be a former HPD officer, appointed Mehau to the state Board of Land and Natural Resources, an influential agency that oversaw a vast empire of state property that included parks and recreation facilities, forest reserves, beaches, shorelines, and prime commercial areas that were leased to private individuals and companies.

In 1973, Hawai'i Protective Association landed its first major government contract, a $1.4 million, one-year job to provide security at airports around the state. The work previously had been performed by off-duty police officers.

The HPA bid for the airport contract was slightly lower than competing offers from national firms Wackenhut Corp. and Burns Security.

The next time the contract was put out to bid, Burns won the job but immediately found itself under intense scrutiny from state officials, who alleged that the company was not meeting specifications of the contract and threatened to cancel it. Burns officials cried foul, and eventually the Federal Aviation Administration had to step in, ordering the state to back off and allow Burns time to become operational.

HPA won back the airport work in 1977. The contract had grown to a two-year deal, and HPA was paid $1.7 million per year.

Then, in 1979, HPA was the sole bidder for the new, $10 million, four-year contract. Officials of both Wackenhut and Burns told me they didn't bother to bid because they felt the contract specifications had been written in such a way as to exclude bids from anyone but HPA, the incumbent contractor.[13]

Gerry Freeman, by then the head of another local security guard firm, disputed that contention, saying anyone could have competed fairly for the contract. But Freeman acknowledged that he hadn't bid for the work and still held a minority interest in HPA.

HPA was also the sole bidder for security work at the state's Aloha Stadium facility.

George Ariyoshi, then in his first full term as governor, was forced to publicly defend the HPA contracts, saying that his personal and political friendship with Mehau played no role in the contract awards. "There has been a great deal of talk of my friendship with the man who has the airport security contract," Ariyoshi said at a news conference. "But I want to make one thing clear, no one buys my friendship. I do what I believe is right for the state and its people."

The contract was awarded fair and square, he continued. "I don't want anyone to believe there was anything shady because there wasn't."[14]

Mehau had been Ariyoshi's state campaign coordinator when he was elected lieutenant governor in 1972. When Governor Burns died in office in 1975, Ariyoshi became governor and then won his first full term in the office in 1976.

By 1978, the godfather allegations about Mehau were in full throat.

They were first made in February 1977 by a local television reporter, Scott Shirai, who charged that an unnamed member of a state board was connected to a heroin sale that had been busted by federal agents and police at the Punchbowl National Memorial Cemetery of the Pacific.[15] "Several meetings were held between this state board member with those arrested in the bust, sometimes at the apartment of a well-known Waikiki entertainer," Shirai alleged.

That was a plain reference to Don Ho and was strikingly similar to testimony delivered several years earlier in a federal court trial by syndicate member Roy Ryder, who said he had attended a meeting of mob members in Ho's apartment.

Ho later said that, while some mobsters were "friends of mine from before" and his door was "always open to them," he had no involvement in criminal activities.

In addition to alluding to Ho, Shirai's report also made clear references to George Ariyoshi and to newly resigned Honolulu police officer Raymond Scanlan, one of the men arrested and later convicted in the heroin case. "One of those arrested worked for this entertainer and was also directed to act as a bodyguard for a candidate for statewide office in last year's election," Shirai's story said.

Scanlan had done part-time work for Ho and provided personal security for Ariyoshi. After he was arrested in the heroin case, Scanlan went to work for Don Ho's television show.

I would write more stories in later years about Scanlan after he got out of prison and went to work in the Teamsters Union production unit, which provided drivers for film and television productions in the Islands.

And I also covered the trial of Scanlan and others accused of participating in the murder of city prosecutor Charles Marsland's son. Scanlan and his codefendants were acquitted in that trial, which was based almost entirely on the testimony of killer Ronald Ching, another man who frequented Ho's dressing room and who also worked with Scanlan and numerous other convicted felons in the Teamsters production unit.

Larry Mehau, above, and Charles Marsland, below, attended an opening-day ceremony of state legislature.
KEN SAKAMOTO, PHOTOGRAPHER; *HONOLULU STAR-ADVERTISER* COLLECTION; HAWAI'I STATE ARCHIVES.

Following the "godfather" newscast in February 1977, a little-known Maui publication called the *Valley Isle* alleged that Mehau was the godfather of Hawai'i's underworld. Several news organizations—not the *Advertiser*—repeated the allegations, as did a member of the state legislature, Kinau Boyd Kamali'i.

The *Advertiser* published a story about the controversy only after Mehau filed a $51 million libel suit. I was deeply involved in covering the Kukui Plaza scandal, and the godfather story was assigned to Walter Wright.[16]

KHON and Shirai eventually settled the suit with a $42,500 payment to Mehau.[17]

The complaint against Kamali'i and other news organizations, except United Press International, was dismissed. UPI eventually settled, reportedly for $35,000.[18]

Mehau defended himself by asserting that he was following the Hawaiian principle of *kokua* when he occasionally helped friends with favors or helped to mediate disputes. *Kokua* is closely related to aloha—the spirit of generosity and openness that permeates Hawaiian culture. To *kokua* means to help someone in need without any expectation of reward or compensation.

Mehau said that, at the request of local law enforcement, he had *kokua'*d by resolving disagreements between factions of organized crime that threatened to become dangerously violent. He knew police, he knew crooks, so he tried to *kokua*.

Mehau pal and sometime employee Herbert Naone once said that complete strangers would occasionally seek Mehau's *kokua* with personal problems like overhanging tree branches in their backyards.

Mehau became the subject of a lengthy criminal investigation, called Operation Firebird, that was conducted by HPD and the U.S. Drug Enforcement Administration. A separate investigation of Mehau by the IRS, called Operation Koko, was also undertaken.

While those probes were underway, I turned out the Hilo airport guards story in May 1979.[19]

That story was followed two weeks later by another about close Mehau associate George Perry, one of the special Hilo guards and a Don Ho pal, who was a principal in a company that was making more than $6,000 a month in illegal "sandwich lease" deals on state waterfront property.[20]

The company, GRG Enterprises, held the master lease on the property, at Kewalo Basin near Aloha Tower, and had subleased to a variety of other companies at substantially higher prices than what GRG was paying the state. Terms of the master lease required GRG to obtain advance approval of such subleases, but it hadn't done so.

A partner with Perry in GRG was another Mehau friend, former Detroit Lions football player Rockne Freitas, who would later become a high-ranking official of the University of Hawai'i and of Bishop Estate and Kamehameha Schools.

State officials told me they were investigating the situation and contemplating legal action against GRG.

That never happened.

Two decades later, in July 1999, *Advertiser* Capitol Bureau Chief Kevin Dayton reported that the state had decided to write off $541,000 in back rent owed to the state by GRG.[21] The decision was made after Freitas told the state that if GRG was required to pay the money, it would declare bankruptcy. The company's only asset was the leasehold waterfront property, which the state owned. And the state also decided to waive another undetermined amount of environmental cleanup costs that GRG was obligated to pay because underground fuel storage tanks had leaked and contaminated the site.

In mid-1979, I was tipped about the Arthur Baker kidnapping-murder case. I wrote the Baker disappearance story without mentioning Ronald Ching—I had nothing on the record to tie him to it.[22]

Six years later, the story came back to life when Arthur Baker's bones were exhumed from the sands of Makaha.

When the Firebird and Koko investigations were quietly closed with no charges in 1980, I wrote the story: "If anything, the investigations may have served to broaden the mystique which has built up around the physically-imposing Mehau."[23]

"Investigators found Mehau to have established a remarkable network of personal ties with rich and powerful figures of high and low repute throughout Hawaii and the Pacific Basin," I reported.

One of the law enforcement officials who oversaw the criminal investigations, U.S. Organized Crime Strike Force attorney Daniel Bent, later testified that Mehau was "a significant organized crime figure with substantial influence in state government." Bent also said under oath that he believed the Firebird investigation would have resulted in a criminal indictment of Mehau if witnesses had not been frightened for their lives.

Bent's sworn deposition testimony was delivered in preparation for the 1992 state court trial of an invasion of privacy lawsuit filed by Mehau against Rick Reed, one of the original disseminators of the godfather allegation through the *Valley Isle* newspaper on Maui back in 1977.

Reed had become a public relations assistant to Honolulu prosecutor Charles Marsland, and in 1985 Reed once again leveled the godfather charges, publicly releasing many investigative records compiled during Firebird by the DEA. That brought the lawsuit, which was repeatedly delayed but finally went to trial in 1992.

Bent's testimony was not heard by the jury in the *Mehau v. Reed* trial. Circuit Judge Wilfred Watanabe ruled that it depended on information not disseminated by Reed.

The trial jury voted to dismiss the complaint against Reed, but Watanabe overturned the jury's decision and ordered a new trial. The jury's verdict came despite a "great weight of credible evidence" to the contrary, Watanabe ruled.

Reed and Mehau settled the case after Reed issued a tepid apology for invading Mehau's privacy. But Reed refused to recant the godfather charge.

I found myself writing another obituary of the godfather controversy in the aftermath of the trial. "There was no 'smoking gun' in the trial to confirm, as federal agents alleged in a 1977 Firebird memo: 'Larry Ehukai Mehau is considered the single most important figure in the organized crime hierarchy in the state of Hawaii,'" my story said.[24]

While the jury did not hear Bent's testimony, it did hear from former HPD Chief Francis Keala and prosecutor Keith Kaneshiro, who testified that they knew of no evidence to support the godfather charge.

John Y. Y. Lee, head of the Honolulu DEA office during the Firebird probe, testified in another deposition that his agents followed Mehau everywhere he went and sought information about his business dealings and associates around the globe.

At one point, Lee noted, DEA agents followed Mehau to a meeting in Los Angeles with Marcus Lipsky, a one-time Chicago syndicate figure who had settled on the West Coast to pursue investments and philanthropy.

Among Lipsky's business interests was a management deal with Don Ho, so it was hardly surprising that Mehau would have the occasional sit-down with Lipsky.

The DEA agents also tracked Mehau to a major Democratic Party fund-raiser in Los Angeles. Given Mehau's warm ties to U.S. senators Daniel Inouye and Daniel Akaka, as well as a multitude of other politicians, the fund-raiser appearance was hardly sinister or even surprising.

"He did meet with Marcus Lipsky [and we] put him at a thousand-dollar-a-plate dinner for a National Democratic Convention," Lee testified. "That's it. Couldn't see anything with dope or anything else. He knew a lot of people. He knew governors and he knew law enforcement people from rank and file up. This guy knows everybody. I think we all agree to that. He knows good guys and he knows bad guys," the agent testified.

But the investigators couldn't make a criminal case against Mehau, Lee said. "We did put him together with ex-felons and Marcus Lipsky in L.A., but we couldn't tie anything into Larry Mehau, his associations with these people, whether he was involved in criminal activities. If we had that information, I assure you Mr. Mehau would be behind bars today," Lee said.[25] IRS agents conducted what's known as a "net worth" investigation of Mehau—a painstaking examination of his personal and business financial records to assess whether his expenditures were within his income.

What they found was *kokua* in action. Mehau frequently didn't pay for anything. Friends or acquaintances who saw the chance to show him a little *kokua* would pick up the tab for him. Maybe they were reciprocating a previous kindness; maybe they were just acting out of the goodness of their hearts. Whatever it was, it didn't fit within the construct of an IRS net worth investigation.

The trial had its lighter moments. Reed, who was not an attorney but represented himself in the case, at one point was exploring Mehau's widespread connections in politics and entertainment.

In my recap of the trial, I wrote that Mehau "was well-known for producing annual opening day entertainment for the state Senate at [Senate President Richard] Wong's request. With Mehau standing in the wings, stars such as Don Ho, Al Harrington and others would show up to give the session a musical kickoff.

"Mehau said at the trial the entertainers didn't like getting up that early, but didn't know how to say no to Wong.

"There were jokes that the entertainers didn't know how to say no to Mehau.

"During the trial, Reed asked Mehau about those legislative parties. Reed related the story of ventriloquist Freddie Morris causing his wooden dummy 'Moku' to say that he didn't want to entertain the senators but 'he'd rather do what Mehau asked than end up a part of [Governor] George Ariyoshi's desk.'

"Mehau didn't remember the line, but said, 'That's pretty good.'"

One of Mehau's main attorneys in the trial, Stacy Moniz, later lost his license to practice law after he was convicted of federal tax crimes. During that tax case, Moniz himself filed evidence showing that Honolulu police considered Moniz to be a member of organized crime affiliated with Mehau associate George Perry and Teamster Union movie driver Blaine Kaakimaka.

While the Reed trial was underway, I finally managed to turn out a story that was originally written six years earlier but wasn't published at the personal request of HPD Chief Douglas Gibb.

In 1985, while reviewing new business filings, I came across a new partnership formed by several of Mehau's close associates and a couple of law enforcement agents who were close to Marsland. Called Circle Six, the partnership was formed by ex-HPD officer Herbert Naone Jr., who went to work for Hawai'i Protective Association after he left the police force because of his involvement in the 1975 armed robbery of an illegal gambling game on Kauai.

Circle Six was formed as a cattle-ranching venture on Central Oahu property owned by Amfac, Inc., a very large business conglomerate involved in agriculture, real estate development, hotel operations, and retailing. HPA had a contract to provide security services for Amfac, and Mehau was a personal friend of Amfac chief executive Henry Walker, who made the property available to the Circle Six partners.

Besides Naone, other partners included two of the Hilo airport special deputies: convicted felon and longtime close Mehau associate Gabriel "Gabe" Aio and Theodore "Joe" Hackbarth, a Carpenter's Union aide who at the time was facing a felony assault charge in a union-related beating of a building contractor. (The charge was later reduced to a misdemeanor.)

HPD Criminal Intelligence Unit officer Arthur Nishida and former HPD officer Frank Perreira, who was then working as an investigator in Marsland's office, were also among the partners.

So I had a story demonstrating that Nishida and Perreira, while investigating organized crime for police and prosecutors, were in business with convicted criminals.

But Gibb told me and *Advertiser* editors that Nishida's participation in Circle Six was "viewed as an excellent intelligence operation" that had brought the police "closer to Mehau than ever before." He asked us to withhold publication of the story. If the story ran, he said, HPD would have no choice but to tell Nishida to pull out of the business. I argued that such publicity might in fact push Nishida further into the confidence of Mehau and company, and I argued to my editors that we had a story in hand and ought to run with it.

I lost. We didn't publish.

Six years later, Nishida and Perreira testified as character witnesses for Mehau in the Reed libel trial. Nishida said he believed Marsland's office had unfairly targeted Mehau for investigation. Perreira testified that he did not believe the godfather allegations about Mehau.

I wrote a story revealing their past personal business ties to Mehau, Naone, Aio, and the others.[26]

The Circle Six arrangement demonstrated both Mehau's ability to *kokua* and his far-flung network of connections throughout Island society.

He testified at trial that he personally worked out the deal with Henry Walker of Amfac. By subleasing 3,000 acres of its agricultural land to Circle Six for ranching purposes, Amfac saved some $200,000 in annual property taxes, Mehau said.

It also brought several of Mehau's close, felonious associates into business with two police officers who were investigating organized crime. Those two officers later testified on Mehau's behalf in court.

In 1989, another tantalizing tidbit about Mehau and his mob connections came to light with the announcement that he was part of a group that planned to start a new interisland air cargo business called Hawai'i Pacific Air, Inc. I read *Advertiser* reporter Kit Smith's article about the venture with interest. He reported that Mehau's partners in the deal were local tour company owner Robert Iwamoto Jr. and a "Las Vegas investor" named Alvin Baron.

I could hardly believe my eyes. Alvin Baron?

Baron had once been the assets manager of the scandal-ridden Teamsters Union Central States Pension Fund and had served time in federal prison for helping to loot that fund. In his fine book *The Teamsters*, author Steven Brill described Baron as "a notoriously uncouth mobster" who had served for years as a protégé to infamous Chicago "Outfit" figure Allen Dorfman.[27]

Baron replaced Dorfman at the Teamsters pension fund after Dorfman, a close associate of Jimmy Hoffa, was sent to prison for a separate kickback conviction. (In the film *Casino*, the "Andy Stone" character played by actor Alan King was based on Dorfman.)

Dorfman was a regular visitor to Hawai'i, usually timing his trips to coincide with the Hawaiian Open golf tournament. He was regularly surveilled by police and FBI agents during those visits, and the watchers saw Dorfman socialize with a wide variety of local residents, often at Matteo's restaurant on Kuhio Avenue in Waikiki.

The Hawai'i jaunts stopped after Dorfman was gunned down in a mob hit outside Chicago in 1983. The murder occurred shortly after Dorfman, Chicago mafia capo Joseph "Joey the Clown" Lombardo, and Teamsters International President Roy Williams had been convicted of the attempted bribery of U.S. Senator Howard Cannon of Nevada.

In a 2011 book about the Chicago mafia, *The Last Dance*, former Chicago police officer James Jack said Dorfman and Lombardo were such close friends that they used to take golfing vacations together to Hawai'i.[28]

I talked to Kit Smith about his story, and we worked together on a follow-up article. I found a very good source who said that Mehau had been "a friend or at least an acquaintance" of Baron's for several years. Two businessmen who had met Baron during a recent visit to Hawai'i told Kit that Baron more than once had mentioned his past ties to the Central States Pension Fund but said nothing about his criminal past.

The attorney for Hawai'i Pacific Air, Tom Foley, gulped when I told him about Baron's background, saying, "That's news to me." He wondered if it might cause the venture licensing problems with federal transportation authorities.

Mehau as usual wasn't talking, but I did manage to speak briefly with Baron in a phone call to Las Vegas. After I explained who I was and what I was calling about, he said, "I don't talk to reporters" and hung up. He was pretty couth about it, though.[29]

The air cargo business never got off the ground and was dissolved a few years later.

A year after the Alvin Baron story, *Advertiser* reporter Andy Yamaguchi and I found Mehau and Iwamoto—the other partner in Hawai'i Pacific Air—involved in a tangled real estate deal on the Big Island that had infuriated state official William Paty.[30] It seemed that a large piece of prime oceanfront property on the Kona coast that the state wanted to acquire for a beach park had been sold three times in two weeks, with the price increasing by leaps and bounds in each transaction.

The first sale, to Iwamoto, had a price tag of $17 million. Iwamoto "flipped" the land on the same day to a Japanese-owned company called Tenzan Corp. for $23 million.

Tenzan Corp. turned around and sold the property 12 days later to another Japanese-owned company, Blue Point Land Development, for $30 million.

Larry Mehau was chairman of the board of directors of Blue Point. A Japanese national named Chiyoko Isayama was the president of both Blue Point and Tenzan. The companies shared the same business address, a home on Kahala Avenue in Honolulu owned by Isayama.

The attorney who represented the original seller was Tom Foley, the same lawyer who had handled legal matters for Mehau, Iwamoto, and Baron in Pacific Air Cargo.

Foley told me that he had disclosed his Iwamoto conflict to the seller, who waived it and told him to proceed. I also found that a lawyer in Foley's firm had represented Tenzan Corp. in another real estate matter, but Foley said he was unaware of that.

Foley said there was a lot of demand for the land, and the various sales were arm's-length and legitimate.

That's not how Bill Paty, chairman of the state Department of Land and Natural Resources, saw it. He accused the parties of colluding with each other to drive up the price the state would eventually have to pay for the property.

"It would appear [that there] was collusion," Paty told me. "It's land speculation at the expense of the people."

Ironically, Mehau had once served on the board of directors of Paty's department. Paty went on at some length about the bad smell wafting up from the land deals.

"It looks like an in-house arrangement of some sort to pump up the price. It's got to be some kind of nefarious-type scheme," he said. "I'm real unhappy about it and I think the people of the state of Hawai'i ought to be unhappy, too."

Paty and the state refused to negotiate a purchase of the property from Blue Point, choosing instead to file condemnation proceedings in court.

At the close of that case, the state agreed to pay $23 million for the land: the middle-ground price paid by Tenzan to Iwamoto but $7 million short of Blue Point's price.

That resolution preserved the $6-million-in-one-day profit of Mehau's in-state business associate, Iwamoto, but washed away the paper profits of the Japanese investors.

Patricia Tummons, founder and editor of *Environment Hawai'i*, a highly regarded publication headquartered on the Big Island, later reported that documents filed in the condemnation case showed how the Foley-Iwamoto-Mehau connections worked.[31]

Foley was representing the original property owner in sales talks with the state when Iwamoto, also a client, heard about the purchase opportunity. Iwamoto knew that Mehau was showing Big Island properties to Japanese investor Isayama, Tummons reported.

So Iwamoto assembled a deal, offering to buy the land for $17 million and sell it for $23 million. Both offers were accepted and booked on the same day, but nobody told the state, which had been on the verge of offering $17.1 million for the property—$100,000 more than Iwamoto paid, Tummons said.

Mehau described himself as a facilitator who introduced Iwamoto to Isayama.

"I just wanted to help," Mehau said in a deposition, Tummons reported.

Isayama told Mehau that she wanted to build him an oceanfront house on the property, but he assured her that wasn't necessary, Tummons reported.

Kokua.

While the condemnation case was being litigated, Foley became the target of an unrelated criminal case. Already convicted once of drunk driving, Foley was charged with the same offense in 1990.

That case was dismissed in 1993, but two years later, Foley did it again. His BMW smashed into another car at midnight on a Honolulu street. The driver of the other vehicle was killed, and his wife was seriously injured.

Foley's blood-alcohol level was triple the legal limit. He was convicted of negligent homicide and sentenced to 10 years in prison.

Foley served several years of that term before Governor Ben Cayetano granted him a full pardon in 2000. Cayetano said Foley had been a model prisoner, had accepted full responsibility for his crime, and worked very hard to help the family of the man he killed.

While Foley's legal problems melted away in the new millennium, new legal actions were being undertaken in federal court that would result in prison terms for other associates of Larry Mehau and a revival of the organized crime allegations that had swirled around him for the previous three decades.

One case, a police detective's whistle-blower lawsuit filed against HPD, eventually yielded thousands of pages of records about organized crime in Hawai'i and the Honolulu Police Department's connections to the mob.

Much of the material was originally sealed from public view, but the *Advertiser*, at my urging, sought access to the records. Over four long years, the secret records were gradually opened to the public in federal court.

The first batch was unsealed in 2003 but was heavily redacted at the insistence of HPD, which claimed the material contained confidential details of ongoing investigations and other law enforcement matters.

More disclosures followed as the *Honolulu Advertiser* and its attorneys, led by Jeffrey Portnoy, disputed and disproved those claims to confidentiality.

Still, the department and attorneys for the city fought on, even after the lawsuit, brought by Detective Kenneth Kamakana, was settled with a $650,000 payment to the officer and his lawyers.

The final secrets that the department had fought so long and so hard to keep were disgorged in 2006 after the U.S. Ninth Circuit Court of Appeals ruled in favor of the *Advertiser*.

They centered on Larry Mehau and his associates, George Perry Jr. and Gabriel Aio, who were repeatedly identified as suspected organized crime figures by officers in HPD's elite Criminal Intelligence Unit.

The material also revealed that some CIU officers, including the captain in charge of the unit, Milton Olmos, had alarmingly close ties to Mehau's associates. Other officers and FBI agents were so distrustful of the CIU that they believed ongoing organized crime investigations had been compromised by leaks from the unit.

The records were contained in a lawsuit filed by Kamakana against Police Chief Lee Donohue, Olmos, and HPD after Kamakana was forced out of the CIU and investigated by HPD's Internal Affairs office.

Included in the unsealed records were sworn depositions from CIU officers Alexander Ahlo, Llewellyn Kaeo, Tenari Maafala, Wesley Wong, and Kamakana himself that said Mehau and Perry had been identified as organized crime figures.[32]

The records also showed that Olmos was a personal friend of Perry.

"I've known him for many years, [he's] been my friend before I became a police officer," Olmos testified about Perry. Olmos said he knew of no evidence that Perry was an organized crime figure.

Olmos was asked by Kamakana's lawyer, Mark Bennett, if he had "ever seen any intelligence indicating that [Perry is] an organized crime figure."

Olmos replied, "Allegations." But he said none of the allegations caused him any concerns about having Perry as a friend.

I interviewed Olmos, who told me that Perry had "always been a fair person with me and I've never had any problems with him."

The police "haven't had any kind of confirmed documentation" linking Perry to organized crime, Olmos said.

"It's like Larry Mehau," Olmos continued. "He's been regarded as organized crime, [the] godfather, and we've had a lot of investigations into those types of allegations and we've never come up with anything to directly tie him into any type of organized crime."[33]

Donohue and Olmos denied any wrongdoing in the Kamakana civil suit and were dismissed as defendants shortly before the city settled the case in 2003.

"We were investigated by Internal Affairs, the FBI and the prosecutor's office and not one investigation found us guilty of any type of wrongdoing," Olmos said.

Donohue said of the Kamakana case: "It just seems like it never ends, it never goes away."

Donohue and Olmos went to work for a private security guard firm (not Hawai'i Protective Association) after retiring from HPD.

The release of the Kamakana case files about Mehau came not long after the FBI publicly identified Mehau as a "long-time Hawai'i organized crime figure." The information was contained in the records of a criminal investigation that snared Mehau's friend and colleague Herbert Naone Jr. in a public corruption case.

Mehau refused to talk to me about the Kamakana or Naone allegations.

His daughter, Dana Mehau-Vericella, noted that her father was "never charged with anything." Perry did not respond to requests for comment.

Copies of the Kamakana case allegations were given to Perry by private attorney Eric Seitz, representing Perry's son Bruce, whose name also appeared in the Kamakana case records.

"I didn't hear back from them," Seitz said after he had given the paperwork to the Perrys. "They don't want to say anything."

Seitz said the allegations made in the Kamakana case records are "just rumor and innuendo. I suggest to you that these are not the [type of] facts that stories are made of."

Another close associate of Mehau and Perry who was repeatedly identified in the Kamakana case files as an organized crime figure, Gabe Aio, also declined comment. Aio was supplied copies of the allegations against him in the Kamakana files, but his attorney, Reginald Minn, said Aio "prefers not to comment."

Aio was a central figure in several events that led to Kamakana's ouster from CIU and the filing of the whistle-blower lawsuit.

Records in the case disclosed that CIU officer Alexander "Charley Boy" Ahlo shocked the local law enforcement community when he unexpectedly brought Aio and convicted mob killer Henderson "Henny Boy" Ahlo (half-brother of Alex Ahlo) to a statewide police intelligence conference at a Waikiki hotel.

At the time, Aio was the target of a joint FBI-HPD undercover investigation of illegal gambling operations in Chinatown. Henderson Ahlo was on parole for the 1977 gangland murder of gambling figure Benjamin Madama on the Big Island.

Several officers attending the conference quickly left the hospitality suite when Detective Ahlo and his two guests arrived, according to case files.

Former CIU captain Harry Auld said he was "appalled" by the appearance of Gabe Aio at the conference.[34] Auld said of Aio: "Without a doubt he was an organized crime figure."

Aio at the time "had a legitimate job" as head of security at the Matson shipping container yard, Auld said, "but he was definitely an organized crime figure going back to his youthful days and his association with Mr. Larry Mehau on the Big Island and his control, not promotion, but control of gambling games in the downtown Honolulu area."

Officer Ahlo said he brought Aio to the conference at the request of a Maui police executive, an assertion that was later denied by the Maui official, according to the records.

Ahlo later apologized for his action and was "counseled" by Olmos about it.

After Aio was indicted in the gambling case, fliers advertising a "Golf for Gabe" legal fund-raiser for Aio were distributed around HPD, according to the court files.

Detective Ahlo told FBI agent Dan Kelly that he "did not believe any current members of HPD would go to this tournament, but he expected retired members to attend," Kelly reported.

"Detective Ahlo acknowledged that he has golfed in the past with Aio . . . [and] advised that there was also a luau fundraiser being planned to raise money for the Aio defense fund," Kelly reported.[35]

In the Chinatown case, police officer Earl Koanui pretended to be a corrupt detective and collected "protection" money from gambling figures like Aio. The investigation was code-named "Ikapono" and was jointly conducted by the FBI and officers from HPD's narcotics-vice unit.

Officials involved in the investigation had attempted to exclude the CIU from the case because of concerns about the loyalty of some officers there, according to the Kamakana files.

"There were some CIU officers who we felt we could not trust," HPD officer Gerrit Kurihara testified.

Koanui, the HPD officer who masqueraded as a corrupt cop, worried that if CIU officers knew about his role in the case, the investigation might be compromised and his life would be endangered, according to deposition testimony from Kurihara.

"Did Earl ever indicate to you that because of the CIU officers' relationships with some of the targets, he had concerns for his safety?" Kurihara was asked by Mark Bennett. "Oh yes, sir," Kurihara said.

"In general it was decided early on that we will not inform CIU and we requested our command not to inform CIU of what Ikapono was designed to do," Kurihara testified.[36] Shortly before a scheduled meeting between Aio and Koanui, agents and police officers who had arranged to secretly videotape the meeting were alarmed to see a car with five CIU officers arrive on the scene. The car was driven by Lee Donohue Jr., the son of the chief, and the passengers included Alexander Ahlo and Olmos.

The watching videotape team, concealed in a van outside a bar part-owned by Aio, hurriedly called Koanui and told him to delay his arrival at the meeting.

They then videotaped the CIU officers, who were met on the sidewalk by Aio associate Steve Crouch. One or two of the officers "embraced" Crouch, and there were "handshakes, back-slapping kind of thing" before all the men went into the bar, Kurihara said. The officers stayed inside for a half hour and then left.

The Koanui meeting then took place without incident, said Kurihara.

One of the CIU officers told Kurihara the next day that the meeting was one of several visits the five officers had made to "various places" the previous evening because they were "using up excess overtime," the Kamakana documents show.

Asked to explain, Kurihara said, "If you don't use what [overtime] you're allocated this year, then next year you get less."

After Aio, Crouch, and numerous other defendants were indicted in the Chinatown gambling case, CIU officers including Olmos and Ahlo met with and secretly tape-recorded one of the defendants, Mari Rose Tangi, despite express notification from the FBI that meeting Tangi without her lawyer present would be improper.

Olmos and Ahlo later testified that they met with Tangi because she had asked for the meeting and they were worried about possible threats to the life of Koanui. Before the meeting, some of the officers involved also expressed concern that the meeting might be a "setup" arranged by the FBI, the records show.

Kamakana had his own explanation of the CIU-Tangi interview, according to the unsealed court records.

"The actual purpose in meeting with Tangi was a particularly corrupt one—to try to develop 'evidence' that Earl Koanui was a dirty cop," Kamakana argued.

That evidence would benefit "Ahlo's friend, organized crime figure and indicted defendant Gabrel Aio, who was associated with George Perry, an organized crime figure who was Olmos' friend," Kamakana said in the suit.[37]

When Kamakana found out about the Tangi meeting, he told FBI agent Kelly about it, who in turn notified the U.S. Attorney's office, according to the records.

Assistant U.S. Attorney Florence Nakakuni, the prosecutor in charge of the Chinatown case, asked the CIU for an explanation and for a copy of the tape. She was originally denied a copy and then was given an edited version. Kamakana obtained an unedited version, which he gave to Kelly.

Kelly later testified that some prosecutors in the U.S. Attorney's office wanted to pursue criminal obstruction of justice charges against the CIU officers involved, but others did not.

"My understanding is that it was not a unanimous decision, but the decision was that criminal offenses or criminal charges would not be pursued in the matter," Kelly said in a sworn deposition.

Kamakana also removed from CIU the records of a long-running investigation of waterfront racketeering, called the "Harbor Rats" case, and delivered them to agent Kelly.

Shortly after that, he was transferred out of CIU and placed under criminal and administrative investigations by Internal Affairs at HPD. The city prosecutor's office declined to accept the criminal case, according to the Kamakana files. The Harbor Rats case included an investigation of narcotics trafficking, according to court files.

Kamakana testified under oath that George Perry and his son Bruce were known to be friendly with two Hawai'i Kai brothers who were targets of the drug-trafficking probe. Kamakana and another CIU officer, Melvin Nakapaahu, both testified that they were reluctant to notify Olmos about developments in the Harbor Rats case because of his friendship with George Perry.

The Hawai'i Kai suspects in the case were never charged because they stopped talking to undercover officers and informants for unexplained reasons, according to the files.

Another man identified as a Mainland drug supplier in the Harbor Rats case, Jacob Sanchez, was convicted of methamphetamine trafficking in 2000, according to court records. An affiliate of the Hells Angels motorcycle gang, Sanchez was sentenced to 14 years in prison and died behind bars in California in 2002.

Bruce Perry was a member of a group of Honolulu stevedores known as the "Perry Boys" that was investigated by the FBI and HPD in the mid-1990s, according to court records contained in civil and criminal cases filed against Bruce Perry.

The younger Perry was tried twice on a charge of felony assault of fellow stevedore Quentin "Rocky" Tahara in 1994 at the Matson container yard on Sand Island. Both cases ended in mistrials after juries could not agree on verdicts. Tahara, who suffered a fractured skull and was blinded in one eye during the affray with Perry, won a $2.3 million civil judgment against Perry.

Eric Seitz, attorney for Bruce Perry, said allegations made against his client in the assault case and in the Kamakana files were "absurd."

Within weeks of turning over the Tangi tape and Harbor Rats files to Kelly, Kamakana was transferred out of CIU, the first officer to ever be involuntarily transferred out of the unit for a nondisciplinary reason, according to testimony in the case.

Kamakana secretly tape-recorded a meeting with Olmos, then the acting captain in charge of CIU, when he was notified of the transfer. Olmos said the move had nothing to do with the quality of Kamakana's work but said CIU was "moving in a direction where we're gonna need people that are faithful to myself and the chief."

Kamakana was reassigned to HPD's auto theft detail, described by witnesses in the case as a demeaning, "entry-level" job for a seasoned detective. He alleged in his lawsuit that the transfer and the Internal Affairs investigations of him were illegal retaliation prompted by his whistle-blowing activities.

Kamakana was represented in the case by two attorneys who later occupied important legal positions in state and city government: Mark Bennett, who became Hawai'i attorney general, and Carrie Okinaga, appointed corporation counsel for the city and county of Honolulu.

Federal Magistrate Judge Leslie Kobayashi conducted a painstaking review of the records and eventually ruled that the vast bulk of them should be thrown open. Allegations in the case, Kobayashi ruled, "raise issues about the conduct of state and federal law enforcement officials, and therefore, the court concludes that the testimony and documents concerning the matter are of significant public concern."

In upholding Kobayashi's rulings, the U.S. Ninth Circuit Court of Appeals lauded Kobayashi's "decision to carefully review every document" and said the government arguments for secrecy were "somewhat tepid and general."

Honolulu Advertiser attorney Jeffrey Portnoy said HPD fought for years to keep the Kamakana records sealed, not because they contained legitimate law enforcement secrets, but because the information in them was "embarrassing" to the department. The attitude continued a long pattern of secrecy at HPD, Portnoy said.

"It's clear that over the past decade or more HPD has gone to extraordinary lengths to keep from the public all information the department considers embarrassing or that will cast it in anything other than a favorable light," said Portnoy, then the president of the Hawai'i Bar Association.

Editors of the *Advertiser* refused to publish the stories I wrote that were based on the unsealed Kamakana revelations about Mehau and Perry. Marsha McFadden, the managing editor of the newspaper, repeatedly said that the stories couldn't be printed because the allegations about Mehau and others were "not proven."

I argued unsuccessfully that the information was based on sworn testimony from police officers that we spent countless thousands of dollars to obtain.[38]

I suggested repeatedly that we consult with attorney Portnoy, a nationally recognized expert on First Amendment issues and libel laws, about her concerns over legal issues raised by the records. She refused, saying there was no reason to seek legal advice on the matter.[39] Mark Platte, by then risen to editor-in-chief of the newspaper, wouldn't talk to me about the stories.

MEHAU TIMELINE

1929	Born, Hilo, Hawai'i.
1945–1948	Kamehameha Schools, Honolulu.
1948–1950	University of Hawai'i, Hilo.
1951–1952	Hawai'i County police officer.
1953–1964	Honolulu police officer.
1964–present	Rancher, security guard company owner.
1970	Appointed to state Board of Land and Natural Resources by Governor John Burns.
1973	Hawai'i Protective Association awarded statewide airports security guard contract.
1974	Reappointed to land board by Governor George Ariyoshi.
1975	Charles "Chuckers" Marsland murdered by Ronald Ching. Eric Naone tells police he was at Don Ho's dressing room with Ching, Larry Mehau, and George Perry Jr. at the time of the murder.
1975	Hawai'i Protective Association loses airports contract. State intercedes for HPA. Federal Aviation Administration overrules intercession.
1977	Television reporter Scott Shirai airs "godfather of organized crime" allegation. *Valley Isle News* on Maui repeats and expands on the allegations. Mehau sues.
1977	U.S. Drug Enforcement Administration memo says Mehau "is considered the single most important figure in the organized crime hierarchy within the state of Hawai'i."
1978	Joint DEA, IRS, and Honolulu Police investigation of Mehau code-named "Operation Firebird" begins.
1978	Mehau ex-employee and DEA informant Arthur Baker is kidnapped and murdered by Ronald Ching.
1978	HPA submits sole bid for five-year airports contract. Some competitors say contract specifications favored HPA.
1978	Mehau arranges VIP airport treatment for his friend, Japanese racketeer Kaoru Ogawa.
1979	Hawai'i Protective Association hires George Perry, Cyril Kahale, and others as "special deputies."

1979	George Perry, Rockne Freitas sandwich lease deals on state waterfront property.
1979	Police investigate Don Ho rape charge. Reporters Walter Wright and James Dooley meet with Ho and Mehau.
1980	Operation Firebird closed with no charges filed.
1981	Police and federal agents raid Ronnie Ching's apartment, seize guns, explosives, drugs, and cash.
1982	Japanese racketeer Kaoru Ogawa says Mehau is his friend, admits he once identified Mehau as "godfather" in Tokyo magazine.
1984	Ching admits murders of Senator Larry Kuriyama (1970), Charles Marsland Jr. (1975), Arthur Baker (1978), Robert Fukumoto (1980).
1984	Mehau and Cyril Kahale accuse prosecutor Charles Marsland of vendetta. Kahale files and later wins false arrest suit.
1984	Mobster Henry Huihui testifies Mehau had advance knowledge of 1977 Joe Lii syndicate slaying.
1985	Charles Marsland aide Rick Reed releases details of Operation Firebird investigation. Mehau sues.
1989	Mehau partners with Chicago and Las Vegas mobster Alvin Baron in Hawai'i cargo airline venture.
1989	State official William Paty accuses Mehau of involvement in "nefarious" land scheme.
1992	*Mehau v. Reed* trial. Former U.S. Attorney Dan Bent calls Mehau "a significant organized crime figure with substantial influence in state government." Police chief, prosecutor defend Mehau.
1992	*Mehau v. Reed* jury verdict in favor of Reed is set aside by trial judge. Case later dismissed after Reed apologizes for invading Mehau privacy.
1999	Mehau attorney Stacy Moniz files police affidavits in court that identify Moniz and George Perry Jr. as organized crime figures. Moniz convicted of tax crimes, surrenders law license.
2000	Detective Kenneth Kamakana files whistle-blower lawsuit, calls Mehau and associates George Perry Jr., Gabriel Aio organized crime figures. Papers filed under seal.
2002	*Honolulu Advertiser* intercedes in Kamakana case, seeking public access to records.

2002–2006	Kamakana case records gradually unsealed. Mehau, Perry records kept confidential.
2006	FBI affidavit names Mehau and associate Herbert Naone as "longtime organized crime figures."
2006	Final Kamakana case records unsealed. Police detectives identify Mehau and Perry as organized crime figures. Criminal Intelligence Unit chief admits friendship with Perry, defends Perry and Mehau.
2006	*Honolulu Advertiser* editors suppress Kamakana case records concerning Mehau and Perry.

CHAPTER SIXTEEN

End of the Line

The death spiral of the newspaper business in Honolulu followed a pattern played out across the country.

The decline first struck afternoon newspapers, which withered away as readers turned to television stations for evening news. Locally owned publications were consolidated or killed off outright.

The surviving publications were still cash cows, earning solid financial returns that attracted carnivorous conglomerates like Gannett looking first to cash in and then to cash out.

In Honolulu, Gannett Co., Inc., first bought the afternoon *Star-Bulletin* from its local owners in 1971. Dwindling subscriptions and advertising revenues at the *Star-Bulletin* were shored up by a joint operating agreement with the morning *Advertiser*.

Under this arrangement, the two newspapers shared printing facilities and advertising sales personnel but retained separate and competitive reporting and editorial staffs. Similar JOAs were reached in other cities around the country under the aegis of the Newspaper Preservation Act, a federal law enacted in 1970 that waived the antitrust nature of the deals in the interest of preserving independent editorial voices in metropolitan centers.[1]

The Gannett managers could do little to stave off the continuing malaise at the *Star-Bulletin*, so they struck a new deal in 1992, agreeing to buy the *Advertiser* from its local owners and sell the *Star-Bulletin* to a little-known and lightly regarded chain, Liberty Newspapers, based in Arkansas.

Liberty's chief executive, Rupert Phillips, was a frequent partner in newspaper deals with Gannett, usually buying and sometimes selling. Occasionally he shut down the publications after buying them from Gannett.

In September 1999, Phillips announced that he would close the *Star-Bulletin* the following month, prompting a community uproar. Loud public protests were staged, and lawsuits were filed. Just weeks before the scheduled shutdown, a federal judge enjoined Phillips from closing the newspaper. Phillips was forced to offer the publication for sale, and in 2001, Canadian newspaper publisher David Black stepped forward and bought the *Star-Bulletin*.

The joint operating agreement was dissolved, and Black moved the newspaper to new headquarters.

Simultaneously, the Internet was revolutionizing society and ravaging the finances of newspapers around the world, including those in the middle of the Pacific Ocean. Classified and display advertising linage shriveled as websites like Craigslist offered free distribution of, and access to, want ads, used-car listings, and real estate deals. Print subscriptions plummeted, so publishers fatefully decided that the only way to keep customers and attract new ones was to offer their news stories on websites of their own, free of charge.

It was a bad business model. Subscribers kept cancelling. Why pay for something when it was available online at no charge? Advertisers cut back again. Why buy ad space when the customers had disappeared?

Owners, desperate to maintain executive salaries and stockholder dividends, began cutting expenses. Employees were fired or laid off or squeezed into early retirement. "More with less" became the industry mantra. Reporters who survived the cutbacks were tasked with additional duties: shooting video, posting stories online, feeding twitter accounts.

The number and quality of newspaper stories plummeted. Some major newspapers ceased publication on a daily basis.

More subscribers cancelled. Why keep paying for a clearly inferior product?

Start-up news websites proliferated.

The dinosaurs were dying.

By 2010, the Gannett overseers decided that their Hawai'i plantation was just about barren, so they cashed out by selling to David Black, the Canadian newspaper minimogul who had purchased the *Star-Bulletin* nine years earlier and owned string of mostly weekly newspapers and free shopping guides, primarily in the Pacific Northwest. Although the *Advertiser* was much healthier financially and still turning a profit, its assets were sold to Black and subsumed into his newspaper, which was renamed the *Honolulu Star-Advertiser*.

Employees of the *Advertiser* were interviewed for jobs at the *Star-Advertiser*, and a great many were hired. I spent a good deal of time in my employment interview speaking ill of the editors of the *Advertiser*. One of them, Marsha McFadden, had already signed on as the new city editor of the *Star-Advertiser*. What did I know?

The *Star-Advertiser* bosses never called back.

When the *Advertiser* shuttered its doors and the *Star-Advertiser* declined to hire me, I took several months off to lick my wounds, take stock, and begin writing this book.

But money was tight, and I missed the daily joys and aggravations of the news business. I took a job at an online news site, *Hawai'i Reporter*, operated by gadfly local journalist Malia Zimmerman.

Malia's politics were demonstrably right-of-center, but she assured me that what she wanted from me was no-holds-barred, politics-be-damned, investigative reporting. She was true to her word, and that's what she got.

It was a blast while it lasted.

We covered stories that were largely ignored by the traditional media: human trafficking of immigrant farm laborers from Southeast Asia, sex trafficking of underage girls, bountiful contracting preferences afforded by the federal government to Native Hawaiian-owned businesses.

We shot undercover video of an illegal lottery business operated in Chinatown. I shot more hidden-camera video when I posed as a customer for the "Volcano Girls" escort business operated from the apartment of a University of Hawai'i professor. We raised pointed questions about the effectiveness of Project HOPE, a nationally touted criminal probation program created by a Hawai'i state judge.

After a two-year run, the grant money Malia had found to finance my salary dried up, and I eased my way into retirement. Malia soldiered on.

In researching this book, I have spent countless hours in the archives of Honolulu newspaper stories maintained by the Hawai'i State Library.

It can be a maddening, time-consuming process. Finding stories on specific subjects or individuals that were published before 2000 is a hit-and-miss affair because the library indexes are so thinly organized. (Post-2000 stories are much more accessible because they are contained in a computer-generated database or available online.)

To locate older news items about, say, organized crime, a researcher must first consult bound volumes that hold listings of stories published by the *Advertiser* and *Star-Bulletin* in specific years. Each volume covers only a one- or two-year period, so there are numerous books to consult.

Stories specifically about organized crime are probably listed in these books, but others that touch the subject tangentially are probably excluded.

Specific story citations in the indexes list the headline, date of publication, and page of the newspaper the story appeared on. The researcher must then retrieve a roll of microfilm for that date from a large bank of storage cabinets, thread the film into a reader, and wind it to the appropriate page. Each microfilm roll contains two weeks' worth of newspapers, so there can be a lot of winding and rewinding involved. Sometimes the microfilm image is blurry or distorted. The reading machines are cranky and balky. Sometimes the printer function on the reader is broken or otherwise malfunctioning. Sometimes all the readers are in use.

I have described this very clunky process in some detail to make a point. There is a much better archive of Honolulu newspaper stories in existence, but as of this writing it is unavailable to the public and even to reporters currently on staff at the *Honolulu Star-Advertiser*.

The collection is what used to be called "the morgue" or "the library" by employees of the *Advertiser* and *Star-Bulletin*: a collection of tens of thousands of microfiche cards painstakingly assembled over decades by librarians who worked for the two newspapers.

The cards are organized alphabetically in two sections: one covers individuals, and the other covers general subjects. The individual cards contain photocopies of all stories written about specific people. The subject cards carry all stories written about generic subjects.

The collection is a one-of-a-kind, richly detailed history of Hawai'i and its people from 1950 to approximately 2000.

It was jettisoned by the owners of the *Honolulu Star-Advertiser* when that newspaper was born in 2010.

The hybrid newspaper retained the staff of the old *Star-Bulletin* and hired some new personnel from the *Advertiser* but discarded other assets of the morning paper, including many employees and the irreplaceable morgue.

This archive contained all the past work of not just the *Advertiser* but also the *Star-Bulletin*. Out it went. The past didn't matter. History was dead.

The state library took ownership of the microfiche collection but found that the records were in such jumbled disarray that they could not be made available to the public until extensive review, analysis, and cataloguing were undertaken.

That process has taken years and is still incomplete.

A similar fate befell the huge photographic library of the two newspapers. The surviving *Star-Advertiser* electronically scanned copies of a large number of the photographs and kept them for its own use, then dumped the badly jumbled collection on the office of the state archives.

They have been stored in the basement of the archives: 559 banker's boxes full of photographic prints and countless more cartons of negatives. Archivists, like library personnel, have undertaken a time-consuming preservation of this glorious resource, sorting and cataloguing the huge number of photographs that represent a priceless pictorial history of modern-day Hawai'i.

In my visits to the state library's microfilm room, I have occasionally encountered *Star-Advertiser* reporters searching for copies of old stories that their own newspaper could have kept for them but callously tossed aside.

Hawai'i academic and newspaper historian Helen Geracimos Chapin called newspapers "the memory of a community."[2]

The shrinkage of statewide newspapers, coupled with the disappearance of the morgue, has forced a collective amnesia on the state. Memories and records of people and events have been erased altogether or at least rendered all but inaccessible.

For those of us who lived through it, the demise of newspapers was a wrenching, agonizing process.

Those reporters lucky and talented enough to have survived so far still face foreboding questions about the future.

Posting, tweeting, and shooting video are the new imperatives, eating into that most perishable of commodities in the news business: time.

The Internet is a fabulous creation that saves journalists a great deal of the time they used to spend on research. But time saved on research must then be devoted to meeting the constant demands of ravenous websites.

Start-up online news sites struggle to attract revenue while offering indecently low wages and minimal job security.

The work will always be the same: find good stories and share them. Landing a gig that gives you time to do that and pays enough money to feed the kids is the hard part.

H. L. Mencken, the curmudgeonly columnist and satirist who wrote scathingly and incisively about American culture in the first half of the 20th century, famously called journalism "the life of kings."

Those words will always be true, but the kingdoms are in decay.

Notes

Chapter 1: "A Culture of Corruption"

1. *People Magazine,* Don Ho profile, July 2, 1979. http://www.people.com/people/article/0,,20074030,00.html.
2. FBI Special Agent Timothy Beam, wiretap application affidavit, Misc. No-04–00199, U.S. District Court, District of Hawai'i.
3. Federal civil case 00–00729, *Kenneth Kamakana v. City & County of Honolulu et al.,* U.S. District Court, District of Hawai'i.
4. Walter Wright, "Honolulu Memories Return Only as Nightmares," *Honolulu Advertiser,* July 16, 1979.
5. Ibid.
6. Dave Donnelly, *Honolulu Star-Bulletin,* June 3, 1981.
7. FBI Special Agent Timothy Beam, wiretap application affidavit, Misc. No-04–00199, U.S. District Court, District of Hawaii.
8. "FBI Ties Security Chief to Organized Crime," *Honolulu Advertiser,* May 26, 2006.
9. "Schutter Says Ching Confession Part of Vendetta against Mehau," *Honolulu Advertiser,* July 31, 1984.
10. FBI memo, May 5, 1979.
11. "Broken Trust," *Honolulu Star-Bulletin,* August 9, 1997.
12. Ibid.

Chapter 2: Kukui Plaza

1. "Kukui Developers Get Parking Revenues," *Honolulu Advertiser,* March 25, 1976.
2. "Documents Show Devens Did Kukui Plaza Work," *Honolulu Advertiser,* April 8, 1976.
3. "Aoki Ordered to Answer Charges," *Honolulu Advertiser,* November 20, 1985.
4. "Kukui Insurer Is Son of Fasi Treasurer," *Honolulu Advertiser,* May 5, 1976.
5. "Sapienza Lived Free in Oceanside Project," *Honolulu Advertiser,* July 7, 1976.

Chapter 3: Organized Crime

1. Author and Gerald Kato, "Loomis and Chung Accused of Lying as Kukui Trial Opens," *Honolulu Advertiser*, December 9, 1977.
2. "Syndicate Thrived on Gambling—and Numerous Murders," *Honolulu Advertiser*, August 7, 1988.
3. Hawai'i Crime Commission, "Organized Crime in Hawaii," August 1978, 13.
4. Ibid.
5. Ibid., 14.
6. Author, "Gambling Bill Dies Again," *Hawai'i Reporter*, April 29, 2011.
7. Gene Hunter, "$100,000 Cost Nets $140 in Fines," *Honolulu Advertiser*, April 18, 1974.
8. Ibid.
9. Author, "The Case of the Missing Bouncer," *Honolulu Advertiser*, March 18, 1979.
10. Gene Hunter, "Syndicate Silences Open Mouths," *Honolulu Advertiser*, July 20, 1970.
11. Author, "Taking Bull by the Horns, Leota Eyes Governorship," *Honolulu Advertiser*, February 18, 1978.
12. Hawai'i Crime Commission, "Organized Crime in Hawaii," August 1978, 4.

Chapter 4: Yakuza

1. "Complex Tale of 'Yakuza' Puzzled Out by Isle Police," *Honolulu Advertiser*, February 8, 1978.
2. "Takagi Has Syndicate Escort," *Honolulu Advertiser*, February 9, 1978.
3. http://www.youtube.com/watch?v=TF6tjuXH_5Y, "DocJon Talks about the Yakuza."
4. "Double Murder Case Still Unsolved," *Honolulu Advertiser*, March 20, 1978.
5. "Japanese Tourist Special—Hotel with Love for Sale," *Honolulu Advertiser*, March 21, 1978.
6. Ibid.
7. "'Floating' Prostitution in Oahu's Finest Areas," *Honolulu Advertiser*, August 9, 1979.
8. "Ring Promoter Ringed by Yakuza," *Honolulu Advertiser*, February 20, 1979.
9. Charles Turner, "Furlough Is Justified, Says Corrections Chief," *Honolulu Advertiser*, July 2, 1973.
10. James Dooley and Robert Bone, "Lee Gets the Maximum—Plus," *Honolulu Advertiser*, December 17, 1980.
11. "Secret Videotape Turns Out to Be 'Who's Who' of Organized Crime," *Honolulu Advertiser*, December 15, 1980.
12. "Fishing Scheme Called Front for Smuggling," *Honolulu Advertiser*, March 30, 1981.
13. Kim Murakawa, "Man, 53, Guilty in Drug Case," *Honolulu Advertiser*, March 12, 1997.
14. U.S. Attorneys' *Bulletin*, vol. 45, no. 04.
15. "Rubber Tip Leads Customs to Finger Yakuza," *Honolulu Advertiser*, September 28, 1988.
16. "And Now the 'Sokaiya,'" *Honolulu Advertiser*, January 10, 1982.
17. "Japan Crime Figure in Bank Suit," *Honolulu Advertiser*, August 15, 1982.
18. "Ogawa's Business Feeling Heat," *Honolulu Advertiser*, August 15, 1982.
19. "Informant Paid by U.S., Yakuza Associates," *Honolulu Advertiser*, March 14, 1986.
20. "Two Japanese Crime Figures Held without Bail," *Honolulu Advertiser*, September 11, 1985.
21. "Yakuza Witness Was Arrested in Extortion Case," *Honolulu Advertiser*, October 23, 1985.
22. Ibid.

23. "Last Yakuza Not Convicted; Jurors Criticize Case," *Honolulu Advertiser,* May 3, 1986.
24. Ibid.
25. "Acquitted Yakuza Figure Is Dying of Cancer," *Honolulu Advertiser,* April 23, 1986.

Chapter 5: Yakuza, Inc.

1. "New Turtle Bay Owner Booted in Visa Fraud Case," *Honolulu Advertiser,* August 5, 1988.
2. "Golf Course Developer Seen Departing Soon," *Honolulu Advertiser,* January 28, 1989.
3. "Real Estate Business an Easy Crime Target," *Honolulu Advertiser,* August 23, 1988.
4. "Yakuza Close to Top Japanese Leaders," *Honolulu Advertiser,* August 23, 1988.
5. Ibid.
6. "Yakuza Gang Has Hawaii Connections," *Honolulu Advertiser,* August 24, 1988.
7. "Ken Mizuno Called Foe of Yakuza," *Honolulu Advertiser,* July 19, 1982.
8. "Yakuza Close to Top Japanese Leaders," *Honolulu Advertiser,* August 23, 1988.
9. Ibid.
10. "Yasuda Blows $100 Million on Vegas Hotel," *Honolulu Advertiser,* August 20, 1989.
11. "Money Issues Take a Backseat to Cars for Yasuda Pal," *Honolulu Advertiser,* August 21, 1989.
12. Ibid.
13. "Owed $6 Million, Bad Debt Collectors Shop for Picassos," *Honolulu Advertiser,* December 10, 1989.

Chapter 6: Vegas

1. FBI records concerning Ash Resnick released under the Freedom of Information Act are available online at http://vault.fbi.gov/irving-resnick/.
2. Ibid.
3. Ibid.
4. UPI, "Ariyoshi and Fasi Help a Gambler," *Honolulu Star-Bulletin,* May 26, 1978.
5. Gerald Kato, "Vegas Gambler Backed at Probe by Ariyoshi, Fasi," *Honolulu Advertiser,* May 26, 1978.
6. Ibid.
7. Walter Wright and James Dooley, "Duke Reportedly Pays Off $32,000 in IOUs to Vegas," *Honolulu Advertiser,* June 8, 1978.
8. Walter Wright and James Dooley, "Kawasaki's Casino Debts Doubled," *Honolulu Advertiser,* September 26, 1978.
9. "Vegas Casino's Rep No Longer on the Payroll," *Honolulu Advertiser,* March 20, 1979.
10. "Sukamto Again Loses Big at Casinos in '93," *Honolulu Advertiser,* February 24, 1994.
11. "Sukamto Staff Aids Campaigns," *Honolulu Advertiser,* February 22, 1994.
12. Gary Thompson, "Asian Whale Arrested on Bad Check Charges," *Las Vegas Sun,* October 23, 1998.
13. "Jones Asks Judge to Be Lenient with Sia," *Honolulu Advertiser,* March 21, 2002.
14. "Hawaii Bankruptcies Still Active Years Later," *Honolulu Advertiser,* November 19, 2007.
15. Ibid.

Chapter 7: Bishop Estate

1. "Billions of Dollars Make Big Estates Big Business," *Honolulu Advertiser,* May 6, 1984.
2. "Justice Lum Has Ties to Bishop Estate," *Honolulu Advertiser,* March 22, 1989.

3. "How a Justice and a Huge Land Trust Became Associated," *Honolulu Advertiser*, March 22, 1989.

4. "Justice Lum Has Ties to Bishop Estate," *Honolulu Advertiser*, March 22, 1989.

5. "Lawyer Also an Investor with Lum," *Honolulu Advertiser*, March 22, 1989.

6. "Bishop Trustees Rode Along on Texas Deal," *Honolulu Advertiser*, February 26, 1995.

7. Ibid.

8. "Bishop Estate Staff Did Zoning Work for Trustee," *Honolulu Advertiser*, March 5, 1995.

9. "Estate's Uneasy Link to Posh Golf Club; Bishop Investment in Virginia Enclave Raises Questions," *Honolulu Advertiser*, April 30, 1995.

10. David Waite and James Dooley, "Hard Time at Halawa," *Honolulu Advertiser*, September 6–10, 1995.

11. "Purge of Union-Mob Ties Looks at Local Labor Leader," *Honolulu Advertiser*, February 9, 1996.

12. "Broken Trust," *Honolulu Star-Bulletin*, August 9, 1997.

13. "Jervis Investigation," KITV4News, March 11, 1999.

14. "Kamehameha Schools Settled Lawsuit for $7 Million," *Honolulu Advertiser*, February 8, 2008.

Chapter 8: Ronnie, Henry, and Royale

1. Vickie Ong, "How State Senator Was Slain," *Honolulu Advertiser*, August 8, 1989.

2. "Arsenal Seized with Felon's Arrest," *Honolulu Advertiser*, March 3, 1981.

3. "Tam: Was 'Threatened' by Ching," *Honolulu Advertiser*, March 5, 1981.

4. "Arsenal Seized with Felon's Arrest," *Honolulu Advertiser*, March 3, 1981.

5. "Witnesses Afraid to Implicate Mehau, Bent Says," *Honolulu Advertiser*, January 9. 1992.

6. FBI memo, December 11, 1981, "Ronald Kainalu Ching Information Concerning Unity House."

7. Ibid.

8. "Friend's Evidence Undid Ching," *Honolulu Advertiser*, August 9, 1985.

9. Lee Catterall, "Hitman Ching Expands on Dealings with Police," *Honolulu Star-Bulletin*, June 6, 1985.

10. "Ching Links 2 Lawmen with Slaying," *Honolulu Advertiser*, June 4, 1985.

11. "Marsland Trial Drama: Missing Gun Produced," *Honolulu Advertiser*, June 13, 1985.

12. "Underworld Saga of Huihui," *Honolulu Advertiser*, August 19, 1984.

13. "Huihui Says Mehau Knew of Lii Fate," *Honolulu Advertiser*, December 5, 1984.

14. Letter dated January 1, 1985, copies sent to federal and county law enforcement agencies and defense attorney David Bettencourt.

Chapter 9: Three Dogs and a Vet

1. "Maple Garden Donate," KITV4 News, September 26, 2000.

2. Rick Daysog, "Prosecutor Lauds Fines for Towill Executives," *Honolulu Star-Bulletin*, June 5, 2004.

3. Rick Daysog, "Donors from Firm Fed Harris $319,000," *Honolulu Star-Bulletin*, October 12, 2003.

4. Jim Dooley and Malia Zimmerman, "University of Hawaii Professor Tied to X-Rated Escort Service," *Hawaii Reporter*, January 25, 2012.

5. Jim Dooley and Malia Zimmerman, "Prostitution Bust at University of Hawaii Professor's Apartment," *Hawai'i Reporter*, January 27, 2012.

6. "Lucrative Weddings at War Memorial," *Honolulu Advertiser*, June 26, 2005.

Chapter 10: Pay to Play

1. "Key Kukui Word: Favor," *Honolulu Advertiser*, December 19, 1976.

2. "$150,000 No-Bid Grows to $51 Million," *Honolulu Advertiser*, April 6, 1992.

3. "Non-Bid Contracts," *Honolulu Advertiser*, February 23, 1992.

4. "A 'Special' Lease," *Honolulu Advertiser*, May 14, 1982.

5. "FBI Raids State Environmental Agency," *Honolulu Advertiser*, August 14, 1990.

6. "How Miura Awarded a Big Contract," *Honolulu Advertiser*, August 16, 1990.

7. "Miura Political Gifts Came from Recipients of No-Bid Contracts," *Honolulu Advertiser*, August 18, 1990.

8. "Miura Invoked Prominent Names," *Honolulu Advertiser*, June 14, 1993.

9. "Mainland Firm Says It Never Got a Chance to Bid," *Honolulu Advertiser*, August 18, 1990.

10. "Miura Singled Out, Attorney Says," *Honolulu Advertiser*, June 4, 1993.

11. "No Competitive Bidding Used in Office Spruce-Up," *Honolulu Advertiser*, November 29, 1992.

12. Ibid.

13. "Kiyabu Says Parceling Was Cheaper," *Honolulu Advertiser*, December 4, 1992.

14. "Kiyabu Quits Job," *Honolulu Advertiser*, December 13, 1992.

15. "Non-Bid Contracts," *Honolulu Advertiser*, February 23, 1992.

16. "Airport Contracts Part 1," KITV4 News, May 1, 1996.

17. "DOT Contracts Part 2," KITV4 News, May 2, 1996.

18. "DOT Contracts Part 3," KITV4 News, May 6, 1996.

19. "DOT Contracts Part 5," KITV4 News, May 7, 1996.

20. "Airport Sublease," KITV4 News, May 16, 1996.

21. "DOT Investigation Follow," KITV4 News, July 19, 1996.

22. "UH/Korean Building," KITV4 News, December 25, 1997.

23. Memo July 9, 1992, Gov. Ben Cayetano to Chief of Staff Sam Callejo, "Subject: Jim Dooley."

24. "State Probes Airport's Construction Contracts," *Honolulu Advertiser*, June 2, 2002.

25. Gordon K. K. Pang, "3 More Get Prison for Airport Bid-Rigging," *Honolulu Advertiser*, October 5, 2007.

26. "Hawaii Firm Got $7.3 Million in Nonbid Work," *Honolulu Advertiser*, September 2, 2007.

Chapter 11: Pearl Harbor

1. "The Harbridge Connection, Part 2," *Honolulu Advertiser*, July 17, 1983.

2. April 29, 1983, letter to Thurston Twigg-Smith from Joseph Petrillo.

3. "The Harbridge Connection, Part 7," *Honolulu Advertiser*, July 23, 1983.

4. Ibid.

5. "The Harbridge Connection, Part 2," *Honolulu Advertiser*, July 17, 1983.

6. Ibid.

7. "The Harbridge Connection, Part 3," *Honolulu Advertiser*, July 19, 1983.

8. "The Harbridge Connection, Part 5," *Honolulu Advertiser*, July 17, 1983.

9. "The Harbridge Connection, Part 6," *Honolulu Advertiser*, July 22, 1983.

10. "Navy Drew Line on Harbridge House," *Honolulu Advertiser*, October 16, 1983.

11. "Anadac Got Navy Sole-Source Contract," *Honolulu Advertiser*, October 31, 1983.

12. "Condo Interest Involves 2nd Navy-Harbridge Link," *Honolulu Advertiser*, November 6, 1983.

Chapter 12: Huis

1. *Honolulu Advertiser* and Journalism Department, University of Hawai'i, "James Dooley as Detective of Documents: The *Hui* Connection," 1982.

2. George Cooper and Gavan Daws, *Land and Power in Hawai'i* (Honolulu: University of Hawai'i Press, 1985).

3. "Delays Boost 'Gap Group' Housing Cost" and "Who's the Man behind Project at Kuliouou?" *Honolulu Advertiser*, April 20, 1980.

4. "Maui—Maybe Death Should Take a Holiday," *Honolulu Advertiser*, February 2, 1980.

5. "Yakuza Subject of Top Law Meet Here," *Honolulu Advertiser*, January 29, 1980.

6. "Release Breaks Given to Inmate by U.S. Marshal," *Honolulu Advertiser*, March 22, 1980.

7. "Marsland Roars into Prosecutor's Race," *Honolulu Advertiser*, March 12, 1980.

8. "Marcos Friend Pays $800,000 in Cash toward Purchase of Estate Here," *Honolulu Advertiser*, April 19, 1980.

9. "Conjugal Visits at Halawa Jail," *Honolulu Advertiser*, March 27, 1980.

10. "Maui Gamblers 'Involved' in Land Investment," *Honolulu Advertiser*, June 15, 1980.

11. Ibid.

12. Ibid.

13. "Unregistered *Huis* Keep Landowners Secret," *Honolulu Advertiser*, June 15, 1980.

14. "Maui Realty Firm's Door Leads to Key Posts," *Honolulu Advertiser*, May 12, 1980.

15. "Questions Arise about Maui Hotel," *Honolulu Advertiser*, May 8, 1980.

16. Ibid.

17. "Maui Realty Firm's Door Leads to Key Posts," *Honolulu Advertiser*, May 12, 1980.

18. "Unregistered *Huis* Keep Landowners Secret," *Honolulu Advertiser*, June 15, 1980.

19. Cooper and Daws, *Land and Power*, 349–350.

20. "Tidy Profits in Maui Land Developments," *Honolulu Advertiser*, June 15, 1980.

21. "Peeling Away Layers of Nukoli Purchase," *Honolulu Advertiser*, October 26, 1980.

22. Cooper and Daws, *Land and Power*, 351.

23. "Peeling Away Layers of Nukolii Purchase," *Honolulu Advertiser*, October 26, 1980.

24. "Ewa Developer Went Broke in Style," *Honolulu Advertiser*, October 15, 1989.

25. Ibid.

Chapter 13: Death and Taxes

1. "Maui—Maybe Death Should Take a Holiday," *Honolulu Advertiser*, February 10, 1980.

2. "Refashion Med Examiner System," *Honolulu Advertiser*, February 11, 1980.

3. "Bulgo's Prices Subject of Tourist Complaint; State, County Checking," *Honolulu Advertiser*, February 10, 1980.

4. "Funeral Trusts Take 30 Percent off the Top," *Honolulu Advertiser*, May 20, 2007.

5. "Big Island Burial Businesses Went Under during the 1980's," *Honolulu Advertiser*, July 23, 1990.

6. "Greenhaven: Peaceful Repose?" *Honolulu Advertiser*, July 23, 1990.

7. "Pre-Need Funeral Plan Sales Fill Coffers, Fuel Controversy," *Honolulu Advertiser*, July 22, 1990.

8. "Abercrombie Revises Campaign Report to Add Services, Cash from Felix Firms," *Honolulu Advertiser*, July 22, 1980.

9. Ibid.

10. "Problems Stem from Plan to Redirect Trust Funds," *Honolulu Advertiser*, May 10, 2007.

11. *Department of Enforcement v. Lance C. Newby*, National Association of Securities Dealers Disciplinary Proceeding C01030019, April 8, 2004.

12. "As State Slashes Away at Budget, Millions in Taxes Go Uncollected," *Honolulu Advertiser*, March 7, 1993.

13. "Travel Firm Folds; Hefty Tax Debt Goes Uncollected," *Honolulu Advertiser*, March 8, 1993.

14. "State Tax Chief Says Department Is Looking into Regal Travel Case," *Honolulu Advertiser*, March 8, 1993.

15. "Regal Owner Also Heads Tour Bus Operation," *Honolulu Advertiser*, March 8, 1993.

16. "Firm's Tax Debt Gets 300,000 Fix," *Honolulu Advertiser*, October 30, 1994.

17. "What the Mayor Left Unsaid," *Honolulu Advertiser*, July 17, 1994.

18. "Improper Tax Clearance Issued to Many 'Hostess Bars,'" *Honolulu Advertiser*, March 9, 1993.

19. "Department's Computer in Itself 'Taxing,'" *Honolulu Advertiser*, March 7, 1993.

20. "Tax Audits on Rise, Reviews Add $23 Million," *Honolulu Advertiser*, March 7, 1993.

21. "Ohai Family Patriarch Knows about Surviving," *Honolulu Advertiser*, April 24, 2005.

22. "Boat Loan Project a 23-Year Bust," *Honolulu Advertiser*, April 24, 2005.

23. Ibid.

Chapter 14: Teamsters

1. Consent decree, *USA v. International Brotherhood of Teamsters et al.*, U.S. District Court, Southern District of New York, March 14, 1989.

2. Charles Turner, "Syndicate Here to Blame, Says Teamster Boss," *Honolulu Advertiser*, May 30, 1975.

3. Ibid.

4. Charles Turner, "Ex-Isle Union Aide Kidnapping Suspect," *Honolulu Advertiser*, September 3, 1975.

5. Gene Hunter, "Kidnapping Suspect Heir to $1 Million?" *Honolulu Advertiser*, September 8, 1975.

6. "Naone: Bought Bullets for Philippines General," *Honolulu Advertiser*, October 19, 1976.

7. "Naone Gets 18 Months for Ammunition Violation," *Honolulu Star-Bulletin*, November 23, 1976.

8. "HPD: Movie Fund Aide Involved with Syndicate," *Honolulu Advertiser*, November 20, 1981.

9. Ibid.

10. "$1 Million Rutledge Fund to Aid Films Here," *Honolulu Advertiser*, November 20, 1981.

11. "Group Fights 'Voluntary' Teamster Fee," *Honolulu Advertiser*, May 8, 1989.

12. "Teamster Feud May Hurt Isle Film Industry," *Honolulu Advertiser*, May 7, 1989.

13. "Shoot in Hawaii, Hire Lots of Drivers," *Honolulu Advertiser*, May 7, 1989.

14. Ibid.

15. "Mehau Is Playing a Role in Teamster Turf Battle, Tony Rutledge Believes," *Honolulu Advertiser*, May 10, 1989.

16. "Teamster Discord Visible on Fat Man Set," *Honolulu Advertiser*, May 7, 1989.

17. "Teamsters Settle Feud over Film, TV Production Drivers," *Honolulu Advertiser*, May 11, 1989.

18. "More Teamster Trouble Erupts during Filming of TV Series," *Honolulu Advertiser*, August 11, 1989.

19. "Kamekona Sentence," KITV4 News, February 22, 2000.

20. FBI memo, June 16, 1998, 5–8.

21. Rod Ohira, "Movie Supply Executive's Jaw Broken in Beating," *Honolulu Star-Bulletin*, May 20, 1994.

22. "Teamsters/Walden," KITV4 News, August 6, 1999.

23. Joe Tavares legal memo filed April 23, 1999, in federal criminal case #99–0078 (*USA v. Tavares*).

24. Ibid.

25. FBI memo, June 16, 1998.

26. "Teamsters/Moniz," KITV4 News, August 7, 1999.

27. "Moniz/Organized Crime," KITV4 News, November 29, 1999.

28. Motion to reconsider filed November 19, 1999, in federal criminal case 96–240 (*USA v. Stacy Moniz*).

29. Ibid.

30. Sally Apgar, "Alleged Shooter Has Roots in Old Isle Underworld," *Honolulu Star-Bulletin*, February 9, 2004.

31. "Sheriff Admits Dealings with Two Felons 'Look Bad,'" *Honolulu Advertiser*, March 3, 2004.

32. "Murder Guns Got Melted Down, Trial Witness Says," *Honolulu Advertiser*, February 5, 2009.

33. "Gotti Lawyer on Murder Case," *Honolulu Advertiser*, January 29, 2009.

34. "Pali Suspect Sought Control of Gambling," *Honolulu Advertiser*, March 7, 2009.

35. "Hawaii Murder Defendant Says He's Entrepreneur, Not Mobster," *Honolulu Advertiser*, March 11, 2009.

36. "Gotti Lawyer on Murder Case," *Honolulu Advertiser*, January 29, 2009.

37. "Pali Suspect Sought Control of Gambling," *Honolulu Advertiser*, March 7, 2009.

38. All information in this section was contained in a story that was spiked by Mark Platte on May 20, 2005. "There is no reader interest in a story like this," Platte said.

39. Federal criminal case 05–026, *USA v. Aiwohi et al.*

40. Ibid.

41. Federal criminal cases 05–206 (*USA v. Aiwohi, Audwin, et al.*) and 06–525 (*USA v. Aiwohi, Randolph*) in Hawaii District Court.

42. Debra Barayuga, "Bodybuilder's 1989 Slaying Brings 10-Year Term," *Honolulu Star-Bulletin*, November 26, 2002.

43. 2005 author interview of Mel Kahele.

44. Ibid.

45. Federal criminal cases 03–200 (*USA v. Farias*); 04–171 (*USA v. Paahao*); 01–184 (*USA v. Mataele*).

46. Federal criminal case 99–257 (*USA v. Duarte et al.*); State criminal case 1PC98-0-1277 (*State of Hawaii v. Duarte*).

47. *Wood & Tait Inc. v. William Duarte*, Case # 1SP03-1-00026.

48. State criminal case 08–1-132, *State of Hawaii v. Matthew Higa*.

49. Ibid.

50. "Driver for 'Lost' Pleads Guilty," *Honolulu Advertiser*, January 4, 2010.

51. State criminal case 08–1-132, *State of Hawaii v. Matthew Higa*.

52. "Borge, Called Key Crime Figure, Gets 20 Years in Drug Trafficking," *Honolulu Advertiser*, April 30, 2005.

53. "Driver for 'Lost' Pleads Guilty," *Honolulu Advertiser*, January 4, 2010.

54. Ibid.

55. "Hawaii Five-0 Teamsters Official Killed by Police," *Hawai'i Reporter*, May 14, 2012.

56. Tim Sakahara, "1.4 Million Settlement Reached in Honolulu Police Custody Death," Hawaiinewsnow.com, May 7, 2014.

57. "Hawaii Movie, TV Drivers Have a Long History of Drugs and Violence," *Hawai'i Reporter*, May 14, 2012.

58. State criminal case 1PC10–1-1389, *State of Hawaii v. George Cambra Jr.*

59. State criminal case 1PC14–1-221, *State of Hawaii v. George Cambra Jr.*

Chapter 15: Larry Mehau

1. "Very Special Deputies: 3 Felons, an Ex-Cop," *Honolulu Advertiser*, May 6, 1979.

2. Honolulu Police Department employment application, May 16, 1953.

3. One Year Probationary Report, May 21, 1954, written by Asst. Chief Arthur Tarbell.

4. "Police Take to the Air in Waikiki Aikido Show," *Honolulu Advertiser*, October 3, 1957.

5. Honolulu Police Department memo, February 25, 1969, summarizing "sweetening case" investigation conducted June–August 1958 by Asst. Chief Leon Strauss.

6. "Two Officers Suspended in Vice Probe," *Honolulu Star-Bulletin*, October 9, 1958.

7. "Vice Squadsman's Demotion Cancelled," *Honolulu Advertiser*, October 18, 1958.

8. Dan Katz, "Police Study Informer Role in Vice Raids," *Honolulu Star-Bulletin*, August 12, 1958.

9. "Procuring Charge Filed against Police Informer," *Honolulu Star-Bulletin*, September 24, 1958.

10. Mehau memo to HPD Chief Dan Liu, April 30, 1962.

11. Ibid.

12. Personnel memo, February 19, 1963, HPD Asst. Chief Dewey Mookini.

13. "Airport Contract Bidding Unfair, Losing Firm Says," *Honolulu Advertiser*, May 9, 1979.

14. Gregg Kakesako, "Airport Security Pact Defended by Ariyoshi," *Honolulu Star-Bulletin*, May 12, 1979.

15. Scott Shirai, KHON Television, February 2, 1979.

16. Walter Wright, "Mehau Sues for $51 Million, Denies He's Crime 'Godfather,'" *Honolulu Advertiser*, June 24, 1977.

17. Ken Kobayashi, "KHON Agrees to Pay Mehau, Kealoha in Defamation Suit," *Honolulu Advertiser*, July 12, 1978.

18. "After 13 Years, Mehau Settled His UPI Lawsuit," *Honolulu Advertiser*, July 10, 1990.

19. "Very Special Deputies: 3 Felons, an Ex-Cop," *Honolulu Advertiser*, May 6, 1979.

20. "Public Land Subleased without OK," *Honolulu Advertiser*, May 18, 1979.

21. Kevin Dayton, "Freitas Property Deal Questioned," *Honolulu Advertiser*, July 4, 1999.

22. "The Case of the Missing Bouncer," *Honolulu Advertiser*, March 18, 1979.

23. "Mehau—No Black Marks in Two Probes," *Honolulu Advertiser*, December 5, 1980.

24. "Mehau Is a Man of Vast Connections," *Honolulu Advertiser*, February 9, 1992.

25. Deposition of John Y. Y. Lee, January 3, 1992.

26. "Ex-Officer Who Testified for Mehau Was in Ranch Hui," *Honolulu Advertiser*, December 15, 1991.

27. Steven Brill, *The Teamsters* (New York: Simon and Schuster, 1978), 36.

28. James Jack and Eldon Ham, *The Last Dance* (Bloomington, IN: Xlibris, 2011), 263.

29. James Dooley and Kit Smith, "Ex-Convict in on Mehau Airline Venture," *Honolulu Advertiser*, November 5, 1989.

30. Andy Yamaguchi and James Dooley, "Paty Terms Triple-Sale of Parcel at Kona 'Nefarious-Type Scheme,'" *Honolulu Advertiser*, October 10, 1990.

31. Patricia Tummons, "Anatomy of a Speculation: The Many Flips of Mahai'ula," *Environment Hawai'i*, April 1995.

32. Federal civil case # 00–00729, *Kenneth Kamakana v. City & County of Honolulu et al.*, Hawaii District Court. Ahlo deposition, 144–146; Kaeo deposition, 24–25; Maafala deposition, 89–92; Wong deposition, 14; Kamakana sworn declaration.

33. Ibid., Olmos deposition, 360–361.

34. Ibid., Auld deposition, 81–85.

35. FBI Special Agent Daniel Kelly, 302 reports, 2.

36. Federal civil case # 00–00729, *Kenneth Kamakana v. City & County of Honolulu et al.*, Hawaii District Court. Kurihara deposition, 41–45.

37. Ibid., Kamakana sworn declaration, September 5, 2002.

38. Memo, author to Marsha McFadden, October 3, 2006.

39. Notes of October 10, 2006, meeting with Marsha McFadden.

Chapter 16: End of the Line

1. In some localities, including Honolulu, joint operations between competing newspapers were undertaken before enactment of the Newspaper Preservation Act. The federal law was shepherded through the U.S. Senate by Senator Dan Inouye, and Congressman Spark Matsunaga of Hawai'i sponsored companion legislation in the House of Representatives.

2. Helen Geracimos Chapin, *Shaping History: The Role of Newspapers in Hawai'i* (Honolulu: University of Hawai'i Press, 1996).

Index

About the Author

Raised in San Francisco and the Bay Area, James Dooley worked as a United Press International reporter in Honolulu in 1973 and a year later joined the staff of the *Honolulu Advertiser,* where he was an investigative reporter for nearly two decades. After five years at Honolulu's KITV News, Dooley returned to the *Advertiser* in 2002 and moved to online reporting at Hawaiireporter.com in 2010. He retired in 2012.

Production Notes for Dooley | *Sunny Skies, Shady Characters*

Composition by Westchester Publishing Services, with display type in Palatino LT Std Bold and text type in Palatino LT Std Roman

Printing and binding by Sheridan Books, Inc.

Printed on 55 lb. House White Hi-Bulk D37, 360 ppi.